The Only Woman

at

Gallipoli

John Howell

The Only Woman at Gallipoli

All Rights Reserved

Copyright © 2013 John Howell

Reproduction in any manner, in whole or in part,
in English or any other language, or otherwise,
without the written permission of the copyright holder is prohibited

First Printings of First Edition 2014
Second Edition September, 2015

ISBN: 978-0-9923422-2-7

Published by The Mickie Dalton Foundation
Kempsey, NSW
Australia

For information address mickiedaltonbooks@lycos.com

www.theonlywomanatgallipoli.com

INDEX TO CHAPTERS

	PAGE
Introduction	1
Chapter 1 - Charles Doughty-Wylie	4
Chapter 2 - Lilian Doughty-Wylie	13
Chapter 3 - World War One Starts	18
Chapter 4 - V Beach	22
Chapter 5 - The Naval Campaign in the Dardanelles	30
Chapter 6 - The Land Campaign on the Gallipoli Peninsula	35
Chapter 7 - April 26 at V Beach	49
Chapter 8 - The Other Woman	62
Chapter 9 - Years of Over-Active Distraction	68
Chapter 10 - A Love Affair	75
Chapter 11 - The Journey to Hayyil	93
Chapter 12 - Gertrude Bell and Lilian Doughty-Wylie In The Early War Years	103
Chapter 13 - The End of The Gallipoli Campaign	109
Chapter 14 – If Only...	112
Chapter 15 - Both Women Learn Of the Death Of Doughty-Wylie	120
Chapter 16 - A Book Unopened	133
Chapter 17 - The Arab Bureau	138
Chapter 18 - The Means and Opportunity To Visit The Grave	142
Chapter 19 - Morphia and Such Things	147
Chapter 20 - A Visitor to the Grave on Hill 141	153
Chapter 21 - With Gertrude for the Duration	171
Chapter 22 - Lilian Sees Out the War Years	180
Chapter 23 - The Arab Uprising	182
Chapter 24 - The Paris Peace Conference of 1919	191

PAGE

Chapter 25 - Faisal, Oil and Iraq					202
Chapter 26 - The Cairo Conference of 1921			205
Chapter 27 - Creating Modern Turkey and Becoming Ataturk	210
Chapter 28 – Lilian's Later Life					213
Chapter 29 - Did Lilian Imagine a Gallipoli Visit?		226
Chapter 30 – Evidence Emerges					238
Chapter 31 - Gertrude Bell and T. E. Lawrence			246
Chapter 32 - Gertrude Bell and the Early Days of Iraq		257
Chapter 33 - Cutting a Strong Thread				263
Chapter 34 - Family Knowledge					278
Afterword							285
Notes								293
Bibliography							315

Dedication

To my darling wife Lia, who believed in this project from the very first.

Acknowledgements

For the many letters and other items of Gertrude Bell and Charles Doughty-Wylie quoted throughout this book, I thank the Robinson Library Special Collections, Newcastle University, UK. Information is used by permission of the Librarian, Robinson Library, Newcastle.

For this unfettered use I also thank sincerely the family of Gertrude Bell.

The photos of Lilian Doughty-Wylie, and her letters, poems and diary extracts are from her file in the Imperial War Museum, and I thank the trustees.

The picture of Doughty-Wylie with Sir Ian Hamilton (p.25) and Lawrence's rifle (p.184) are copyright IWM and published under licence 6163.

The sketch of Hill 141 (p.57) and the Doughty-Wylie window (p.284) were provided by Tony Preston of Suffolk, and are used with his permission.

The picture of HMS *Louis* (p.228) was provided by Michael Griffith of Melbourne and is used with his permission.

The poem: 'The Anzac on the Wall' was provided by the author Jim Brown, and is used with his permission.

The picture of Lilian Doughty-Wylie's headstone (p.224) was provided by Ray Burrow in Cyprus, and is used with his permission.

The picture of Gertrude Bell's grave in Baghdad (p.277) was supplied by Rich Galen, and is used with his permission.

The balance of the pictures and maps are my own, or from the AWM, or were published when taken, and so are in the public domain under Australian copyright laws.

Special thanks to Sir Timothy Daunt, who helped me more than he realised.

Thanks also to Charles Smith who helped me put all this into a sensible shape, Rob Fairbairn who helped polish the shape, and Michael Davies who skilfully turned it all into a book.

The Only Woman at Gallipoli

Introduction

One day during the disastrous 1915 invasion, a woman set foot on the Gallipoli Peninsula. The troops of the British Empire and France clung to small footholds of land from April 25th for a mere eight months. In the middle of this carnage, a lone woman made a visit to the Peninsula. She stayed ashore for only an hour or two, as she had arrived with a single task.

The woman came to lay a wreath. She walked from a beach to a single, lonely grave on a battle-scarred hill.

I have walked this same path. I walked alone from the beach through the ruins of a fort. Behind the fort are the steep uphill lanes of a village. They take you to the higher ground and the grave.

I was there in July. The streets were dusty and the higher ground was covered in beautiful golden yellow sunflowers that came up to my chin. This was not the scene when the woman made the uphill walk. It was November. Cold winds blew and rain had turned dust into mud. War had obliterated all local foliage. What wasn't blasted away had been scrounged for camp fires.

Once on the high ground, she gently laid her wreath on the wooden cross of the grave. She then spoke some silent words to the man she had loved, and cried some more tears. Her time at the graveside was only minutes, as a war was raging all around.

That sad woman then walked back down to the beach and left on the same boat that had brought her to Gallipoli.

We have a photo of the wreath on the cross of that grave, but who was this woman dressed in mourning black?

The Only Woman at Gallipoli

This is the true story of this woman, the man in the grave, and another woman. Unavoidably, it is also a story of world events before, during and after this time of war.

The lives of all three people are inseparable from the period that encompasses what we call The Great War, and the opposite is also true. Each of them left their own imprint on the world and the war history.

There are shelves full of books written about Gallipoli. Some were published during the war, and many immediately after the war. A steady stream continues to this day. This book is different. It is more than just a summary of war history.

The Gallipoli campaign is an important episode within this story; but the story of the three people involved is also necessarily a story from before, during and after those brief events of 1915.

Chapter 1 - Charles Doughty-Wylie

The man in the grave was Charles Hotham Montagu Doughty-Wylie. He was born in Suffolk, England on July 23 1868, and was 46 when he died. This meant he was double the age of most of the men who went ashore.

He grew up in a wealthy family, and their home was Theberton Hall, just out of the village of the same name. The village church is St. Peters, and the family has a long connection with it. Charles is commemorated there with a beautiful stained glass memorial window, and plaques recall earlier family members, including a famous uncle.

To his parents Henry and Elizabeth, and friends and family, he was Dick Doughty. This text sometimes calls him Charles, and sometimes Dick.

He won a scholarship to the famous and ancient Winchester School, and then joined the army, graduating from Sandhurst Military College in 1889. At 21 he was commissioned as a second lieutenant in the Royal Welch Fusiliers, and this was the start of a distinguished and varied military career.

By 1891 he had his first war wound, when he was shot in the knee.

In 1895 he fought at the Relief of Chitral on the north-west frontier of India, where he was a junior transport officer. The death of a local chieftain led to a power vacuum and tribal fighting in a conflict over succession. The British sent in a small force commanded by an officer named Townshend to quell the violence, but were themselves attacked.

After heavy losses, Townshend, Doughty-Wylie, and the remaining 400 troops sought refuge in the old Chitral Fort. They were besieged by Pathan tribesmen from

March 4 to April 20. By the time a relief column fought its way to them, food and ammunition were nearly gone. A third of the occupants of the fort were killed or wounded, but it was looked back upon as a heroic defence. Townshend was hailed as a hero. (His name crops up again in the Great War, and he plays a part later in this book.)

The following year Doughty-Wylie served on Crete as part of an international government. The Ottomans had declared war on Greece for encouraging insurrection in Crete. Britain, France, Italy and Russia intervened, and governed until an autonomous Crete was created.

In 1898 and 1899, he fought in the Sudan War as a Brigade Major, with Kitchener's army. In 1900 he went to the Boer War, but was badly wounded at Vredefort. He recovered from his wounds sufficiently to be transferred to China to join the China Field Force. It was still 1900 when he was in Tientsin, with forces sent to subdue the Boxer Rebellion. He was now the commander of a corps of mounted infantry. Again he was wounded, and again he was decorated.

By 1903 he was back in Africa, commanding a unit of the Camel Corps in Somaliland. The young officer had gained a lot of experience in only twelve years, in a broad range of roles in different lands. He was now a Captain, with as many decorations as wounds.

He married Lilian Adams-Wylie in India in 1904. She was a military nurse, and it might well be that they met as nurse and patient. (With his record of wounds, there was a lot to be gained from marrying a nurse.) He had been born a simple Doughty, but at this time adopted Lilian's maiden name for them to become the Doughty-Wylies. The marriage signalled the start of a decade for Charles that was less eventful than the previous one.

There followed an assortment of diplomatic postings, including becoming a military vice consul in Turkey. Charles and Lilian were sent to a town called Konya, in central Turkey in 1907. Nearby was another town called Adana.

The Ottoman Empire was a large but stagnant entity in the early 1900s. On the scene came the Young Turks, and they were talking up patriotic nationalism. Enver, Djemal and Talaat finally deposed the last Sultan in 1909. They were assisted by a group of ambitious young lieutenants, including a Mustafa Kemal.

The Only Woman at Gallipoli

ABOVE: A DOUBLE FRAME WITH LOVELY PHOTOS OF CHARLES AND LILIAN

The picture of Charles may have been from around 1900, as he had little hair by the start of the War.

AT LEFT: CHARLES DOUGHTY-WYLIE

He is looking much more the gentleman vice consul, but has much less hair.

LILIAN AND CHARLES DOUGHTY-WYLIE AT A 1908 GARDEN PARTY IN TURKEY
To friends and family, and in their correspondence, they were often called Judith and Dick

The Canakkale War (the name the Turks gave to the Gallipoli invasion) would make Kemal a national hero, and elevate his profile. This and his later actions enabled him quite rightly to leap-frog all other contenders and became the first president of modern Turkey.

A side effect of this new nationalism was racism, and religious tension between the many ethnic groups who made up the old Empire. The Christian Armenians were one group who saw this as a time to seek their independence, and had armed themselves. Turkish over-reaction was to attempt to completely crush the Armenians, and it was turning into a racial massacre in and around the southern town of Adana.

Charles Doughty-Wylie put on his old army uniform and led a small detachment of Turkish soldiers to intercede in the massacre. He had no real authority to act, and certainly no authority over Turkish troops, but he couldn't bring himself to stand back and watch.

Although as many as 2000 Christian Armenians died in Adana, he eventually took control of the town. He had saved thousands of lives. Once more he was wounded by gunfire when a bullet broke his right arm. He was shot by one of the Armenians he was trying to save. Not surprisingly, the terrified Armenians took the uniformed officer careering into their midst to be a Turkish aggressor. Again it was clear that it wasn't the style of Charles Doughty-Wylie to lead from anywhere but the very front.

The Only Woman at Gallipoli

The artist at THE GRAPHIC came up with this very dramatic scene.
It is actually a very good likeness of our hero, with his wounded arm in a sling.

There was rioting and death in the coastal town of Mersina too, and the British sent HMS *Swiftsure* to encourage peace. Further encouragement was provided when they were joined by warships from Germany, France, Austria, Russia and Turkey.

A young officer on *Swiftsure* was Richard Bell Davies. He would have a long and distinguished career, and later won a Victoria Cross and rose to be a Vice Admiral. He wrote that:

"We duly arrived and anchored off the town. The massacre there had been stopped, largely due to the efforts of Colonel Doughty-Wylie, the British consul."

He went on to describe the scene from aboard:

"... during the disturbance, numbers of dead Armenians had been thrown into the river and the corpses had drifted out to sea. For many days after the arrival we had to keep a boat ready to tow floating corpses clear of the ship."

Another eye-witness account was published in the New York Times. The issue of May 3, 1909 included a long article about the experiences of a young American missionary caught in the Adana crossfire, with some girls from a missionary school.

Miss Elizabeth Webb explained graphically the terror and uncertainty faced by the teachers and their students. The only steadying influence amongst the chaos was the arrival of Doughty-Wylie. He arrived at the blockaded school at night, and she said:

"Finally about 9 o'clock there came a knock at the gate, and in walked the English Consul. You can imagine our relief at the sight of him. ... The consul is Major Doughty-Wylie. He could stay only a moment, but he left three of his own guard of Turkish soldiers to take care of us."

The chaos in town was complete. Of course, the three Turkish guards weren't *"his own"* and they soon fled the school. He passed by again and left another man, who also disappeared! Turkish leaders in the town were confused as to just what was right and patriotic. In their uncertainty they did nothing and mobs ruled the town until Doughty-Wylie bluffed them into believing he was in control.

His brave actions at Adana saw Charles awarded the Sultan's Imperial Ottoman Order of Medjidieh, a medal rarely awarded to a foreigner.* His own King also made him CMG – a Companion of the Order of St. Michael and St. George.   [see note page 293]

In late 1912 and 1913 Charles was working for the Red Cross, and was with Turkish forces fighting in the Balkans Wars. By the end of the wars, he was the Director of a British Red Cross hospital in Constantinople, and Lilian was the Nursing Superintendent. The hospital was nursing wounded Turkish soldiers returning from the fighting – the very soldiers who became the defenders of Gallipoli only two years later.

What sort of a man was Doughty-Wylie?

He was a tall man, and was solid and physically imposing. His blue eyes had a direct gaze and he had a direct manner. His whole adult life had been devoted to Sandhurst Military College and his career in the army. Promotions and experience made him a senior officer in all senses of the term. As well as this he was an educated man, and always maintained a flat in London and his club memberships. He was fascinated by the ancient civilisations of the Ottoman Empire, and liked nothing better than to discuss their history over an after dinner port. He spoke French, and some German, Turkish and Arabic.

We get more understanding of Doughty-Wylie the gentleman (as distinct from the officer) when we read of his life as a diplomat in Turkey during peaceful times.

Herbert and Helen Gibbons were newly-wed American teachers in Turkey at a missionary school. They were soon spending weekends and more in the Doughty-Wylie household, and give us personal insights into Charles the man. In Helen's 1917 book

---

*Texts agree that Doughty-Wylie received the Order of Medjidieh. Some have it for his deeds at Adana, and some for his service with the Red Cross in 1912 and 1913. All agree on the irony that he should end up fighting and being killed by the Turks only a few years later.

'The Red Rugs of Tarsus'* she captured the essence of him when she recalled:

"speculating on the mysterious phenomenon of the best of England's blood, content always to live away from home."

She wrote also of rushing to enjoy the little oasis of English life when invited to the winter consulate in Mersina. Her eagerness to enjoy the contrasts between the world within the consulate and the Turkish world outside was summarised by her rhetorical question:

"Wouldn't you have done so to be able to wake the next morning at nine, and have a maid push back the curtains while you sipped tea and munched thin toast?"

She appreciated the very 'Britishness' of the atmosphere of the consulate, where days of leisure could drift by with:

"Ten o'clock help-yourself-when-you-want-breakfasts, a morning canter, siesta after lunch, and whiskey-and-soda and smokes in the evening."

Life was enjoyably formal and upper-class, as life in a vice-regal establishment should be. Lilian even bought a tiara for 350 pounds to wear on official occasions, and Helen Gibbons fondly recalled that:

"At the Doughty-Wylie's, I am able to dress in the evening, and Herbert always looks best to me in his dinner coat."

[Only an American would call her husband's dinner jacket a coat!]

The consulate was only a building, and only a building in a regional town. Imposed upon this Turkish stonework was the world of Charles the stylish and educated English gentleman. Here he had created a lifestyle as anyone would have wished it to be in England. The consulate was a British oasis in a foreign land, where Helen Gibbons felt that:

"we are thirty miles only from Tarsus, and yet three thousand. We are back in an English country home. We can smell the box and feel the cold and fear the rain – so strong is the influence of the interior."

---

*Mersina (now Icel) is on the coast and Adana is inland. Tarsus is between the two.

Chapter 2 - Lilian Doughty-Wylie

For Edwardian times, Lilian was far more than just an officer's wife. She was an independent woman and a highly trained career nurse.

For some reason, her family often referred to her as Judith. Even a family member who knew her well couldn't explain why. At times she even signed her own letters in that name.

Lilian Oimara Wylie was born in Devon in 1878, but grew up in Glasgow. She was the daughter of John Wylie and his housekeeper Jean 'Minnie' Woods. Thus Lilian and her younger sister Vi were born illegitimately. The family recollection is that the parents were convinced to marry when the girls were toddlers. As part of the ceremony, Lily and Vi hid under their mother's wedding dress. The family felt that the priests blessing now 'legitimised' not only the union, but also the two giggling girls.

John Wylie was part of a prosperous cabinet-making business named Wylie & Lochhead in Glasgow. He died in 1888, and so the marriage ceremony ensured that Jean, Lilian and Vi were now wealthy. Lilian used her money wisely, and while she spent money all her life, she also left a lot in her eventual will. The majority of it went in duties, and to a fund now called the Colonel Doughty-Wylie Fund. It operates in several countries still today.

When Lilian met Charles Doughty, she was the widow of Lt. Adams-Wylie of the Indian Medical Services. She had trained in Edinburgh, and here she met Doctor Charles

Henry Benjamin Adams. They married in 1899 when she was 21 and he was 26. Soon after they founded and ran what they called the Adams Wylie Hospital in Bombay. The hospital was certainly run on some of Lilian's money, and it soon developed a good name for the treatment of leprosy. The hospital and the name still exist today, but the involvement of Charles Adams was unfortunately short. He died less than two years later during the Boer War.

Not everyone in war dies a heroic death, and it seems that Lt. Charles Adams-Wylie was an example of this. One report has him being killed in an accident with a bullock wagon, but another one claims he died of enteric fever on June 2, 1900. Lilian also nursed in the Boer War, and the Queen's South African medal was the first of many she would be awarded.

Two years after Adams' death she met Charles Doughty in Bombay, and they married in 1904, when he returned to India from fighting in the Boxer Rebellion. They had a brief honeymoon in the cooler north of India, but then Charles had to return to his regiment in Agra. A more extensive honeymoon came in the March of 1905, when leave became available. The couple embarked on a tour of archaeological sites in Turkey and Mesopotamia, as they made their way back to England and family.

It says something about the proud and assertive nature of Lilian, that both husbands incorporated her maiden name of Wylie into their own. This was a most uncommon thing in those times of sexual inequality, and we must assume that it was never the husbands' idea. Charles Doughty and Lilian had married in the May of 1904, but it was the following December when he changed his name by deed poll to Doughty-Wylie. It appears he took some convincing.

It seems to me that Lilian was spirited in a positive way, but not everyone is of the same opinion. Virginia Howell's 'Daughter of the Desert' is a fairly hagiographic biography of a fascinating woman of the time named Gertrude Bell, and Lilian and Charles feature in it. The book is harsher on Lilian and calls her *"His volatile and ambitious wife"* and claims Charles transferred to the diplomatic field at *"Judith's insistence."*

Different and more informed opinions than mine (or my namesake) can be found. Helen Gibbons, in her book *'The Red Rugs of Tarsus'* begged to differ, and said:

"Mrs. Doughty-Wylie is a little woman full of life and spirits... Frank and outspoken, you never know what she is going to say next. She is as vehement as the Major is mild, as bubbling over as he is cool, as Scotch as he is English."

She also revealed that Charles got the diplomatic posting not at his wife's insistence, but to recuperate from the health effects of his many wounds. It seemed also that Charles thought this foray as a diplomat was only a temporary thing, as he still saw himself as a soldier.

Helen Gibbons' comments can only be based on conversations with Charles and Lilian and so can be taken as their opinions passed on to her. She wrote that:

"The Major is still in his thirties but has had a whole lifetime of adventure crowded into fifteen years of active service in India, Somali-land, Egypt, and South Africa. He has not been robust of late, and was given this consular post temporarily."

It was ironic that he found himself in the midst of fighting in Adana. This was supposed to be a time of physical recovery, but again he ended up being shot! The belated honeymoon and tour that Charles and Lilian took in 1905 may well have also been part of the break he needed from the Army to resume his former strength. His diaries of this are mostly about shooting game and archaeological sites, but he also mentions his walking stick and his physical limitations when hunting.

While Lilian's second husband had been forced to resume his military ways to quell the massacres at Adana, Lilian had saved many lives also. The continuing Turkish political and racial upheavals caused a flood of refugees to arrive in Armenian towns such as Konya, Adana and Mersina. Lilian showed her training and capabilities as a career nurse, by establishing three makeshift hospitals to deal with the large numbers of sick and wounded. Richard Bell Davies left *Swiftsure* at Mersina, because Charles Doughty-Wylie felt a 'be seen' policy for uniformed officers would help keep the peace.

Davies' report shows graphically what a dirty business it all was:

> *I visited Adana for a day and went around the mission hospital. It was not a pleasant spectacle and showed up the Turk's most fanatical and brutal side; the sight of children who had been cruelly assaulted infuriated me."*

The biography of Gertrude Bell mentions Lilian and Charles, at the time when Bell's travels took her near Konya. It was only two months after the time of the racial riots. Bell had also met the Doughty-Wylies in Turkey a few years before, and a letter sent home on 27/6/1909 puts some scale on the happenings, and the real achievements of the couple:

> *"Dearest Mother, I wish I could have seen Major Doughty. I'm capable of running over Taurus and spending a couple of days with him, but I expect I should only give him trouble. I hear he still has 15,000 in relief camp and she has 70 in her hospital."*

She knew of Charles' family as simply Doughty, and so without thinking she dropped the Wylie from his surname, and didn't seem to recall Lilian's name at all.

Only three years after the incidents at Adana, Lilian Doughty-Wylie found herself running a Red Cross hospital in Constantinople.

That Lilian was seen as a dedicated and successful nurse is emphasised in the British Journal of Nursing, of July 12, 1913. British nurses who had served overseas for the Red Cross in the recently ended Balko-Turkish War (as the journal described it) were presented to Queen Alexandra at Marlborough House, for the presentation of the Red Cross Badge. Lilian, as a Superintending Sister, was obviously held in the highest esteem by those in authority. She also was presented with what the Journal described as:

> *"a beautiful gold watch subscribed for by those who recognised the value of her work. The watch is studded with diamonds, rubies and pearls, The Red Cross being in rubies."*

The terrible conditions of the Red Cross hospital in Constantinople illustrate to us how really capable Lilian must have been as the wounded were rushed into her care. This was not a hospital in one of the world's great cities as we would imagine it. It was set up in an unused part of an old museum. Mattresses were thrown on the floor, and soldiers treated there for the first few weeks. Eventually some canvas and timber was scrounged, and stretchers were made up. In the midst of this chaos of wounded men, there were outbreaks of typhoid and cholera. A British orderly named Moore died from typhoid, with his cause of death given as 'enteric'. These were conditions only a little better than the ones at Adana, where the corpses of slaughtered Armenians were left where they fell.

Dick Doughty-Wylie had seen a lot in his time, but wrote in his diary of:

"carts full of dead and dying... without exception the most dreadful sight I have ever seen."

Lilian and the overworked doctors and staff coped and eventually triumphed. She well and truly earned her medal and the jewelled watch.

In the years before World War I, Lilian and Charles spent some time in Albania and Abyssinia. In Albania he was on the International Border Commission, and in Addis Ababa he was a consular official. These were times when she might have relaxed, and simply enjoyed the privileged lifestyle of the diplomat's wife. This was not her way. Having done a course in midwifery in England, she promptly started teaching her new-found skills to the women of Addis Ababa.

Chapter 3 - World War One Starts

Several early versions of this book were provided to male and female friends for comments and feedback.

One interesting aspect was that many were intrigued by the title and were keen to read the drafts. When I asked them about Gallipoli, only a few had ever read a true account of what really happened. Their only knowledge was the odd feature article in a newspaper, or television documentary. These had been typically read or viewed around Australia's Anzac Day on April 25 each year.

My original intention was not to produce another summary of the start of the war, or of the Gallipoli Campaign. I felt that so many previous books had done it well, and it wasn't necessary. Friends convinced me otherwise. Brief pages about both topics were worthwhile, as they provided some necessary background.

These next few pages set a stage on which a man and two women perform.

In 1914, the European nations had an interwoven arrangement of conditional treaties and over-lapping pacts. A single event meant that they found themselves going to war like falling dominoes.

On June 28, 1914 Arch-Duke Franz Ferdinand and his wife Sophie were assassinated in a motorcade in Sarajevo. Franz Ferdinand was the heir to the Hapsburg Empire of Austria-Hungary. We know this snippet, almost as the answer to a trivia question, but wonder how this brought the world to the greatest war it had ever known.

Although Sarajevo was in Bosnia and the assassins were Bosnian, it was the Serbian secret society the 'Black Hand' that was blamed. It all became another reason for Austria-Hungary to continue acting aggressively towards Serbia. This they did with overt German encouragement.

In the decades before, countries had gradually established what were supposed to be protective alliances. Germany's Chancellor Bismarck had forged an Austro-German alliance, because he had fears for their future, sitting between Russia and France. Russia and France had their own alliance, because they feared for themselves if left alone to fight a war against any combination of Germany, Austria-Hungary, and Italy. Russia was racially aligned with Serbia, as they all saw themselves as Slavs. Britain had her own pacts, including one with Belgium.

European leaders, royals, and diplomats were all on summer vacations that July, but their peaceful actions were all pretence. They were all secretly mobilising their armies.

On July 23, Austria-Hungary sent an ultimatum to Serbia, with a list of unreasonable territorial and diplomatic demands. Germany was in the background pushing this along, as they had their own agenda. They wanted to attack Russia, but wanted it to be seen as Russia's fault for standing by Serbia.

Serbia caved in to the demands on July 25, as they were a minnow compared to their aggressive neighbour. Their reply was irrelevant, and gained them nothing. Austria-Hungary declared war on July 28 and the next day shelled Belgrade.

Germany now felt free to act, and the dominoes started to fall. On August 1 they declared war on Russia, and the next day invaded Luxembourg. The day after that, they declared war on France. (France was about to act on their alliance with Russia anyway.)

On the 4th, Germany declared war on Belgium and immediately invaded. Britain's treaty with Belgium meant they must immediately go to war with Germany, and this automatically brought in Australia, New Zealand, Canada, and South Africa.

Two days later, Austria-Hungary declared war on Russia, and Serbia declared war on Germany.

The next day was August 7. On this day France invaded the Alsace-Lorraine region and the British Expeditionary Force landed in France.

It was only *nine days* since Austria-Hungary had attacked Serbia!

The summer of unofficial mobilisation meant that nations could move at this breath-taking pace. By August 23, Japan had declared war on Germany, Germany had captured Brussels, and Russian forces had marched into East Prussia.
The world was at war.

Turkey found herself as the largest nearby nation that hadn't been caught up in this world game of toppling dominoes. Turkey's entry to the war could also carry the name of a game, but the players were Germany and Britain. Their game was called Battleships.

The Ottoman Turks had large numbers of men in their armed forces, but had little in the way of modern armaments. As part of moves to catch up with the modern nations, they had ordered two new warships, and they were being built in British shipyards. They were so close to completion that the Turkish crews were at Tyneside waiting to take delivery.

Winston Churchill was First Lord of the Admiralty, and he couldn't let these two brand-new warships sail over the horizon at the start of a war. Both were seized and became HMS *Agincourt* and HMS *Erin*. They were now the newest ships of the world's largest navy.

While Churchill had no choice, the Turkish government and the ordinary Turkish man in the street were incensed. Much of the three million pounds had been raised by public donations. To Turkish people these two vessels were far more than ordinary purchases from their savings and government funds. They were part of a ticket for their country's journey to modernity.

During the previous month as war emerged, Germany had two modern warships cruising in the Mediterranean. The *Goeben* was a battle-cruiser and the *Breslau* was a light cruiser. In a master-stroke they were ordered to steam to Turkey, and were soon signalling the fort at Seddulbahir for permission to enter the Dardanelles. Permission was granted and their next stop was Constantinople.

As a neutral country, Turkey should have impounded both ships, but neither Turkey nor Germany wanted that. It was announced that Turkey would 'buy' the two vessels. No-one expected money to ever change hands, but it allowed Germany to pull Turkey closer, without forcing Turkey to declare war on anyone. This situation muddled on until late in October.

Four months of bitter trench war in Europe were enough for Germany to realise that the war would last years, and that they needed Turkey as an ally.

On October 28 the *Sultan Selim* and the *Medilli* (as the German ships were now named) sailed north into the Black Sea and shelled the Russian ports of Odessa and Sevastopol. These so-called Turkish ships, with so-called Turkish crews (of fez-wearing Germans!) had brought Turkey into the war.

Turkey declared war on Russia on October 31. Russia made a formal declaration of war against Turkey on November 2.

Chapter 4 - V Beach

At the southern end of the Gallipoli Peninsula is the village and ruined medieval fortress of Seddulbahir.

From the fort you can look easily across the Dardanelles. The lands on the opposite side of this narrow stretch of water are the fabled plains of ancient Troy, and the Dardanelles are the ancient Hellespont.

Whether the legend of Troy was on the mind of British military planners in 1915 is not known, but part of the invasion plan for the southern end of the peninsula around Cape Helles included something reminiscent of the Trojan Horse.

To the west of the fortress is a small curving beach, and then some high cliffs and a headland. On the headland today is the British Memorial To The Missing, and just behind the small beach is one of the many war cemeteries of Gallipoli.

On these cliffs in 1915 were fortifications much newer than the medieval fort. The British invasion plan for the southern end of the peninsula called for simultaneous landings at several locations, including this small strip of sand. It was to be called V Beach.

(The other landings around Cape Helles were at beaches called S, W, X and Y. Further to the north was Anzac Cove where the Australians and New Zealanders landed, and the French crossed the Dardanelles to land at Kum Kale on the Asiatic side. What happened at these landings is mentioned later in this story.)

The Only Woman at Gallipoli

General Sir Ian Hamilton[*] was in overall command, and Major-General Aylmer Hunter-Weston was to take command of things that happened ashore. In the early days he based himself on HMS *Euryalus* which was stationed off W beach. No matter what happened elsewhere, Hunter-Weston's focus remained obsessively on W Beach.

V Beach was an obvious place to land, and this was plain to both sides. The Turks and their able German advisors also made good use of the weeks available while the Allies got prepared. The sheer size and number of warships assembled signalled clearly that operations in Turkey were to be more than a mere diversion.

[*]Hamilton was 62 years old when appointed as overall commander. He had joined the army in 1873, so that by the outbreak of WW1 he had been in uniform for over 40 years. A description of him at the outbreak of war was that he had been: *"gliding into a dignified and agreeable retirement."*

There would be no element of surprise to aid any of the landings on the Peninsula either. The Allied build-up was being mentioned regularly in newspapers in Egypt, Italy, and even at home. [see note page 293]

By early 1915 there were barbed wire entanglements in the shallow water and above the beach. Well-sited guns and the natural topography would allow a small number of defenders to dominate any approach from the sea.

An old collier called the *River Clyde* was to be the Trojan Horse. Smaller boats were to lead the *River Clyde* in close, until it ran aground on V Beach. Troops would pour out of hatches cut in the sides of the ship and scramble across the small boats to the shore. Covering fire would come from machine guns set up in the bow, with heavier support fire from warships offshore.

By early 1915, Dick Doughty-Wylie had been seconded from the diplomatic service back to the General Headquarters staff. The force was being assembled to invade Turkey, and Dick was a rare commodity: an English military man with knowledge of Turks and Turkey.

According to some, he was supposed to be on the battleship HMS *Queen*, safely offshore as an Intelligence Officer. According to others, he was to accompany the Australians and New Zealanders on their landings to the north. In reality, he did neither of these things. He spoke to Sir Ian Hamilton at the eleventh hour. The military commander had authorised his request. Dick was to transfer to the *River Clyde*. All on board the *River Clyde* must have known that their real chances of survival would be slim, so this was no easy request to make.

What happened at V Beach on April 25th was a fiasco, and a lethal disaster.

Machine guns from the fort and the cliffs had an open field of fire to sweep the beach. Successive waves of troops were mown down as they bravely tried to go ashore. One modern aspect of this campaign was that there would be some air support. A small detachment of the Royal Naval Air Service was part of the invasion force. They flew mainly from a simple strip prepared on nearby Imbros Island.

General Sir Ian Hamilton (on left) talks to Doughty-Wylie at the Rail of HMS *Arcadian* in Mudros Harbour, Mid-April 1915.

Ships of the invasion fleet are anchored in the background. Was this the fateful moment when Charles got permission to transfer to the *River Clyde*?

The Royal Naval Air Service leader was a Commander Charles Samson. On the morning of the first assault he flew overhead and reported the horror below. He wrote that:

"the sea was red with blood for 50 yards," and that the smaller boats drifting around the *River Clyde* were full of dead and dying soldiers.   [see note on page 293]

Valiant and heroic efforts were made to save the wounded men and organise the drifting boats. Six men were awarded the Victoria Cross for actions in front of the *River Clyde* that morning. Testimonials to some of the six were later found on dead soldiers, scribbled in the boats before they died. One VC winner was 18 year old Midshipman Wilfred Malleson. He was the youngest VC winner of the campaign.

A large number of the men who steamed into V Beach were men of the Royal Dublin Fusiliers. Their statistics illustrate this carnage of the first days. As the *River Clyde* grounded off the beach there were 25 officers and 987 other ranks of the 'Dubs' on board. Thirty six hours later there remained only one functioning officer and 374 other ranks.

When the beach was finally evacuated in January 1916, there remained only eleven men from the original force of the Royal Dublin Fusiliers.

As night fell, there were a few hundred soldiers sheltering against a small bank on the narrow beach, and in the shadows of the stone walls of the fortress. Many of them were wounded. Photographs from the bow of the old collier show many soldiers. What you can't tell is that all those on the small boats off the bow of the *River Clyde* are probably dead, as are those on the water's edge. The shallow waters were also full of dead men either shot or drowned, and they cannot be seen. A survivor told his son after the War that every man who jumped from the wooden gangplanks to avoid the hail of fire was quickly lost. Each was sadly destined to be *"held in a watery grave by his 90 pound pack."*

The Only Woman at Gallipoli

The *River Clyde* aground on V Beach

The photo was taken a week after the landing. Stores are being transferred ashore. The canvas covers on the sides cover the sally ports that were cut into both sides of the ship. Soldiers were supposed to emerge from the ports and run down ramps to a string of barges leading to the shore.

During the following weeks a road of stone and rubble was built out to the bow of the old ship.

Aboard the *River Clyde* that night there remained about a thousand more men, including the 46 year old Lieutenant-Colonel Charles Doughty-Wylie. He was a staff officer with the title of Liaison Officer, Intelligence.

He had more experience than anyone else aboard, and his mood was somehow different to that of the others on the ship.

Events of the next day would make him famous.

The Only Woman at Gallipoli

V Beach As It Looks Today

Beyond the small crescent of beach are the ruins of the fort, and the village of Seddul Bahir. Seddul Bahir is Turkish for 'Barrier of the Sea.'

The fort was built by Sultan Mehmet IV in 1657. Little remains now except the outer walls. It was never repaired after being extensively damaged during the Gallipoli campaign.

On the hazy horizon to the right are the plains of ancient Troy.

On the left foreground you can see most of the V Beach cemetery. 696 servicemen are buried there, but only 216 of these are identified.

The curved line of rubble under the water is what is left of the roadway that was built out to the *River Clyde*.

After the War the ship was re-floated and went on for many more years as a collier. At the end of its life there were moves in the UK to preserve it as a memorial to all those who died around it. The money wasn't forthcoming and the old ship was eventually scrapped.

Lieutenant-Colonel Charles Hotham Montagu Doughty-Wylie
He is wearing the bright red dress uniform now in the Wrexham UK archives of the Royal Welch Fusiliers, and some of his many medals.

Commander Charles Samson, RNAS
Pistol in hand and a cigarette on his lips, he stands beside his Nieuport 10 biplane. It is said he feared being captured and tortured, and told new pilots to always keep the last bullet in their pistol for themselves.

Chapter 5 - The Naval Campaign in the Dardanelles

Before any soldiers landed on Turkish soil, an attempt was made to defeat Turkey using the Royal Navy alone. Russia had wanted Britain and France to open a second front. This would distract and occupy some of Germany's forces making inroads against Russia. For Britain and France, an attack on Turkey seemed an attractive alternative to the stalemate developing in the trenches of Europe.

Britain also had fears that Turkey might move on Egypt and threaten the Suez Canal, or try to seize their new oil refinery at Abadan. To fight the Turks nearer Constantinople would certainly distance them from these options.

The more the idea was discussed, the better it seemed. The Allies (with Churchill at the forefront) envisaged that the arrival of a battle fleet in Constantinople would be a knock-out punch. Turkey could be out of the war within months of being lured in. Months before, Royal Navy ships had unsuccessfully chased the *Goeben* and *Breslau* through the Mediterranean when they had escaped into the Dardanelles. Churchill's frustration and urge for revenge was another motivating factor for him.

The Dardanelles is a narrow and strategic strait that links the Mediterranean to the Sea of Marmara. At the other end of the Sea of Marmara is the Bosphorus Strait that leads to the Black Sea and Russia. [See maps on p.23 and p.39]   Straddling the Bosphorus is Constantinople (now Istanbul.) One half of the city is seen as being in Europe, with the other half in Asia. From Roman times when it got its name as the Polis of Emperor Constantine, it has been one of the world's greatest cities.

THE FLEET AT THE DARDANELLES.

The allies knew that if a fleet of warships could destroy the old forts along the Dardanelles, the way to Constantinople was open. Initial discussions had included the idea of troops landing behind the fleet to occupy the shore and the blasted forts, but this just didn't seem to happen. [See note on page 294]

There was early encouragement for the Allies in the first days of Turkey's war. Ships of the British fleet shelled Kum Kale and Seddulbahir forts on November 3, 1914 (even though Britain had not yet formally declared war on Turkey). These two old forts were the gate-posts of the entrance to the Dardanelles. A shell had a lucky hit on a magazine at Seddulbahir, and the huge explosion left the fort in ruins. Six weeks later the British submarine *B11* sank Turkey's old battleship *Messudieh* a little further up the straits, and things were looking too easy. There was then a respite, while the allies assembled for attack, and the Turks prepared their defence.

When Admiral Carden led his allied fleet to the Dardanelles in the February of 1915, it was the greatest collection of naval firepower ever assembled. It included eighteen major battleships from Britain and France, plus battle cruisers, destroyers and minesweepers.

Carden however, was proven to be an overly conservative commander. His caution led to half-hearted attacks by only a few of the ships at his disposal. Isolated damage was caused to some of the old forts, but with little overall effect. On top of this, a lot of the effective fire from shore was from mobile artillery, which was impossible to destroy from the sea.

This approach continued for a month, until mid-March when Churchill pushed Carden for more decisive action. An all-out assault was planned for March 18, but only a few days before it was Carden who succumbed to the pressure. He stepped aside under the guise of ill-health, and was replaced by Vice Admiral De Robeck.

The plan called for an assault by three rows of the largest ships. The second row would be close enough to fire over the first, so that many guns could fire against the old forts.

Real progress was made. By 2 pm the forts were enveloped in their own dust, and their firing had fallen away. Guns had been destroyed and others had used all their ammunition. British mine-sweepers were busy and the fleet was set to advance.

The second half of the afternoon went horribly wrong.

During the previous month Allied ships had sailed up the straits to shell the forts, and then swung to starboard into Eren Keui Bay to allow following ships their own sea room. The Turks had noticed this.

Under cover of darkness a few nights previously, the Turks had sent out the (relatively) tiny vessel *Nusrat*. The Turkish mine-layer laid a string of mines in Eren Keui Bay where none had been before and none was expected.

The bay had supposedly been swept the night before, but failure to clear mines was an on-going issue in the Dardanelles.

Suddenly, as the French battleship *Bouvet* turned at speed into the bay there was a massive explosion. Before she had even slowed down, she rolled and sank with all but 45 of her crew of 600 trapped aboard. Eyewitnesses said it was all over in fifty seconds.

At 4 pm the British HMS *Inflexible* was next to hit a mine, and also sustained some major damage from the guns on shore. Ten minutes later it was the turn of HMS *Irresistible*.

Inflexible limped away to the nearby island of Tenedos, but *Irresistible* had damaged steering gear, and was a lame duck. Shore batteries soon found the range of the easy target.

HMS *Ocean* came in to try and tow *Irresistible* to safety, but couldn't close in the shallow water. She stayed nearby and kept up fire on the forts and shore batteries, until she too hit a mine at around 6 pm.

HMS *Inflexible* fires on the Turkish forts in early March.
They also put a landing party ashore at Seddul Bahir with demolition charges, but it met fierce resistance. On March 18 she hit a mine in Eren Keui Bay. She limped away for major repairs, and eventually fought in the English Channel later in the War.

At 7.30 that night the *Irresistible* went down, and at 10 pm was followed by *Ocean*.

While all this was happening, two more French ships were severely damaged. *Gaulois* limped away from the scene, and was eventually run aground to save her from sinking. *Suffren* became the sixth ship of the afternoon to be either sunk or very severely damaged.

The consequence of the long and disastrous day of March 18 was more or less inaction. What was left of the fleet after that day was still a mighty force, but they were never sent in again as a battle fleet. Forts were shelled, and defences were tested, but the naval-only phase was over in the hearts and minds of all concerned.

HMS *Majestic* (see above) and HMS *Triumph* (see below) were two ships that survived the naval stage of the campaign in March.

After the landings they were stationed off the Peninsula to use their firepower against Turkish positions. On May 25 the *Triumph* was sunk by German submarine *U21*, under the gaze of the Anzac troops and the Turkish defenders. Two days later *U21* sank the *Majestic* off Cape Helles, again in plain view of the attackers and defenders. HMS *Triumph* came to be British in a similar fashion to the pre-war takeover of the Turkish ships that became *Agincourt* and *Erin*. A decade before WW1 two vessels were laid down for the Chilean navy, but were taken over by Britain to become *Triumph* and HMS *Swiftsure*.

Chapter 6 - The Land Campaign on the Gallipoli Peninsula

I have set the scene at V Beach, and the happenings there on April 25. There was a lot more to unfold at V Beach, and to Charles Doughty-Wylie and the others huddled aboard the *River Clyde*. We will get to that.

Most books on the campaign are a battle by battle description, with enormous detail of every happening, but a simple summary to keep in mind is by Tim Travers:

"Bravery and panic, blood lust and skulking, malingering and heroism – all had their place at Gallipoli."

The first landing anywhere on the Peninsula was by the Australian and New Zealand Army Corps. The moon had set at 3.30 am and the boats crept in under cover of complete darkness. The water was perfectly smooth and a veil of mist hung over the beaches.

As the first hints of dawn appeared in the sky that Sunday morning, the silence was broken. After hours cramped in the landing boats the Anzacs jumped ashore and sporadic firing broke out.

The Australians and New Zealanders were to land higher up the Gallipoli Peninsula than the southern beaches around Cape Helles. They were to land near a little sea-port on the north coast called Gaba Tepe. As it happened they chose to land even further north, near a small bump of a headland the Turks called Ari Burnu (bee's nose). [see note on page 294]

The attackers were pre-occupied with getting ashore, and only gave names to the beaches each side of Ari Burnu. The small and narrow beach to the south became Anzac Cove, and the wider beach to the north became simply North Beach. [see note on page 295]

From either landing point, the rough terrain inland was nearly impossible to attack and to advance as was hoped. It was heavily in favour of the defenders. Adding to the physical obstacles were the confusions of landing so many men and their equipment on two narrow beaches.

Private Sydney Loch[*] was with an Australian artillery battery, and landed at Anzac Cove during the first afternoon of April 25. He described the chaos that he found himself a part of:

"There seemed no regimental order here. Men of all corps milled about and officers were as numerous as privates. Nobody shot at anything, none flourished swords, there was not an enemy to be discovered. The place was more like the waiting room of a station, a bank or a government office, where everyone is going somewhere and nobody is getting anywhere."

Even more controversial stories were in Loch's book. There was the tale told by his mate Cliffe, who said:

"Later on I met an officer who had lost his way, his men and everything else. He came to me and asked if I could direct him – he was nearly incoherent. There was some shrapnel about at the time and as each shell burst he dived under cover and refused to come out. I spoke to him roughly in the end, though he was senior to me, and finally he started to cry – I left him there."

---

*Loch's account of his experiences was published during the war as 'The Straits Impregnable.' Censorship laws didn't allow the publication of true accounts or diaries, so it was published as fiction with all real names changed. Loch became Charles Lake, but other names were plainly obvious. Red-headed war correspondent Charles Bean became a Carrot! The ruse was soon revealed, and copies of the book were seized from bookshops and pulped.

Loch also tells of his own experiences under fire, including being in a trench when a shell came in. Feeling something hit the side of his foot, he looked down and realised he had been struck by a rolling head.

Reports like these could undoubtedly have come from any of the other beaches on the Gallipoli Peninsula that day.

From a Turkish viewpoint, the coast behind Anzac Cove was impossible to attack, and as a result it was very lightly defended. The Anzac troops scrambled up the slopes, and followed the ridges and gullies, as the outnumbered defenders fell back. Within hours there were troops on the highest points, and they could see across the Peninsula to the waters of the Dardanelles.

At this time the Turkish commander of this part of the Peninsula arrived. What Mustafa Kemal apparently then did was recklessly brave, and was what effectively stopped the Anzacs from rapidly capturing the narrowest part of the Peninsula. If they had been allowed to continue, they would have also isolated the out-numbered Turkish forces to the south.

Legend has it that Kemal ordered his fleeing troops to stop retreating, and lie down as if to fight. No matter that they were outnumbered, and had fired most of their ammunition. Immediately the Anzacs did the same, and their advance was halted. The Allied troops were strung out, and were forced to retreat to consolidate. Turkish reserves were rushing to the front, and the Allies were soon pushed back towards the coast.

Anzacs never held these heights again. The consolidation turned an attack on a Peninsula into the defence of a beachhead.

Eight months of constant fighting never got them back to where they ran to on that first day. Kemal would become the greatest modern hero of Turkey, with that morning's actions as a major building block to his eventual status. His orders to the defenders also became legend: *"I don't order you to defend, I order you to die!"*

Author's Note:

In 2005 I went to Anzac Cove on a drizzly day, and had the whole area to myself. From what is now Beach Cemetery on Hell Spit I walked up a steep ridge to Plugge's Plateau. To my right I looked down into Shrapnel Valley and Monash Gully, with the high ground of Quinn's Post on the other side. A stumble in that direction would have seen me roll uncontrollably downhill through the spiky undergrowth, to finally stop at the bottom with a thousand scratches.

I made my way across the Razor's Edge to Russell's Top and walked to the back of The Sphinx. The Razor's Edge was so sharp, with sides so steep that I crossed with arms outstretched to balance like a tight-rope walker. From the Sphinx the view to the beach far below was like that from a light plane. At times I had to scramble through old trenches, and barbed wire and star pickets. I saw bones sticking out of the sandy soil, and was startled from my solitude by a tortoise trundling by.

After some confusing bush-bashing through the scrub I found myself climbing out of the old Australian trenches and walking across that narrow strip of green that is The Nek.

When I stopped in the quiet and looked all around at all that was behind me, uncontrollable and unexpected tears rolled down my face. No description of the steepness of the barren terrain had prepared me for the absolute impossibility of it.

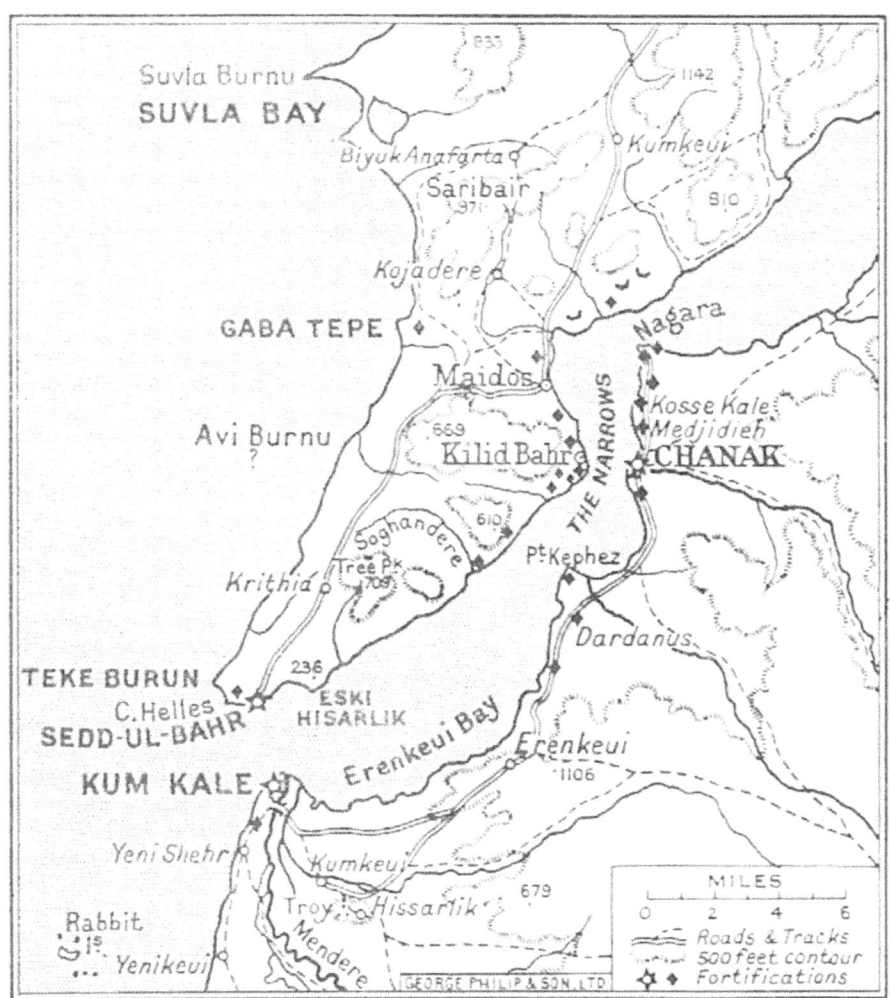

WHERE THE ALLIED TROOPS LANDED AT THE DARDANELLES: THE BRITISH ARE ATTACKING IN THE GALLIPOLI PENINSULA AND DISEMBARKED AT THREE POINTS BETWEEN CAPE HELLES AND GABA TEPE; THE FRENCH ARE ATTACKING ON THE ASIATIC SIDE, AND LANDED NEAR KUM KALE.

Map from the May 5, 1915 edition of *'The Illustrated War News.'*

It is an excellent map, but has one sign of being hastily prepared. Ari Burnu (Anzac Cove) is shown as Avi Burnu, and is floating and with a question mark off the coast. It should be just north of Gaba Tepe.

Back down near Cape Helles on April 25, the British were also having some mixed results.

At Y Beach there were soon 2,000 troops ashore, and observers on the ships offshore realised that there was no fighting. What they could see was men diligently ferrying water, supplies and ammunition from the sand to the cliff top. The landing at Y had in fact outflanked those Turkish defenders rushing south to V, W and X Beaches. (see Map on p.23)

Lt. Colonel Matthews of the Marines was the officer in charge, and scouting parties were reporting to him that they had the area to themselves. Matthews and his adjutant strolled into nearby Krithia. The largest town on the southern Peninsula was deserted, and they wandered around alone. Then they returned to the cliff top and settled in.

A Captain Cooper of the Kings Own Scottish Borderers also left from Y Beach. He strolled across the Peninsula until he could see across to Morto Bay and S Beach. He then also retreated to the cliff top at Y!

On the opposite side of the Peninsula it was also progressing. Three companies of the South Wales Borderers were ashore at S Beach, and Hunter-Weston told them to hold their position. With little opposition nearby, they could have also done more.

At X Beach a single platoon of Turkish soldiers were blasted by broadsides from HMS *Implacable* and soon there were two companies of Royal Fusiliers ashore. The landing boats were returning with more men and the place seemed secure.

It was a different and bloodier scene at W Beach. The naval bombardment did little to damage the wire on the beaches and in the shallows. There were only three platoons of Turkish defenders, but they were well-sited and held their fire until the boats were only a hundred metres from shore.

In fierce fighting a beach-head was established, but at terrible cost. 950 officers and men were put ashore from HMS *Euryalus*, and the day ended with 533 casualties. One third of these numbers were dead that morning, and six Victoria Crosses were later awarded.

Nevertheless, by lunch time the forces at X Beach had fought their way to join the men at W, and they now outnumbered the local defenders by ten to one.

The Turkish vacuum at Y Beach was destined never to last. Turkish defenders arrived and there was heavy fighting through the night. Matthews suggested to his fellow officers that they try to fight their way along the coast to join up with the Royal Fusiliers at X Beach. He was talked out of this. Ammunition was low and his plan meant abandoning the growing numbers of wounded to the chasing Turks. They would stay and fight.

He then saw his forces evaporate before his eyes. Wounded men were being carried to the beach, and able-bodied men were following. They were all being ferried to the ships offshore. Without the Turks knowing, and without them even doing a great deal, they had won the day at Y Beach.

At S Beach there was another bout of the early inaction seen at Y. The British forces essentially camped there and did nothing.

The French had landed on the Asian side of the Dardanelles on the morning of April 25, to stop the enemy from transferring troops across the water to the Gallipoli Peninsula. A second reason was to capture the fort of Kum Kale, so that its guns couldn't fire on the British ships landing troops at S Beach.

By late morning, Kum Kale fort was captured, as was the surrounding village. As night fell a second wave of troops were ashore, and settled into defensive positions. It was as well that this second lot were ashore and that the French also had some field artillery, because the Turkish attacked relentlessly throughout the night.

There was an unusual incident the next morning. Sixty Turks came forward under white flags and laid down their arms. Others then came forward, but kept their weapons. In a strange scene in a Kum Kale cemetery, the forces of both sides intermingled.

Suddenly, a French soldier, Capitaine Roeckel disappeared within a group of enemy, and shooting broke out. It was several hours of confused fighting before the French consolidated their lines and regained proper control. It was decided that the first group had genuinely surrendered, but that the others had followed them into the French lines in an opportunistic ruse.* As a punishment, the captured Turkish commander and eight of his soldiers were lined up and shot as war criminals.

By the end of April 26, there was some panic on the Turkish side. The French were holding five hundred prisoners, and the Turkish commander General Weber Pasa was calling for reinforcements. Further French advances could have been made if more men were landed, but this had never been part of the overall Allied plan.

As night fell on April 26, the French transport ships were called back in, and all were disembarked during the early hours of April 27. They had spent less than forty eight hours ashore. As V Beach was now secured, they were landed there and assumed a position at the right hand end of the British lines. V Beach became essentially the French supply base, as W Beach became for the British. (Eye-catching rows of barrels of French wine can be seen in the later photos of V Beach.)

Here at Cape Helles, the French were in the thick of much fighting, both attacking and defending. At times their morale was low, as on the night of May 1, when the Senegalese** troops broke and ran during a Turkish attack. British troops of the Royal Naval Division and the Worcester Regiment were rushed to shore up the line, and only left some days later when low on food and ammunition.

By the middle of May, French losses from Kum Kale and Gallipoli were horrific. Their original official combat strength was 334 officers and 22,116 men. After only 3 weeks fighting, they were reduced to only 88 fit officers and less than 10,000 men.

As stated previously, books with the full detail of the campaign abound. It will suffice to say here that the trends of the first days continued for the rest of the campaign.

*The first 60 men to surrender weren't Turks as such. They were conscripted Greeks and Armenians. While I generally describe the enemy as Turkish, it would be more precise to call them Ottomans. The army was composed of troops from all over the Empire.

**French forces also came from all over their empire. As well as Senegalese there were Zouaves (North African Berbers) and the Foreign Legion Battalion.

Hunter-Weston finally realised that the Turkish defenders weren't strong enough to overrun the troops ashore, and he ordered an attack for April 28. This became known as the First Battle of Krithia.

The net result was a waste of resources and lives. Tired troops attacked with poor maps and inadequate briefing. They were met by reinforced forces. His hesitation allowed fresh troops to man the Turkish trenches just in time.

Thus the campaign continued. The Second and Third Battles of Krithia came and went, and were marred by Hunter-Weston's insistence on near impossible frontal attacks against well-prepared positions. Hamilton did little, and in fact was accused of spending too much time on his yacht, and too little time near the action.

These British attacks were interspersed by some Turkish attacks. These only served to prove that the folly of frontal attacks was the same for both sides.

Fighting continued at Anzac Cove, where the Turks also had their turn at attacking. They charged bravely but recklessly on May 19 and 20, and were cut down by the waiting Anzacs. Such was the slaughter that a ceasefire had to be called on May 24. Anzacs and Turks mingled in no-man's land to bury thousands of bloating bodies. [see note page 295]

In an effort to break what had become a stalemate on all fronts, the British decided to mount a new landing. It was to be north of Ari Burnu, at a place called Suvla Bay. At the same time, it was decided that the Anzacs would break out of their containment and capture the critical high ground of Sari Bair. Fresh but untried troops came ashore at Suvla on August 6 and 7. The newly raised and trained Territorial Divisions were led by 61 year old Lt. General Sir Frederick Stopford. He had been an officer in the Grenadier Guards for 40 years, until his retirement in 1910. During this 40 year career, the man chosen to lead these new troops against the now seasoned and well-organised Turks had *never* commanded troops in battle.

Sadly, the officers below Stopford were further evidence that Kitchener still saw Gallipoli as a sideshow to the main event in Europe.

This panoramic View of The Dardanelles was published in the 'Sydney Mail'

The Allied Men in Charge: Vice Admiral de Robeck and General Sir Ian Hamilton.
This picture was actually taken on October 17, 1915. Hamilton had been replaced by Monro, and was being recalled as a failure, to face England and a Royal Commission. (Monro didn't last as long as Hamilton. He was replaced by Sir William Birdwood.)

Stopford's Chief of Staff was Brigadier General Reed VC, who had been withdrawn from the Western Front. In France he had planned and seen through many set-piece assaults against established German defences. Those Western Front actions had relied on massive artillery bombardments, and it was thought he was pre-occupied with them. Things would be different here. His nerves were not good, and at Suvla there would be little artillery. On arrival in Gallipoli, Reed was briefed by a Colonel Aspinall. After the briefing Aspinall is quoted as saying: *"He had the air of a man who does not think he is going to perform his task."*

The new troops available for Suvla consisted of three Divisions, and they had been tagged as 'Kitchener's New Army.' Kitchener optimistically believed that these woefully under-trained troops with uncertain leadership would soon perform like the seasoned survivors already ashore. How wrong he turned out to be. (There were even suspicions that Kitchener was becoming senile. We will never know, as he died at sea a year later).

The 'New Army' had trained in the green fields of England and Ireland, and many were billeted (and spoilt) in village homes. The scrappy terrain, high temperatures, and meagre water rations hit them hard. Now they were also expected to fight.

The dysfunctional leadership went lower down the chain than Stopford and Reed. The best of the three divisions was supposedly the 11th. (The other divisions were the 10th and 13th). The 11th was commanded by a Major-General Hammersley. Back in 1911 he had been in command of a brigade, until a stage when he was simply not around. It transpired that he had been temporarily committed to a mental asylum!

In spite of all this, the men were fit and keen when they first arrived, and eager to do well. They landed at Suvla at night and the first waves were ashore without fuss. This was perhaps the most positive part of their first 24 hours, as dawn revealed chaos. Men had wandered all night looking for their units (as had happened at Anzac Cove only four months previously). Immediate objectives like Chocolate Hill weren't taken overnight. There was real doubt in the darkness as to where it really was! By the end of a hot day, little was achieved, but Turkish snipers continued to pick off the officers. Groups of men settled down in the heat and were seen 'brewing up.'

In a late action, Chocolate Hill was finally taken by troops so tired, thirsty and disorganised that losses were inevitably heavy.

The 24 hours of inaction had allowed enough time for three battalions of Turkish troops to march in from Bulair, and get a night's sleep.

Ian Hamilton finally could stand by and watch it go wrong no longer. He intervened,[*] and prodded Stopford to attack the adjacent high ground on August 9. It was too late, as the reinforced defenders were there and waiting. Two weeks later Stopford was replaced by Lt. General Sir Julian Byng.

The break out by the Anzacs was also to be on the night of 6/7 August. While this operation and the landing at Suvla were separate events, the combination would certainly stretch and confuse the Turks.

Two main thrusts were planned. The Australians, Indians and some British would attack and capture Hill Q and Koja Cimen Tepe. The New Zealanders would attack Chunuk Bair, the third important part of the Sari Bair range.

The New Zealanders were actually successful. They captured Chunuk Bair on August 8, in some of the most savage fighting of their whole campaign. Their stay was brief. Lt. Colonel Malone was killed and they were driven back by a counter attack at dawn on August 10.

The Australians, Indians and British had even less success. Their night approach was over a longer distance, through even worse ground. Inevitably, the tired men got lost or pinned down, and few were ready for the dawn attack. Some Ghurkas and men from the South Lancashire regiment got to the saddle of Hill Q, but were repelled. Unfortunately, they were defeated by a combination of Turkish attacks and 'friendly' naval fire.

---

*Hamilton had what we see now as an outmoded sense of military etiquette. He thought that it was the job of those below him to make all decisions. For him to actually direct someone to any specific action was a rare event indeed.

While all this was unfolding at Suvla and at Ari Burnu, there were other diversionary attacks on the Peninsula. The British and French attacked at Helles with little real objective other than to straighten the front line and tie down the defenders.

The Australians attacked at Lone Pine and advanced at great cost. In vicious hand-to-hand fighting they captured the Turkish trenches. Seven Victoria Crosses were awarded at Lone Pine.

At 4.30 am on August 7 the fighting was still going on at Lone Pine, when the Australians also charged Turkish trenches at the Nek. Here there was great heroism, but no success. Waves of men from the Australian Light Horse were to charge across open ground at the end of a naval and field artillery barrage. Clocks weren't properly synchronised* and the barrage ended a few minutes early. During these minutes the Turkish machine-gunners were able to return to the parapets.

To ensure that their only goal was the enemy trenches, the Australians were ordered to charge across the open ground with bayonets fixed and rifles unloaded. The Light Horsemen were cut down as four successive waves leapt from the trenches and charged. Their bodies were never retrieved. They lay where they fell until the remains were buried by the Imperial War Graves Commission after the war.

[see note on page 296]

Thus ended the August offensive. This supposed turning point of the campaign never eventuated. Fighting continued, but there was a general stagnation. Disease and weather became the biggest issues for both sides.

---

* More facts emerge from a New Zealand official War Diary. The artillery timetable there says that their field artillery was to range to another target at 4.30, and so stopped firing at 4.27am. The naval guns stopped around this time also, because they feared they would shell the charging Australians. This was probably in addition to some clock issues, as the fatal pause between the barrage and the order to charge is said to be seven minutes.

By September there were up to a thousand sick men a day arriving at Mudros from the various fronts. Primitive or non-existent sanitation left them suffering from typhoid, dysentery and diarrhoea. Total evacuations for September and October were about 50,000 men. 44,000 of these were evacuated not with wounds, but for medical reasons. [See note on page 296]

November was even worse. A New Zealand nursing sister named Lottie Le Gallais[*] wrote in her diary that from the Anzac beaches alone there were barges coming off regularly at 10.30 am and 3.30 pm. These barges of sick men were reducing the Anzac garrison alone by 900 men a day.

---

*Lottie Le Gallais was a nurse on a liner called the *Maheno* that had been converted to a hospital ship. In an amazing coincidence in 2010, I read her diary extract the day before going on a tour to Fraser Island in Queensland. On the island the next day I stood next to the rusting hulk of the *Maheno*.

After an illustrious career, the liner had come to a sad end, washed ashore in a storm while being towed to the ship-breakers.

Chapter 7 - April 26 at V Beach

We left Charles Doughty-Wylie aboard the *River Clyde* on the night of April 25. He was among a thousand men on board, forced to witness the slaughter as the first waves of troops tried to land. Within 24 hours he would become a hero.

The attack went a little better at V Beach on the second day. Things could hardly have been as bad as April 25, when there was such great loss of life for so little gain. British troops nearly overran the old fort, and there was some progress in heavy fighting in the village behind the fort.

In the early hours of the 26th, Doughty-Wylie had gone ashore and spoken to the men, encouraging them and ordering them to cut the wire under cover of darkness. (Some reports had him on the beach early on the morning of the 26th, rather than in the darkness.) On returning to the ship he spoke with Surgeon Burroughes Kelly, who later wrote that:

"Early on the morning of the 26th, Doughty-Wylie left the River Clyde for the beach. He was prominent there throughout the forenoon, and about 11.00 am he returned and drank a cup of tea. I had a chat of about a quarter of an hour with him, and he seemed depressed about the whole affair. Several times he remarked that something must be done."

That morning, a Captain Garth Walford also went ashore to mobilise the forces there. They had formed themselves into three groups, and Walford led one group in some bloody fighting in the village. A second group was pinned down in the centre of the beach. The third group was led by a Colonel Williams but had achieved little at the western end of the beach.

As the fighting stagnated further during the morning, Doughty-Wylie went ashore 'armed' with only his swagger stick. He took command of Walford's group, as by this time Walford and his lieutenant had both been killed. Charles could see himself being forced to repeat his heroics at Adana, seven years earlier. Once again he had to step into a leadership role in dangerous fighting, and once again it was supposed to be someone else's responsibility.

A Photo from the Bridge of the *River Clyde* on April 25.
At the foot of the photo is the bow of the *River Clyde*, covered in dead and dying men. The dark smudge in the barge in front is another group of the same. The large dark patch on the beach and the dark line to the left are soldiers who made it to the pitiful shelter of shore, but they are under deadly fire from the high ground to the left of the photograph.

A junior officer surviving in the village that morning was Lieutenant Guy Nightingale, and he described Doughty-Wylie soon after his arrival ashore:

"He was passing some distance in rear of the gateway, when a bullet knocked the staff cap off his head. I happened to be quite close at the moment,

and remember being struck by the calm way in which he treated the incident. He was carrying no weapon at the time, only a small cane."

Doughty-Wylie was not alone on the Peninsula as an unarmed leader. W Beach had something similar in Captain Richard 'Walking Stick' Willis. He won the VC at W Beach, and went on to live to 90.

An Un-Armed Doughty-Wylie Leads the Troops In a Charge Through the Village.

Many paintings of heroic events are complete fabrications in the mind of the artist. In this case it seems the artist saw photos of the village, or spoke to men that were there.

The streets that run uphill from the old fort are just like this today.

This painting first appeared in a patriotic periodical: 'Deeds That Thrill the Empire.'

Doughty-Wylie's calm manner and extreme bravery inspired his men, and by the middle of the day the village was secured. Doughty-Wylie then called for ships off-shore to bombard the remaining Turkish strongpoint on Hill 141. He watched the bombardment from the ruined fort, and then led all three groups on a charge up the hill. Like men possessed, they cheered and charged the heights with bayonets fixed, to where the Turkish redoubt was surrounded by a dry defensive moat.

The warships anchored just off V Beach were close enough to witness all that went on, like some bizarre diorama. A report from a Major Mure is verbose, but nearly poetic in its admiration of what took place:

"It was a glorious and terrible sight, and I felt as it looked – fearful and exultant. The infantry pushed and tore through the village of Sedd-el-Bahr* up to the fort belching fire and death from the cliff beyond. The blood danced in our veins, as we leaned and looked, our souls fighting with those men struggling in the thick of the carnage. Their bayonets flashed in the dancing eastern sunlight, and as the men rattled on, bleeding, dying, yet persisting, conquering, the glittering sheen they threw before them and about them scintillated like a sea of liquid, burnished steel, more alive than the molten sunlight it mocked and out shone, throwing great swathes of terrible searchlight for yards in front of our straining, suffering infantry, and for yards on either side of them. It was a field of the cloth of living silver. And we could hear the men shouting, 'Go on lads: go on you devils!' and cries much more vitriolic, less episcopal."

Lieutenant Guy Nightingale later wrote his own much briefer summary of the latter stages of the charge, where the defenders finally ran and the attackers eventually triumphed: [see note on page 297]

"The men lined the top edge of the moat, firing down on the retreating Turks. ... It was at this moment that Colonel Doughty-Wylie, who had led his men to the last moment, was shot in the head, dying almost immediately on the summit of the hill he had so ably captured."

---

*Seddulbahir can also be found as Seddul Bahir, Sedd-el-Bahr, Sed Le Bar and more. Language and spelling in the region are fluid things, and many words have many variations.

The Only Woman at Gallipoli

Brave to the point of recklessness, Charles Doughty-Wylie had inspired a group of dispirited men to a great victory. They stood in triumph on the high ground that dominated V Beach, but the man who took them there was dead at their feet.

The original orders for Doughty-Wylie were that he land with the Anzacs as an intelligence and liaison officer, and he had obviously discussed this with fellow officers. When news of his heroics came out, many people therefore assumed that he must have fought and died with the Anzacs. There was even an illustration published in Britain and Australia showing him heroically leading these same Anzacs up the slopes, but people were so keen for news and a hero that such publications rushed into print without the real facts being known.

'The Illustrated War News' was a weekly British magazine that was keeping people informed with their best effort of the latest news and photographs. The May 5 edition had sketchy details, but at least they were essentially accurate. [see note on page 297]

The best that they could say of the Gallipoli invasion was:

"Already we know officially that an army under Sir Ian Hamilton has landed on the toe of the peninsula, … , and that that force, after establishing itself across from water to water, is already making some movement forward…. Landing was affected on several beaches, mainly with success, though at Sedd-ul-Bahr there were difficulties. These were overcome with great dash by our men, and landings were made good in the face of vigorous opposition."

Colonel Williams and his men, who had been pinned down at the western end of the beach, joined up with the others for the final surge. He survived the charge that essentially secured the whole landing at V Beach. He also wrote about arriving at the scene of the death of Doughty-Wylie:

"I came up shortly after he had fallen; the men round about were full of admiration and sorrow. They told me he was first the whole way up the slope and it was only in the last few yards that some four or five men had got up to

and passed him actually over the castle walls; personally, I noticed him on two or three occasions always in front and cheering his men on. As soon as I came up and realised that he was dead I took his watch, money and a few things I could find and had him buried where he fell. I had this done at once, having seen such disgusting sights of unburied dead in the village that I could not bear to have him lying there. This was all done hurriedly as I had to reorganize the line and think of further advance or digging in; we just buried him as he lay and I said the 'Lord's Prayer' over his grave and bade him goodbye. That night when things had quietened down I asked Unwin to have a temporary cross put up to mark his grave."

[I have read this quote from Williams also, but a shorter version. It is said to be from a letter by Williams to Sir Ian Hamilton's Military Secretary.]

Ironically, his brave actions at Adana had seen Charles awarded the Sultan's Imperial Ottoman Order of Medjidieh. His leadership back then had saved so many Turkish lives. Now these same people had caused his death.

Had Charles gone unarmed into battle because of his earlier connection with the men who had now killed him? In Michael Hickey's book 'Gallipoli' he plainly states that he so loved the Turkish people that he refused to bear arms that day.

Charles Doughty-Wylie Wins the Victoria Cross

R. H. Moppet's painting from the 'Sydney Mail' of June 2, 1915. He was in Sydney and shared the misconception that Doughty-Wylie was killed leading a charge at Anzac Cove. Patriotic artwork was rushed into publications, loosely based on scraps of news from the front.

And so Charles was buried that evening on the hill where he fell, and a wooden cross was erected. The next morning a burial service was read at the graveside by the chaplain of the Munster Regiment. It was plain to all that no-one would have been on that high ground, were it not for Doughty-Wylie's fatal heroics. They would still be huddled on the edge of the beach, under withering Turkish fire.

That simple grave on Hill 141 is the only war cemetery on the Peninsula that consists of just a single grave.

The London press were looking for a hero from Gallipoli. Charles Doughty-Wylie became that hero and was front page news, even before his name was officially known. Reporters starved for specific news spoke to wounded men arriving back in Egypt, and papers were soon running the story of April 26 at V Beach as: *'NAMELESS HERO OF SED-LE-BAR'*

Real names soon came out, and Walford and Doughty-Wylie became posthumous heroes, and the first two Gallipoli Victoria Cross winners to be announced. Their awards became official in June and a joint citation was published in the *'London Gazette'* on the 23rd.

Six other Victoria Crosses were subsequently awarded for fighting of the previous day, but their announcements all came later. [see note on page 298]

The explanation of how Charles ended up on the *River Clyde* is further revealed in a letter that has found its way into the archives of Lilian Doughty-Wylie in the Imperial War Museum. The letter was from a Colonel W. L. Williams, and was written to a Captain Pollen, who was Aide de Camp to a senior officer.

Colonel Williams wrote on 22/5/1915:

"Dear Pollen: I send you full particulars of poor old D Wylie, I had always intended writing to his wife, but not knowing the address I have always postponed it; anyhow I feel sure that particulars coming from Sir Ian or someone on his behalf would be more appreciated. I have always felt responsible as I induced him

to come with me in the 'Clyde;' he did not want much inducing naturally and I feel sure he would have met with the same fate had he landed at Anzac which was his original intention."

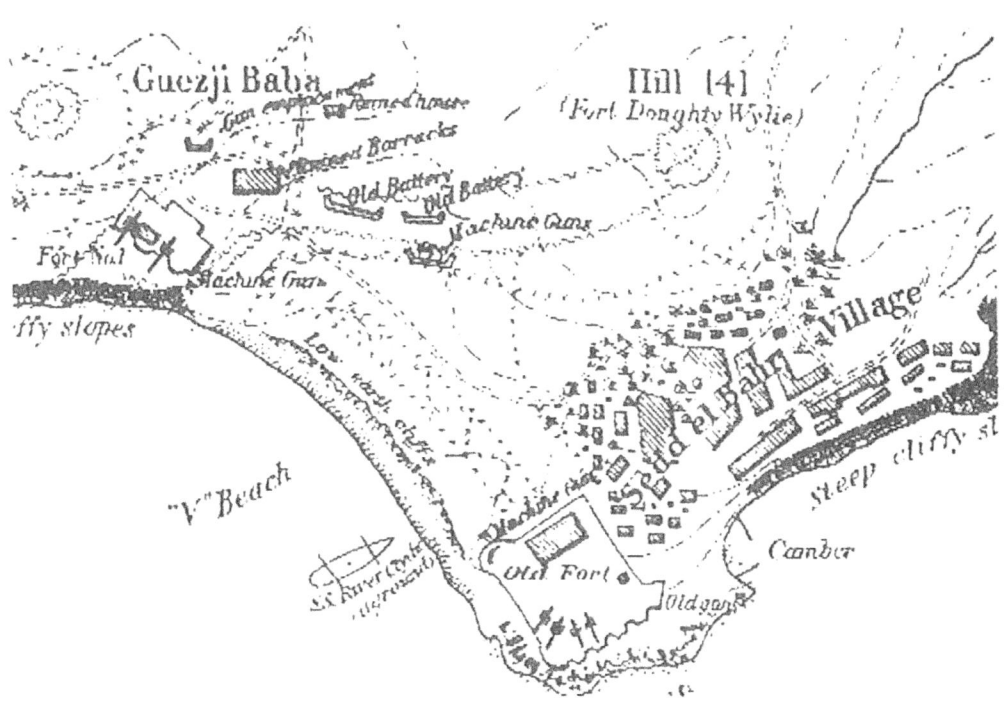

AN EARLY SKETCH MAP OF CAPE HELLES, AND V BEACH.

The old redoubt on Hill 141 was dubbed 'Fort Doughty-Wylie' and retained the name for the duration of the campaign.

General Sir Ian Hamilton was in charge of the overall Gallipoli operation. He knew Charles well, as Hamilton had also been at the Chitral siege in India in 1895, and at the Boer War. [During the Boer War, Hamilton was Kitchener's Chief of Staff.]

Hamilton wrote patriotically and eloquently of the death of Doughty-Wylie in his supposed diary. His entry written that evening of April 26 says:

> *"Hove to off Cape Helles at quarter past five.*
>
> *"Joyous confirmation of Sedd-el-Bahr capture and our lines run straight across from 'X' to Morto Bay, but a very sad postscript now to that message: Doughty-Wylie has been killed leading the sally from the beach."*
>
> *"The death of a hero strips victory of her wings. Alas for Doughty-Wylie! Alas, for that faithful disciple of Charles Gordon; protector of the poor and of the helpless; noblest of those knights ever ready to lay down their lives to uphold the fair fame of England. Braver soldier never drew sword. He had no hatred of the enemy. His spirit did not need that ugly stimulant. Tenderness and pity filled his heart and yet he had the overflowing enthusiasm and contempt of death which alone can give troops the volition to attack when they have been so long under a pitiless fire. Doughty-Wylie was no flash-in-the-pan VC winner. He was a steadfast hero."*
>
> *"Years ago, at Aleppo, the mingled chivalry and daring with which he placed his own body as a shield between the Turkish soldiers and their victims during a time of massacre made him admired even by the Moslems."*
>
> *"Now as he would have wished to die, so has he died."*

Before this long excerpt, I said that it came from Hamilton's 'supposed' diary. By this I mean that I see it as purporting to be a true diary, with daily entries. They are all dated, and in the present tense. (The entry above says that Doughty-Wylie *has* been killed, and is presented as being written that day, just after Hamilton's flagship has *"hove to."*)

The reality is that it was embellished or re-written well after the event. Hamilton's diary* says that Doughty-Wylie was no *"flash-in-the-pan VC winner."* Charles Doughty-Wylie was not a VC winner at all that April day. His award was only official the following June!

Hamilton's 'diary' deliberately re-writes other aspects of the campaign that have more importance than this fairly minor point.   [see note on page 298]

It was hastily written articles like 'VICTORY IN DEATH' (and the painting on page 55) that caused Lilian to write in her diary on May 25:

*Gallipoli Diary was first published by Doran and Company in 1920.

"There is an account in the Daily Telegraph of how Dick was killed. It seems he was disembarking the Australians when they lost a lot of officers & were pushed back. He for some unexplained reason got leave to quit his job and lead them. He led & they got to where they were supposed to get & he was killed. If it's true it's a performance which Dick himself in cold blood would condemn, he condemned the performance which cost young Roberts his life in S.A. & was very strong on men sticking to their own particular job. I can't understand him having done anything so opposed to his own views."

VICTORY IN DEATH.

AUSTRALIANS' CHARGE.

A COLONEL'S HEROIC END.

Details of the death of Colonel Doughty-Wylie during the landing operations in the Dardanelles, which have just reached me (says the "Daily Telegraph's" correspondent in Mitylene), disclose a thrilling story of personal heroism in one of the most glorious charges in our Imperial history.

Colonel Doughty-Wylie, who was on the Staff, had previously been superintending the landing of the Australians. From a transport lying close to the point of disembarkation he was observing their valiant efforts to secure a very difficult position, which they had attempted several times under a terrific fire, and against a strong defence of the well-entrenched Turks.

Many Australians were killed, and the officers were dropping one by one. Colonel Doughty-Wylie eagerly asked permission to lead the charge, and this was given reluctantly in view of his position as Staff officer. Colonel Doughty-Wylie sprang to the head of the Australians, and called them to follow him, which they did with loud cheers.

Under his lead the Colonials, who had lost greatly in numbers, but nothing in spirit, stormed the ridges and trenches, advanced a considerable distance, and captured position after position, inflicting heavy losses on the Turks and enabling the disembarkation of more troops to be effected in comparative safety. The brave Colonel's heroism thus prevented the loss of many lives, in addition to achieving a feat of arms which provided a splendid example, and resulted in a substantial gain.

Having performed this glorious self-imposed mission, Colonel Doughty-Wylie fell at the head of the victorious troops with the satisfaction of knowing that they had reached the goal and consolidated the position.

NAMELESS HERO OF SEDDUL-BAHR IDENTIFIED.

MAJOR DOUGHTY-WYLIE.

CAIRO, May 16.

In a recent despatch from the Press Association's correspondent at Cairo mention was made of a certain colonel who, after the difficult landing operations at Seddul-Bahr and subsequent to the assault on the fortress and the searching of the neighbouring village, led men in a gallant bayonet charge up a hill. The men spoke of this brave man in most eulogistic terms. They said that all he carried was a small cane, and from a band he wore on his arm they gathered that he was a Staff officer. He walked about in the open under continuous fire, talking to the men, cheering them up and rallying them together. Then when they were all ready for the bayonet charge he placed himself in front of them all, and, armed simply with this small cane, led them in a great bayonet charge up a hill. The moral effect of the officer's action was great. The men charged up the hill and cleared the enemy from his position, but, as already recounted, the gallant officer lost his life.

It now transpires that this was Major Doughty-Wylie, and the hill on which he met his death is now known as "Doughty Wylie's Hill." Officers speaking about the major said that no braver man ever lived. He had no business to be there as he was a staff officer, but the loss amongst officers in landing had been so great and the necessity for making headway quickly was so essential, that Major Doughty-Wylie felt that his duty lay in landing the men, and so he went forth fearlessly to his death. The hill will be a lasting monument to his self-sacrifice and great valour.

The right hand article is from the 'Birmingham Mail' of May 26.

It sets the record straight after the earlier headlines such as 'Nameless Hero of Sedd-Le-Bar.' The article at left is typical of the earlier ones rushed into print, where the tale is spun from wrong information.

"DOUGHTY-WYLIE'S HILL."

BRITISH OFFICER'S GALLANT DEED.

A Reuter message from Cairo states that after the landing operations at Sedd-el-Bahr a certain colonel led the men in a gallant bayonet charge up a hill. The men, who spoke of him in the most eulogistic terms, said that all he carried was a small cane, and from a band he wore on his arm they gathered that he was a staff officer. He walked about in the open under a continuous fire talking to the men, cheering them up, and rallying them together. Armed simply with his small cane he led the charge. The moral effect of the officer's action was great. The men charged up the hill and cleared the enemy from his position, but the gallant officer lost his life.

It is now said that this was Major Doughty-Wylie, and the hill on which he met his death is now known as "Doughty-Wylie's Hill." An officer speaking about the major said that no braver man ever lived. He had no business to be there as he was a staff officer, but the loss amongst officers in landing had been so great and the necessity for making headway quickly was so essential that Major Doughty-Wylie felt that his duty lay in leading the men, and so he went forth fearlessly to his death, and the hill will be a lasting monument to his self-sacrifice and great valour.—*Reuter*.

A report of Charles Doughty-Wylie charging to his death, with only his swagger stick.
This is one of the few early reports that didn't have him leading Anzac troops.

The Only Woman at Gallipoli

One day in November, 1915 a woman visited the lonely grave on hill 141.

Think about that scenario. Seven months into a bitter eight month campaign, where men couldn't lift their heads above a parapet for fear of snipers, a woman appeared in their midst.

Soldiers woke to frost on their great-coats, and the first sun of the day brought back the swarms of black flies. Disease was rivalling warfare as a daily threat, and yet a woman came strolling up a path!

Some say there was a pause in the firing, as both sides respected her visit. There has even been conjecture that the Turks stopped firing because they knew whose grave this was – Charles Doughty-Wylie, their decorated hero of Adana. This I find unlikely. In the climate of the time he was now most likely seen as someone who had meddled in Turkey's own affairs.

Also, observers from the Turkish lines may have seen an evening burial back on April 26. Would they have known whose grave it was after the chaos of the second day, or seven months later in November, when the fighting had pushed them further away?

I think not.

The visitor that day may have been his wife Lilian, but I said at the very start that this was a story of a man and two women. The visitor that day may also have been the other woman in Dick's life, because Dick Doughty-Wylie had come to also love another.

There seems no definitive evidence of which woman it was. Moreover, there are conflicting reports and contradictory clues.

This delicious doubt certainly created an enduring mystery!

Chapter 8 - The Other Woman

The other woman in the life of Charles Doughty-Wylie during his final years was in fact Gertrude Bell. Was it Gertrude or Lilian who made the sad journey to that single grave?

Bell was an amazing woman, tackling and triumphing in so many aspects of life that many books have been written to record her achievements. It is difficult to summarise all her life and deeds in anything less than a book, so I will only provide enough of her history to give some appreciation of the woman she was, and to establish her prime place in this story.

Contemporaries described her as the greatest woman of her day, and even our wisdom of hindsight makes this hard to dispute.

Gertrude Margaret Lowthian Bell was born on July 14, 1868. She was born into a family of wealthy industrialists headed by her grandfather, Isaac Lowthian Bell. Isaac and his brothers owned Britain's greatest iron and steel works of the day, and built and operated railways and mines. A family firm manufactured the first 1300 mile long trans-Atlantic cable, and their 'Transporter Bridge' over the Tees remains as a wonder of British engineering

This wealth gave her the independence and means to travel the world throughout her life, endlessly seeking knowledge and adventure.

Her father was Hugh Bell. He later became Sir Hugh, and ran the huge family business when his father and his uncles had all died. Gertrude's birth mother was Mary, but Gertrude did not have the normal pleasure of growing up with her. Mary died just three weeks after giving birth to Gertrude's brother Maurice in 1871. Maurice and

Gertrude were thus brought up by a household of servants and nannies, while Hugh worked six long days a week in the massive family business.

Five years later Hugh re-married. His second wife was Florence Olliffe. Over time Florence became very close to Gertrude, and they loved each other as a mother and daughter. Not surprisingly, Gertrude was also very close to her father, and remained so for her whole life.

In 1878, Florence gave birth to Gertrude's half-brother Hugh, and the following year to a half-sister Elsa. In 1881, Florence completed the new branch of the Bell family with the birth of Mary. Hugh was always called Hugo by the family, and Mary was called Molly.

Gertrude Bell Photographed in Adulthood.

One description has *"Her curls escaping from the pins, to soften the effect of her penetrating gaze."*

Gertrude Bell aged four with her father, Hugh.

Gertrude Bell in her Oxford days, aged only nineteen.

The wealth of the Bells meant that Gertrude could have the best education available. The norm for someone of her station would have been to have home tutoring, followed by some 'finishing' in Europe. Gertrude Bell was one of the pioneers of a more modern path.

In 1886 Gertrude went to Oxford University and took up residence in Lady Margaret Hall. This was a time when most institutions (including Cambridge) were for men only. Seventy years later her arrival was described in a book titled 'Six Great Englishwomen' where she was grouped with Queen Victoria, Charlotte Bronte and Florence Nightingale:

"Just before her eighteenth birthday the new student arrived at Lady Margaret Hall, a striking vivid personality, rather untidy with sharp, straight features, and a mass of auburn hair. And she proceeded to electrify her fellow students by her ease of manner, her self-confidence, her vivacity, her clever talk, and general aptitude for combining physical prowess with intellectual energy."

She then proved the point, doing three years' work in two, and becoming the first woman to win an Honours First in Modern History.

Perhaps it was at Oxford, where she was rapidly growing up and making her place in the world that she took up her lifelong habit of smoking. It would have been a sign that she was a modern and liberated woman. At this time cigarettes weren't seen as harmful, but were clearly the domain of men. If women did smoke, they most certainly didn't do it openly and publicly.

After graduating in 1889, she joined the London whirl of a socialite from a wealthy family, and was presented to Queen Victoria at a debutante ball. Some of her time was also spent travelling abroad, including a stay in Bucharest. She lived there with her uncle Frank Lascelles, a British diplomat.

As the niece of a senior diplomat, she continued to circulate in the highest social circles, even dancing at a ball with King Carol of Romania. She met and talked with famous people. These included Count Von Bulow and Charles Hardinge. Von Bulow would become Chancellor of Germany, and Hardinge became Viceroy of India.

In Bucharest she also met Valentine Chirol. He was a foreign correspondent for *'The Times,'* and they became firm friends. He was considerably older than Gertrude, and she felt able to speak freely in her conversations and correspondence with him. They wrote to each other for the rest of their lives.*

For three seasons Gertrude appeared at all the right functions where a well-connected young lady might meet a suitable and similar young man, but nothing came to be. She was educated, confident, and wanted much more than seemed to be on offer in her age group. Before she knew it, Gertrude found herself being the chaperone of her younger step-sisters Elsa and Mary at the London balls. She was seemingly an old maid in her mid-twenties.

In May 1892 she had a life-changing experience when her uncle and aunt, Sir Frank and Mary Lascelles invited her to stay with them in Teheran. Sir Frank had been transferred from Romania, and was now the ambassador to Persia. Here she could continue to grow and mature, away from the strict social conventions of London that she found so stifling.

Here also, Gertrude saw the desert for the first time, and was cast under a life-long spell by it. She wrote to a friend:

"Oh the desert around Teheran! Miles and miles of it with nothing, nothing growing; ringed in with bleak bare mountains snow crowned ..... I never knew what desert was until I came here; it is a very wonderful thing to see."

It was in Teheran that she had another new experience. She fell in love for the first time in her life. One sunny day Gertrude sat under the shade of the chanar trees in the embassy gardens, and waited for her Uncle Frank Lascelles. There she met Mr. Henry Cadogan.

She wrote home with her early impressions of him, describing him as:

"tall and red and very thin, agreeable, intelligent, a great tennis player, a great billiard player, an enthusiast about Bezique, devoted to riding though he can't ride in the least I'm told, smart, clean, well-dressed, looking upon us as his special property to be looked after and amused. I like him."

---

*This was an age when people wrote letters to each other every day. We are lucky that so many of Gertrude's letters survive. As you would expect the majority are to and from Hugh and Florence.

Henry was a charming 33 year-old First Secretary of the British Embassy. Their relationship soon blossomed into love, and Henry charmed Gertrude in many ways. He was sporting, intellectual and well educated, and even read Persian poetry to her.

Henry Cadogan soon proposed and Gertrude accepted.

She wrote excitedly home with the news, assuming that Hugh and Florence would be as thrilled and excited as she was. Unfortunately, even the grandson of the Earl of Cadogan was deemed unacceptable by her parents. 'Polite enquiries' at home had revealed him to be not good enough or wealthy enough in the family's eyes. He hadn't inherited family wealth, and his salary as a minor diplomat was certainly not at a level to support Gertrude in her accustomed style. His financial issues were further exacerbated by some gambling debts.

Gertrude was summoned back to England, where Hugh and Florence could properly explain their findings and justify their decision (and keep an eye on her!) Surprisingly, for the independent woman that she was becoming, she obeyed the instructions. Talking her parents around may well have been her own reason for agreeing to return.

Henry stayed behind in Persia, and whether they could have got together again at a later date we shall never know. In August 1893, a telegram from Aunt Mary in Teheran was handed to Gertrude. The news was an unexpected bombshell.

Henry Cadogan was a trout fisherman, and had gone up into the cold mountains fishing. Henry had fallen into the icy waters of the river Lar. While he was slim and handsome, he was also slightly built and not physically strong. He caught pneumonia and died.

It was perhaps this grieving for Henry that drove Gertrude in the following years. She put all of her energy into travelling, learning, and adventuring. This became her life now, and she lived it wholeheartedly, trying vainly to distract herself from her sorrow.

Chapter 9 - Years Of Over-Active Distraction

It was now around two decades before World War One was to erupt. For this whole period Gertrude pushed herself in many ways and to many different places. It was as if she feared times when she had an idle body or an idle mind, for this was when she might have been confronted with a certain emptiness of soul. By keeping her every waking moment busy, she sought to avoid any introspection.

For the next seven years she travelled almost constantly, with family or friends. Compared to later years, these were the times of travel to 'ordinary' destinations.

Most of 1898 was spent on a seven month tour with her brother Maurice. It started in the West Indies, United States and Mexico, and then moved on to Hawaii, Japan, China, Hong Kong and Burma. The journey home took in Egypt and Greece, and then went through the Dardanelles to Constantinople.

Either side of this Grand Tour were stays in Italy, Switzerland, France, Austria, Greece again, and Germany. While in Athens she had been to an archaeological dig and spent some time there. She had access to the site because she had an introduction to the chief archaeologist. He was David Hogarth, and Gertrude had been at Oxford with his sister Janet. Gertrude's friendship with both Hogarths was to continue for the rest of her life.

Throughout this whole time, Gertrude was also studying languages. She became fluent in Persian, Arabic, and Latin, and also spoke German and Hebrew.

Her Persian was so fluent, that in 1897 Heinemann published her acclaimed translations of the famous poems of Hafiz. Literal translations were dry and lacked the emotions of the originals. Gertrude had the talent to translate them, and maintain the passions and emotions. One passage quoted in a biography seems even to reflect back on her sorrow at the loss of Henry Cadogan:

> *Songs of dead laughter, songs of love once hot,*
> *Songs of a cup once flushed rose-red with wine,*
> *Songs of a rose whose beauty is forgot,*
> *A nightingale that piped hushed lays divine;*
> *And still a graver music runs beneath*
> *The tender love notes of those songs of thine,*
> *Oh, Seeker of the keys of Life and Death!*

Another passage is even more direct, and perhaps indicates that she was able to colour the translations at times toward her own thoughts and feelings:

My beloved is gone, and I have not even bidden him farewell.

Translations of Persian poetry always had an English readership due to Edward Fitzgerald's popular published translations of the *'Rubaiyet of Omar Khayyam.'*

Omar Khayyam was a mathematician, astronomer, physician, philosopher and poet who lived around the year 1100. Fitzgerald's sometimes liberal translations of the Persian quatrains came out in five well-spaced editions between 1859 and 1889, and were widely read and discussed. They were not only full of tales of the exotic east, but were pitched in a style that we would say today was politically incorrect. The straight-laced Victorians loved them.

Because of her family wealth, Gertrude was able to study seriously in ways beyond normal means. In 1902 she sailed to the eastern Mediterranean port of Haifa and stayed for months. From here she made some excursions to Jerusalem and other biblical places, but the prime purpose was for language study. She hired two tutors, with one teaching her Persian and the other teaching her Arabic. This upper-class, wealthy and single English woman obviously stood out in Haifa. She became a local personality. Her letters to Hugh and Florence show that she enjoyed this new status. Today we might call her a celebrity, but she was happy to simply write home that she had reached the level of a *"Person."*

Her skill with languages allowed her to converse fluently with people she came across in later desert wanderings. Knowing what was really being said allowed her to travel in places considered unsafe for other foreigners and she was able to learn so much more than mere English-speaking travellers. Gertrude was able to avoid the 'Chinese whispers' of interpreters tainting everything with their own opinions, or simply telling her what they thought she expected to hear.

These language skills and her self-confidence often saved her on occasions where she encountered groups of Arab bandits. For some people the encounter would have meant being robbed and possibly killed. For Gertrude Bell it meant giving respect and often gifts to the leader. She was then usually asked to join the camp for the night as an honoured guest. (She never left on a journey without appropriate items like binoculars, to be given as gifts when required. At times she also carried a revolver under her long skirts, but her conversational skills were such that it was never required.)

In the northern summer of 1897, a new aspect of her life developed. The Bell family travelled to Switzerland for a season of Alpine climbing. As was her way, Gertrude took this new interest to a level that far exceeded the rest of the family. She soon left them behind and was hiring personal guides to tackle climbs of ever-increasing difficulty.

Two years later she was back, and climbed for five of the next six climbing seasons. As a wealthy young woman, she could hire the best guides. In her case this meant the brothers Heinrich and Ulrich Fuhrer.

In the 1899 season the three climbed the Meije, and the following year it was Chamonix and the glacial Mer de Glace. In 1901 it was peaks in the Engelhorn, some previously unclimbed, or now climbed by new routes. Gertrude was now becoming famous amongst the climbing fraternity.

Her last season was the late summer of 1904, and the list of conquests finally included Mont Blanc and the Matterhorn. As legacy to the pioneering nature of these seasons of climbing, there are still today two peaks called Gertrudespitze and Ulrichspitze.

Perhaps a brief comparison with the famous English climber George Mallory illustrates that Gertrude's climbing exploits were at the forefront in 1904. She had essentially retired from mountaineering when he climbed Mont Blanc in 1911, and it was the 1920s when he turned his gaze to Everest.   [see note on page 299]

Gertrude Bell in the Alps, with her Father Sir Hugh Bell and their guide.

Gertrude's greatest passion though, was Arabian archaeology. It was this that caused her to keep returning to the deserts. This passion led her to be accomplished in botany, photography, history, sketching and surveying. To get to these places of interest required great treks on camels or horseback. With guides, servants and pack animals she travelled for months at a time through deserts and along ancient trade routes never travelled by westerners (let alone a single woman). In 1913 she was the first woman to be awarded the Gill Memorial Award by the Royal Geographic Society.

More than half a dozen of her books on archaeology were published. UK's Newcastle University also holds an archive of 7000 of her photos, many of which are the first and best records in existence of some of these ancient sites. The photographs are still relevant and useful to archaeologists today, as many were taken before the damaging onslaught of the 'modern' archaeologists of that time.

Gertrude Bell looking very young and new to Archaeology

In 1911 Gertrude was working at a large British archaeological dig at a place called Carcemish. She had arrived expecting her friend David Hogarth to be in charge of the dig, but he had left the site. Instead she met his replacement, another British archaeologist named Leonard Woolley.

As she would with Hogarth, Gertrude would have more to do with Leonard Woolley in later years. The same could be said for the young assistant working with Woolley. He was a slim young man with sun-bleached eyebrows. Under the eyebrows were eyes said to be "*bluer than the waters of the Mediterranean.*"

His name was Thomas Edward Lawrence.

Gertrude never allowed herself a lonely or reflective evening. As well as producing the succession of time-consuming archaeological books, she was always writing. There were letters to friends and family, and articles relating to her travels, discoveries, and photographs. When out in the desert with no mail available, letters were written and carried to the next town with the post. As well as letters there were diaries. They were always carefully kept and full of meticulous detail. In 1907 she published a popular book of her desert travels. The title of the book was *'The Desert and the Sown.'* The title came from one of Fitzgerald's translations of the Omar Khayyam quatrains:

"The strip of herbage strown
That just divides the desert from the sown."

T.E. Lawrence also used the phrase in his *'Seven Pillars of Wisdom,'* when he said:
> *"The difference between Hejaz and Syria was the difference between the desert and the sown."*

Whether he had it in his mind from reading Fitzgerald or Bell we will never know. He was definitely the sort of man to have read both.

Leonard Woolley and T.E. Lawrence at Carcemish

Lawrence wears a pale blazer with the crest of Oxford University's Magdalen College. As a student he lived in at Jesus College, but as a young archaeology post-graduate student he was based in Magdalen. Woolley's blazer possibly has the crest of the New College. The name is a complete misnomer, as the New College was established at Oxford in 1379.

The Only Woman at Gallipoli

A Gertrude Bell Photo of the Palace of Ukhaidir.

This is one of the thousands of pictures she took in the deserts. Keep in mind the practical difficulties. She is travelling the desert by camel or horse, and taking these photos with a large wooden camera and glass plate negatives.

Chapter 10 - A Love Affair

Gertrude Bell had met Charles and Lilian Doughty-Wylie in Konya in 1906. Konya is in south west Turkey and Charles had moved from the army to the diplomatic service as Military Vice Consul. Gertrude called at the consulate to pick up some mail from home when she needed a break from a nearby archaeological dig. During this stay she was not only their dinner guest, but also became a visiting celebrity at consular garden parties. Her travels and achievements were known, and now she could reveal the latest archaeological findings in the region.

Gertrude later wrote to her confidante 'Domnul' Chirol that she had met a "*charming young soldier*" and his "*quite pleasant little wife.*" Her opinions of both are so thinly veiled. Charles she saw as young and charming at 38. (Gertrude was also 38.) Lilian should have been the young one. She was ten years younger than them both!

If Lilian was partially dismissed as just his little wife, she was properly finished off with Gertrude's final comment:

"*He is the more interesting of the two!*"

Whilst Gertrude didn't know the Doughty-Wylies before this, she was already a great admirer of Charles' uncle and namesake. Charles Doughty was a poet, archaeologist, geologist and desert traveller – all things near and dear to her heart. His famous record of his journeys *'Arabia Deserta'* was much read at the time, and Gertrude is said to have always travelled with her own copy.[*]

---

[*]T.E.Lawrence also travelled with a copy of 'Arabia Deserta.' As well as a source of inspiration while travelling in the desert, he said he used it as a textbook on the psychology of Arabs. When a new edition was published after World War 1, Lawrence was honoured to write an introduction to it.

In a letter years later, Charles also mentioned this first meeting with Gertrude. He recalled: *"GB walking in covered in energy and discovery and pleasantness."*

Obviously no ordinary man would have had real attraction for Gertrude. She was a mature woman, intelligent and famous, well-educated and much travelled. In Charles she had now found a man of her own age, who was also well-travelled and a war hero. He shared her love of the Middle East, the desert people, and the rich archaeological history of their civilisations past.

Lesser men were intimidated by her keen opinions and knowledge, but Charles could match her on every front. Here at last was a man, who loved the subtlety of Persian quatrains; who could finish the famous verses she started to recite.

This does not mean that the two became instantly infatuated and inseparable. It was in fact another two years before they had further contact.

In early 1908, Gertrude wrote to Charles with congratulations soon after hearing about his heroics at Adana. This started a regular correspondence. Her letters were initially to Charles and Lilian as a couple, to be read by both.

This of course was the era of letters and the post. It was the era before the telephone, the era that preceded the electronic age of email, Twitter and Facebook that we know today. Luckily for us all, Gertrude Bell was travelling early in her life, and found some fame while still young. She was also friends with many other famous and important people, so that her letters were not like yesterday's shopping list. They were items of interest that her friends and family kept with a knowledge that they would always be interesting. For all these reasons and through the generosity of friends and family there are many of her letters still available to us. We have no in-depth interviews, or scratchy recordings, but much thoughtful and spontaneous correspondence. Parts of some have mundane purposes like seeking a certain hat or piece of material, but then we suddenly get some lines with insights that are a part of history unfolding.

A chance to be alone with Charles was finally engineered by Gertrude in April 1908. Charles was invited to stay at the Bell home at Rounton in Yorkshire. It was nearly three years after Gertrude's visit to Konya and their first meeting. He was a married man, and

Gertrude could divulge to no-one that she had an improper interest in him. Perhaps she wasn't even sure of the strength of her own interest on 18/4/08 when she wrote home before the visit:

"Dearest Mother, … Captain Doughty suggests himself for two nights on Wed. next. It's rather a bore, but I can't say anything but do come for they were exceedingly kind to me. He is a very nice man."

The upshot of his stay was that Gertrude had now confirmed to herself that he was far more than *"a very nice man."* He was to become the man of her dreams, and in her eyes the only really worthy man she had met since the death of Henry Cadogan back in 1893.

Between 1908 and 1912 the passionate nature of her letters had continually escalated, so that they were definitely for his eyes only. A long-distance love affair was being conducted by letter. This was a tribute to the Royal Mail, and other international postal services, as their letters found each other wherever they were.

Realistically, mail was the only way they could have conducted any affair of the heart. Gertrude spent half of 1909 in Syria, Mesopotamia and Turkey. In 1910 she was in Italy and Germany. The next year she was back in the deserts of Mesopotamia to finish measuring the ruins of the palace of Ukhaidir, and to dig some more at Carcemish with David Hogarth and Leonard Woolley. (see photos on pages 73 & 74)

The Doughty-Wylies spent those years mostly in Turkey and Abyssinia, and it was 1912 before Gertrude, Charles and Lilian were all back in Britain.

In the spring of 1912, Charles and Lilian came back to England from his latest posting in Addis Ababa, in what was then Abyssinia. Charles had returned to London to become director-in-chief of the Red Cross Relief Organization. Lilian went on to stay with her family in Wales, and Charles moved into his London flat in Half Moon Street. This was the usual arrangement, because London was uncomfortable for Lilian. Charles briefly explained to Gertrude why the coast was clear when he wrote to her on January 22 saying: *"and tonight I am alone again. My wife does not come here. She quarrelled with my people – all or very near all her own fault."*

On receiving his news, Gertrude hastily left the family home in Yorkshire, and came to stay in her own flat in London. The pretext was that she needed to shop, see her cousins, and had been asked to give a lecture. The real purpose was to be with Charles, something that had been her most secret wish in the preceding years.

This was their first chance to really live and act as a couple, and have what we would now call 'quality time.' There was no need for the pretence imposed last time by the family presence at Rounton. They spent the whole time together going to concerts, to the theatre, and to dinner parties with friends and her cousins.

One imaginative description of the episode said:

> "The flicker and pulse of sexual attraction between them grew stronger with each meeting. The bond was growing – she knew he felt it too."

Inevitably, Lilian returned to London and this brief episode came to an end. Soon after, the Red Cross sent Charles and Lilian Doughty-Wylie off to Constantinople.

Doughty-Wylie in Constantinople in 1912

The Only Woman at Gallipoli

In the summer of the following year (1913) the Doughty-Wylies were back in London again. Gertrude bravely invited Charles to stay again at the family home in Rounton. She apparently chose a time when she could actually invite both Charles and Lilian, knowing that only Charles would be able to come. This wasn't too difficult to achieve, as Lilian dutifully went to her family home in Wales when in Britain.

This visit to Rounton would also create an opportunity for her parents to get to know Charles a bit better. She would need Hugh and Florence on side if the future was ever to be as she hoped.

This was an era when the long driveway of a wealthy family's country estate was travelled constantly by the cars of house guests coming and going. No doubt a house full of other friends had also been invited as a cover for Gertrude's true intentions.

Those summer days were spent playing tennis, touring local sights, and on leisurely picnic afternoons. The evenings found ladies in fashionable dresses from Paris, and men in dinner suits. Polished dining tables were set with the silverware and fine crystal, and the kitchen staff and servants were endlessly busy.

The nights were different at an Edwardian house party. The nights were apparently when a gentleman in a silk robe might knock softly on a woman's door, and the knock was expected and even hoped for. This was a secret and immoral aspect of Edwardian life that Gertrude hardly knew of. In her short adult life, she had spent more nights in a tent, with a camel hobbled outside.

What happened during that country house weekend we cannot know precisely, but their correspondence reveals a lot.

The early letters from Charles were naturally without strong personal emotion. They were as you would expect from correspondence between a couple and their friend.

After 1910, the increasingly emotional level of Gertrude's letters to Charles was plainly evident. In Charles' correspondence, the emotion and the loving talk didn't always follow Gertrude's ever-increasing intensity. She was sometimes perplexed.

Following that weekend in August 1913 when she had bravely invited him again to Rounton, he wrote his thanks. She had hoped and expected a declaration of instant love, and would have been disappointed to read his words. The blandness of his reply fell way short of confirming their future together. Some of her biographers have seen the letter as impersonal, but I see it quite differently. To me it is an opening ploy by Dick. He is testing the waters and leaving it to Gertrude to further increase what is developing between them. Without being too outrageous, he manages to throw in some titbits like *"intimate friends"* and even *"urgent desire."* He wrote on the 15th:

"My dear Gertrude.

I am so very glad you took me to Rounton. I so much enjoyed it – the people, the place, the garden, the room, everything.   And I am so glad you told me things and found you could talk to me. It's that I like – just openness and freedom to say think do exactly what one wants to do. In your mind I think there was a little feeling, natural to first opening of doors. Don't think it wasn't properly appreciated, properly understood. But it was – I love openness – and I've always ever since those early Turkish days wanted to be a friend of yours. Now I feel as if we had come closer, we're really intimate friends. I've gained so much and I want to hold it.

The loneliness – why we are all born alone die alone really live alone – and it hurts sometimes & more hurts the weaker people. But less than others it will hurt you in a way, because you have the courage, the yourselfness, the character that comes through. Is this nonsense or preachments? I don't care. I must write something – something to show you if I can how very pleased I am to be your friend – something to have some meaning, even if it can't be set down, affection my dear & gratitude & admiration & confidence – and an urgent desire to see you as often as possible...   I had to write to you but it's a d.....d bad letter. All the good luck in the world

yours ever CHMDW   [see note on page 300]

Gertrude had to accept Dick's variations in tone, and hope for the best. She would have been in no doubt later, when he placed her on a pedestal above all others including Lilian. He wrote of his innermost feelings:

"You give me a new world, Gertrude, you give me the key to your heart, though I have friends, some of them women, even a wife, they are as far removed from the garden where we walk as east from west."

"The garden where we walk" became a special and meaningful phrase for Dick and Gertrude. For Dick, the garden started out as a place of loneliness, where he fenced himself in to at least find solitude in his unhappy marriage. As time went on he found it hard to change. In a letter to Gertrude he said:

"I who have for years many years lived in my own heart, and have seen the fences around it growing thicker with content. Now I want to take you in, but I can't. You are a bird flying overhead – come and sing in my trees, for in the garden I am always alone."

She had then explained to him that the Persian words for garden and for paradise were one and the same. Walking in the garden together soon meant being with each other and being in paradise.

That their feelings could become so strong, even though this was essentially a relationship being conducted by international mail seems amazing to us today. Just before the war, Charles wrote to Gertrude on one of her treks, not even knowing where or when she might get his letter. She had openly asked for declarations of his love, and would have been pleased to read his tender words:

"A line my dear. I have some minutes, and every minute I miss you... I haven't anything to say – it's only just to be with you a while."

In his mind they were together, even when he was just writing to her. He then opened up his heart and wrote the words she had longed to read:

"I write to you very little. I think I told you why. I can't. But you are great of heart to know even if I don't. Yet you said in the book you wanted to hear me say I loved you. You wanted it plain to eyes and ears – and in the book for me to lean on, you set it down.

I love you – does it do any good out there in the desert? Is it less vast, less lonely, like the far edge of life?

Some day perhaps, in a whisper, in a kiss, I will tell you."

Loving words became the norm as Charles became fully convinced of his own feelings, and he wrote to Gertrude after she posted a personal diary from a desert trek:

"Ah my dear but the book I love is your book. The book of your heart, and I have it now that I am alone held closer….. My dear dream woman – alive you are, but dream woman to me so often and now in Africa – by the book you are evoked and I love it and you….. I am always thinking of you and wanting you."

"When shall I see you? I don't know – like all else it is in the book – only nothing in that hidden page seems quite so important. But the days pass, and I shall be old.

I can't write any more. There aren't any words. But I love you, and kiss your hands and feet.

Dick"

This passionate affair – albeit an affair principally of love letters, naturally forced Charles to be cautious and secretive about mail. Her letters were eagerly devoured. He hung on every word, and they carried him away to the secret garden - but then he was forced by circumstances to destroy these precious things.   In June 1914, he was in Addis Ababa and wrote to Gertrude back in England:

"My dear,   I kept your last letter. I couldn't part with it, not yet at any rate – and I have just been reading it again.   I had a thing to write … a dull thing and it is finished.   And then I wanted you (when don't I want you?) and turned to the locked drawer and the letter – and the spell is said, the charm is strong and I'm floating somewhere out of the world – but I didn't get to happiness & my magic carpet brought me back – only I want you more than ever & therefore write nothing. I have no words to praise your letters – they are magnificent – I love them – and I send them away – it's damnable to live in chains."

Gertrude loved these words of course, but at times her own letters showed she felt some nagging insecurities:

"My dear. Today came your beloved letter written to me on Tuesday to Rounton – the most beloved letter that you have sent me. When I got up this *morning I was hungering for a letter from you – there was none yesterday – that I would not let myself think that there would be one, lest the post should be empty, & then I found that you longed for mine just as much as I longed for yours. Do you understand, it is still so unbelievable that you love me that there are moments when my heart stands still & I tell myself that I must be dreaming."*

She went on about how they would continue to survive those times when war and travels would keep them apart:

"Heart of my heart, let us put doubts behind us. Never for a moment, whatever happens, let us imagine that each of us is not longing for the other longing to pour all thoughts & joys & fears into the other's mind. We shall fade a little from each other's eyes, we shall not remember quite so poignantly the touch of each other's hand; there will be hours and perhaps even days when we shall be thinking of the work we are doing & not each other at every instant; but woven into the intimate consciousness of both of us, wrapped in the deepest fibres of life, each of us carries the other; breathing in the breath of each of us, throbbing in the nerves, beating in the blood."

Gertrude also made it clear to Dick, that for her their relationship must be all or nothing. She would accept no other path:

"We must suffer & we must sorrow, but don't let us give the only unbearable edge to sorrow – uncertainty.

It would be so infinitely foolish, & to tell you the truth I am not sure whether I could endure it…… And therefore I say to you very clearly – I can bear certainty, whether it is the certainty that you love me, or the certainty that you don't love me.

As long as you love me I am triumphant. I don't mind if the paths I walk on are sharp & stony; nothing but my feet feel them. And with all my soul I glory in you & rejoice in you. But if ever it came about that you should love me less, or not at all - then tell me, don't leave me in uncertainty. It would hurt me less to know."

As difficult as this love affair was, it was made even harder by the outbreak of the War. Travel and communication would be more difficult. Charles was acting as a diplomat, but only temporarily. In his heart he was a soldier.

As the World War flared, Charles was sent back to Addis Ababa. His return to Abyssinia was without Lilian, as it was now a dangerous posting. She was soon nursing wounded soldiers in a French hospital in Frevent. Gertrude was also in France, working long hours as a Red Cross volunteer in Boulogne. She had joined their Wounded and Missing Enquiry Department.

Still, their passion raged via the mails. In the middle of November 1914, Charles wrote his most passionate and unreserved letter. Gertrude must have near swooned at the sexual energy it contained:

"Tonight I should not want to talk. I should make love to you. Would you like it, welcome it, or would a hundred hedges rise and bristle and divide? – but we would tear them down. What is a hedge that it should divide us? You are in my arms, alight, afire. Tonight I do not want dreams and fancies. But it will never be. .. The first time should I not be nearly afraid to be your lover?

So much a thing of the mind is the insistent passion of the body. Women sometimes give themselves to men for the man's pleasure. I'd hate a woman to be like that with me. I'd want her to feel to the last sigh the same surge and stir that carried me away. She should miss nothing that I could give her."

Gertrude now truly believed that their future together would happen; that it wasn't just her private dream. She would live with Charles and they would be man and wife.

Around New Years Eve of 1914 she wrote to Charles about the year to come. She saw it as a tumultuous year for two people in love in a time of war:

My dear you said you liked to hear - anything rather than nothing - yes I know. Tonight I should not want to talk - I should make love to you. Would you like it, welcome it - or would 100 hedges rise & bristle & divide? There they might be but we would tear them down in my walls be small - what is a hedge that to [...] a divider [...] its not hedges, not it is [...] [...] is death itself - in dreams in fancy it is not - you are in my arms alight afire - like me - and happy - but Tonight I do not want dreams & fancies - man & woman [created] [...]

Possibly Dick's most passionate Love Letter to Gertrude

"Tonight I should not want to talk. I should make love to you. Would you like it, welcome it – or would 100 hedges rise and bristle & divide?

There they might be but we would tear them down …"

> *"Dearest, dearest, I give this year of mine to you, and all the years that shall come after it. Dearest, when you tell me you love me and want me still, my heart sings – and then weeps with longing to be with you."*

Charles would never again write as openly as he did in November. He was now a soldier and diplomat, and there was wartime censorship. By the 3rd of January he was writing from Addis Ababa:

> *"I hear news that the French are starting a censorship at Jibuti – much good may it do them – but it cramps my style."*

A week later he started to explain in a letter that the nature of his posting might change, when he wrote:

> *"If I sign this treaty then I will be back as Minister instead of the detested ……. (Oh, Lord – I forgot the censor - damn.)"*

Already he was realising he must write in a way that would make sense to Gertrude, but to no one else including the censors. Later in the same letter he wrote metaphorically of their garden paradise again, and said:

> *"for we have never met since except by magic of the garden – loathed censors come not near!"*

For Gertrude it was different. She was so engrossed in her love of Charles that it was simply her everything. Her mind focussed constantly on Charles and their great love, and the rest of her day-to-day functioning felt to her like some sort of charade.

She wrote with passion on January 10, 1915:

> *"Last night I ached for you – it was many days since I had said to you that I love you and live for you; I felt sure that you were beginning to forget but I had to play at being a politician, masquerade and make pretence that I was not the lover which is all I am."*

Two months later, her self-confidence was soaring. She felt so personally liberated by the love growing between them that she cared nothing for the censors. She wrote on March 7:

> *"There's all that parcel of old letters coming to you – may censors be accursed! I don't care. But what will they make of them? Your fragile reputation gone! I laugh, & tears are close behind."*

At the start of March 1915, Charles arrived again in London as a returning diplomat. His departure was to be different. He would be back in uniform and on his way to the Dardanelles. The uniform he would wear was now that of a Lieutenant-Colonel.

His own behaviour reveals more of his own marriage and his depth of feelings. Having precious free days before embarking to join the forces at Lemnos, he made only a brief visit to Lilian on the way through France. He could have brought his wife to London, or if this was impossible, he could have stayed with her in France. He chose instead to spend those days with Gertrude. There is also something unsettling about that earlier letter to Gertrude, and how he positioned Lilian: *"...I have some friends, some of them women, even a wife..."*

Gertrude's status as a Red Cross volunteer gave her more freedom than Lilian. She could run to the man she loved, and she did. On hearing from Charles she left immediately to be with him in London. Her sudden departure surprised the others at the Wounded and Missing Enquiry Department. Her dedication to the task had meant continual days of long, long hours, yet now she suddenly packed and was gone!

After the brief visit to his wife in France, Charles had come back to his London flat in Half Moon Street. They would be in each other's arms again. The four precious days Charles and Gertrude spent together were to be their last, but neither was to know that. The days flew by, and Charles had to leave for the Middle East. Again he made a brief visit to his wife while passing through France.

No sooner had he gone, than Gertrude wrote to him of her loneliness. She was metaphorically near-drowning as it washed over her on the 7th March:

> *"I've been so busy these two days, so intolerably busy. And now I'm alone for an evening – even Tiger has gone away for a fortnight's leave, and I'm alone with you. And lonely in spite of that. It comes over me in waves, desolating*

waves of loneliness. I go under for a bit and then cling to a floating spar of memory, the echo of a phrase, & coming to the surface catch sight across the salt and bitter flood, of some cape or headland of Paradise to which I must win – to which I shall win. I'm going to dine here in my room – I can't stand eyes & faces tonight, nor men, nor talk, nor anything."

Four days later she was less lonely, but more passionate – even erotic – as she referred back to some intimate moments of those recent days together. She regretted being the naive lover that she was. She now saw that she wanted much more:

"I've grown too, in this last fortnight – which hurts me at every point. Let me spread my wings & fly into the sun."

She went on:

"You said passion would spend itself – you'd sleep. Yes, but between my breasts, one arm around me, you're back half-turned to me, & my body part sheath to you, part pillow – I've learnt."

That an affair happened is an obvious confirmation that the Doughty-Wylie marriage was not a truly loving one. Can it have been a happy one from his point of view? Not if only four or five years after marrying, he is developing a relationship with a famous and exciting woman – a woman who makes it clear she wants to take the difficult path. She will be his wife, but never his mistress.

Other signs were there to show that this was no perfect marriage. When Charles and Lilian returned to London from several of their pre-war sojourns, they could have stayed together, or spent time together with each other's families. This was not what happened. Lilian would soon go on to Wales to be with her family and Charles would be alone by choice.

They had met and married in India. It would seem that the surprise of Charles bringing home a wife and a new surname was not altogether pleasing to the Doughty family. Lilian may have even felt unwelcome in Charles' London. One source goes as far as to label Lilian as "*estranged*" from the Doughty family.

Some earlier writings on Charles show a one-sided aspect of the marriage, revealing that:

"it was no secret that the Doughty-Wylies had a difficult marriage. Judith was surely not unaware of his philandering."

Many years later, one of Lilian's own family would mention this philandering. Lilian was the author's Godmother, and I suspect the older family members whispered sometimes of such things, but were publicly in denial. Throwing mud on Dick's reputation would surely have caused some to splash on to Lilian, and there was nothing to be gained from this.

Lilian's godson wrote that in adult life he read an article that said that:

"Dick Doughty-Wylie had a considerable reputation as a philanderer … - but this kind of gossip would not have arisen in my family in which Dick was regarded as a hero."

None of this means that Charles was rushing to end his marriage. Many an Edwardian marriage was loveless, but divorce was no easy or normal path. Gertrude was certainly expecting that Charles would do the right thing and leave Lilian. After he had left London for the last time, she wrote to him. She told him it was his task to do it as soon as possible, and to do it in a socially acceptable way.

If this could be achieved, things would all work out as she hoped. Gertrude wrote on the 9th of March:

"Oh Dick, write to me. When shall I hear! A fortnight since you left – how many fortnights more & then what? I trust, I believe, you'll take care of me – let me stand upright and say I never walked by furtive ways. Then they'll forgive me & you…My people, all people that matter will forgive…. But it's you who should be saying this, should be saying it now, not I. Are you saying it now, realising it, by some divine affinity between us? I'll put a seal on my lips - I won't say it anymore."

Gertrude said she wouldn't say it anymore, because only days previously she had declared her love again. She had also combined it with a virtual ultimatum when she wrote:

"Before all the world, claim me and take me and hold me forever and ever … Can you do it, dare you? When this thing is over, your work well done, will you risk it for me?

It's that or nothing. I can't live without you."

Her cards were on the table. From Gertrude's point of view the next move was surely his.

Gertrude now had a surprise visit from Lilian. Frevent was not far from Boulogne, but was far enough for Gertrude to surmise that Lilian came with more than a social chat in mind. Did she suspect that Gertrude and her husband were more than just friends? Gertrude couldn't have acted her way through any deception if confronted. For her whole life she had called a spade a spade. Lilian too had enough spirit to speak her mind, and may have confronted some of her husband's previous lady friends. An interesting meeting it must have been, but it seems that more was unsaid than said.

What neither woman could have known was that Charles would be dead in a few months. The fight was over before it started. Gertrude wrote to Dick that same night, and she was in real anguish:

"March 10. Today Judith appeared in my office. I asked her to lunch. We talked of nothing save the hospital, but I hated it. Don't make me have that to bear. – Dick, I'm so torn with regret tonight and with desires. They're worse to bear.

I can't keep still or think or speak & I've this night to face, this long night. Don't forget me – you can't hear me? No, not possibly. It's torture, eternal torture, which never loses its edge. Oh my dear it might be ecstasy!"

The visit by Judith (i.e. Lilian) left Gertrude's emotions in a real state, but this certainly wasn't the same for Lilian. We are lucky that in her diary we can read Lilian's take on the same visit. It seems we get to see not just the other side of the proverbial coin, but a coin of an entirely different currency. All is neatly explained in two diary entries:

> *"Miss Moore and Miss Macoy say they won't stay on and nurse another case of Dr. Barrets & I must say I don't blame them but it's a bother for me. I must go to Boulogne to find somebody else tomorrow."* (March 9, 1915)

She then went to Boulogne, and spent a portion of the morning chasing drugs and medical supplies, and wrote:

> *"I went to four shops before I got it. I then went & saw Miss Bell with whom I lunched, She had just been seeing Mr Todd a friend of our Baghdad days..."* (March 10, 1915)

So what was an excruciating episode for Gertrude is just a lunch with a friend for Lilian! While her diaries are obviously less personal than Gertrude's letters of love, it seems plain that Lilian was less suspicious than she might have been.

Gertrude by this time was swamped by work at the Office of Wounded and Missing, as the casualty lists were now in the tens of thousands. Long hours of work were supposed to be her remedy for the frustration of her loneliness, but try as she might to forget, Charles was on her mind the whole time.

Inevitably, a death touched someone in the office one day, but it only caused Gertrude to deflect her own emotions back to her own relationship:

> *"March 12. Since I came back Lil Douglas Pennant has been working in my office. I didn't know her till I came here, we like each other – It's nice knowing her.*
>
> *Today I had to tell her that her brother in the Grenadiers was killed yesterday. I heard late in the evening near 8 o'clock. – We had had a heavy day & were just going away. She was wonderfully brave. She (leant?) on my shoulder & cried a little. She is very reticent – That she should put her arms round me &*

cry on my shoulder meant a great deal. I was so much touched, so much moved – And then she told me about him. She hasn't seen him much these last years. He was restless, travelled a great deal, troubled about the world. "He wasn't happy" she said."

This made Gertrude think about herself and Charles, and she continued:

"Oh Dick, to have lived and died & not been happy. I've had a few resplendent hours – I could die on those & not be pitied. But you – you've not had what you wanted. Live to have it. Let me make you happy … I can give you happiness greater than anything you have ever dreamed. – Soul & body made for you, fitted to you, no flaw in it. Fire to warm you, to heat through you, love to comfort you – take it all from me & make me prouder, more exalted than the most exalted."

Chapter 11 - The Journey To Hayyil

After the end of Gertrude's engagement to Henry Cadogan (too soon followed by his untimely and early death) Gertrude had sought solace through activity. Activity, study and travel seemed to be how she attempted to keep herself from depression, loneliness and sorrow.

Nearly twenty years later she was driven to do a similar thing for a similar reason. In 1913 the World War was a year away. Simmering international tensions were keeping Charles busy and overseas, and Gertrude could endure it no longer.

By late 1913 she had been in England for most of the year. The outward purpose was to finish her latest archaeological book: *'The Palace and Mosque of Ukhaidir.'* More importantly, she was staying at home to be available to Charles, the man she loved. If he could make the time for them to be together, Gertrude would make sure she was nearby.

Their relationship seemed to her to be sometimes uncertain, with some of his correspondence full of philosophy, yet leaving her unsure of his true feelings. The tone of the early letters would wax and wane, so that it seemed that even Charles was unsure of his feelings, and where life might lead. This was not surprising. World affairs were approaching crisis, and he was a married man approaching his own. Separation and divorce from Lilian, followed closely by a relationship with the famous Gertrude Bell would cause huge upheaval. It would completely change life as Charles knew it, and probably end his career as an officer or a diplomat. Why wouldn't he be uncertain?

When the Doughty-Wylies' went to Albania on yet another diplomatic posting, Gertrude found her continued stay in England unbearable. She wrote to a friend: *"If you knew the way I have paced backwards and forwards on the floor of hell for the past few months, you would think me right to try and find any way out."*

She decided to go back to the desert, and back to pioneering archaeology. Perhaps she would also learn more of the mood of the various tribes, so as to be able to report to British authorities in Cairo and India. This would be the longest and most arduous journey she had undertaken, and she would write two sets of diaries along the way. One set was for the authorities, but the other set was solely for Charles. Writing something for him every day was a long way from being with him, but it was all she had.

The journey put her life in real danger, from the elements and from war-like and murderous Arabs. This seemed to be what part of her wanted and needed at this time.

She would journey to Hayyil in central Arabia. This was an ambitious challenge. It was to be a circular trip of 2500 kilometres, and would take many months. From Damascus she would head south through Amman and Ziza. Ziza was a station on the Hajj railway line later targeted so skilfully and relentlessly by Lawrence and his Arabs. When her party crossed the tracks and turned east towards the desolate interior of the Arabian Peninsula, there were three months of emptiness in front of them. This journey would include a long crossing of the sandy desert of the Nefud. It was the desert of Hollywood movies, with endless hills of pure sand. Later, there would also be a crossing of the Nejd desert, which was the opposite. The Nejd was a desert of stones. Some earlier attempts on the Nejd had killed unlucky travellers.

None of this was off-putting to Gertrude. In reality, the opposite was the case. The mental pressures of her world were far more daunting than the physical journeys ahead.

Gertrude knew of the Nejd desert from *'Arabia Deserta,'* the 1888 book by Charles Doughty (Dick's uncle) and it warned all later travellers of the difficult nature of the journey. The Nejd was a tougher place than the deserts of our imagination. There was no vegetation and very little water. In *'Seven Pillars of Wisdom,'* Lawrence was unusually brief when he said it was simply:

"an area of gravel and lava, with little sand in it."

At this particular time, there were new dangers to be faced in the interior, above and beyond the physical ones. A Bedouin tribal war was going on in the Nejd, between the Sauds and the Rashids. Gertrude was well aware of this, and should have used it as the final reason to cancel. Instead, it seems the danger was the final reason she decided to go. The Sauds were being supported by the British, with guns and money. The Rashids had the support of Turkey, and Turkey was getting support from Germany. No-one could foresee the eventual outcome at the time, but Ibn Saud would eventually defeat Ibn Rashid while World War One raged all around.   [A few years later, Ibn Saud was still being actively feted by the British, as they sought to find strong and British-minded leaders amongst the post-war Arabs.]

From Hayyil, the return to Damascus would involve heading north and east to Baghdad, and then north and west to Damascus.

With international intrigue compounding inter-tribal war, neither Turkey nor Britain needed Gertrude Bell to come wandering into the middle of it all. Authorities from both sides were discouraging at best, but could never really stop this determined woman. In one of her early diary entries, it is as if she is chatting to Charles:

"... and what is more, do you know I am an outlaw? Louis Mallet has informed me that if I go on towards Nejd my own government washes its hands of me, and I have given a categorical acquittal to the Ottoman Government, saying that I go at my own risk."

Mallet was the British ambassador to Turkey. His outward discouragement was his duty as an ambassador in a foreign country. In reality, there would have been many British security people keen to hear Gertrude Bell's fresh and detailed accounts of the region.

On 27th November, 1913 Gertrude wrote to Florence to allay her motherly fears. Gertrude would have known very well that it was far from the truth:

"Moreover, it looks as though I have fallen on an exceedingly lucky moment. Everyone is at peace. Tribes who have been at war for generations have come to terms and the desert is almost preternaturally quiet."

Two days later she wrote to her father, and again made light of the journey:

> *"I sent you today a telegram which I fear will rather surprise you, asking you to make the National Bank telegraph 400 pounds to my credit...."*

And then:

> *"there never was a year more favourable for a journey into Arabia than this. The desert is absolutely tranquil, and there should be no difficulty whatever in getting to Hayyil."*

Hugh may well have been surprised at the first part. The money was about three years of wages for one of his steel mill workers, and this was extra money to top up her personal funds. While it is difficult to update money from earlier times to sums of today, it would be realistic to multiply the 400 pounds by about fifty times. This was a major expedition.

The journey was obviously bigger than anything Gertrude Bell had ever tackled. From the starting point in Damascus she had to buy camels and hire experienced guides who knew the area. As on previous journeys her trusted and favourite servant Fattuh was to be by her side. Fattuh was a big man, and was a Christian Arab from Aleppo. His manner was always more of a guardian than a mere servant, and Gertrude trusted him absolutely. This time though he was ill, and the illness threatened to delay the departure of the party. It was thought that he had typhoid. She finally started without him, but planned for him to rejoin the party in Amman. Along the way she would also hire a succession of *'rafiqs.'* These were local tribesmen, generously paid to ensure her safe passage through areas known for murderous thieves.

The logistics were beyond any of her earlier journeys. If she pondered on travelling light, or taking anything and everything she might require, she settled on the latter approach. Apart from Fattuh there were six other men and 17 camels. The camels were loaded with theodolites and survey instruments supplied by the Royal Geographic Society, who had by now made her a Fellow. There were also large supplies of food, cigarettes, clothing, tents, cameras, film, cartography equipment and stationery, medicines, rifles, and binoculars and telescopes for use and also as gifts. As well as these essentials, the camel packs included a small library (with the complete works of

Shakespeare of course), linen tablecloths, silver cutlery and candelabra, evening wear including dresses, bags and a fur, and even a canvas bath!

When Gertrude and her caravan were finally underway in mid-January, she carried the last letter she would receive from Charles for many months. In it he promised imaginatively to: *"sit by your tent and when you sit on your camel and go rocketing away. I'll leave my heart in your lap."*

Gertrude expressed her relief at her eventual departure in her entry to Charles' diary on January 18, 1914. She had finally escaped what she saw as the hellish pacing of her idleness in London:

"But when two days ago I cut myself loose from civilisation I felt as if I had cast down all burdens. And I do nothing now but look onwards, till tomorrow, till next day – no further; but it is far enough."

Fattuh

Gertude's trusted right hand man on many of her desert treks. She wrote: *"Never in the world was anybody given more devoted friendship and service than he gives me."*

She was now alone in the desert with just her diary to Charles. The hired helpers and the camels were part of the everyday journey, but in her heart and mind they didn't exist. In a way it seemed to her that she was alone with him, and the rest of the world was a far-off place.

As always her descriptive letters set the scene perfectly, as in a letter to her father on February 12:

"We watered our camels and filled our water skins and then turned our faces S.E. into the Nefud. The Nefud is a great stretch of sandhills, seven or eight days journey across. Marching through the Nefud is like marching through the Labyrinth. You are forever winding around deep sand pits, sometimes half a mile long, with banks so steep that you cannot descend. They are mostly shaped like horseshoes and you wander along until you come to the end and then drop down into low ground, only to climb up anew. How one bears it I don't know."

Gertrude Bell and her party arrived exhausted in Hayyil at the end of February. They had defied the odds and circumstances, and crossed the sandy Nefud and the stony Nejd deserts.

They were escorted into the ancient fortress city by Rashid's men. Her reception was like that of an arriving queen, and she was accommodated in part of the Royal Palace. Hayyil was still a place of antiquity, and she found herself in a world of slaves, eunuchs, and a harem of wives and concubines. Murderous in-fighting amongst Rashid's own tribe, and with their arch enemy Ibn Saud had led to the death of most of the male line. The current Amir was away fighting with his troops, even though he was only 16! He had come to power because three of his predecessors had been assassinated in recent years.

By the end of the first week of March, 1914 Gertrude realised that her status in Hayyil had subtly changed from being a guest to that of being a prisoner. Her unease at remaining in this blood-thirsty place is evident in her diary entry of March 2, where she says:

"In Hayyil murder is like the spilling of milk … And to the spiritual sense the place smells of blood. Twice since Khalil was here have the Rashids put one

another to the sword – the tales around my camp fire are all of murder and the air whispers murder."

A week later she wrote again of the ruthlessness of the place: *"… when one of the Rashids murders the reigning Amir and takes his place (which frequently happens) he is careful to murder his slaves also, lest they should revenge the slain."*

The time she was held here enabled her to sit with the women of the harems. The women were mere chattels. If their man was killed, the murderer took his wives and his camels. A powerful diary entry summarises the savage existence:

"Here were these women, wrapped in Indian brocades, hung with jewels, served by slaves … They pass from hand to hand … The victor takes them, his hands bloody from murdering their husbands and children."

Suddenly, her situation changed. She was free to go, and money that she had sent ahead from Damascus was finally handed over. The diary entry for March 6th showed a relieved tone when she wrote:

"An hour later came in my camels and after dark Sayyid again with a bag of gold and full permission to go where I liked and when I liked. And why they have now given way, or why they did not give way before, I cannot guess. But anyhow I am free and my heart is at rest – it is widened."

She left the next morning, and the epic journey continued to Baghdad. Here she posted the private diaries to Charles in Addis Ababa, and received some much anticipated letters from him.

Before heading into the desert she had written him a manifesto of their lives together, which she said was her book of Genesis. This new mail gave her his reaction, when she finally read his letter posted nearly two months earlier:

> *"Where are you? It's like writing to an idea – a dream. It's you that are free to wander as a cloud. I'm in prison. How can I write? There are so many things in that book of yours, my queen of the desert, so much that runs in my mind. You are right of course about evasions and deceits…."*

He went on with what he realised was a letter that reflected his love, but also his mood of melancholy that night:

> *"Is it that gloom is so black on me tonight? Or is it regret for things lost, great and splendid things I find in your book – you, your mind & body, and the dear love of you – all lost.*
>
> *No – I know they are not lost – only tonight's all black. Sleep well wherever you are, in your tent, under the stars your friends…. Would you like me to write you a love letter, to say in some feeble whisper what the wind outside is shouting, to say my dear how glad & grateful and humble I am when I think of you, when I read the book – but all that belongs to the garden – it will never be said, not adequately – it cannot be… I'll go to bed. Send me a short cut of your desert and we'll dream dreams. Dick"*

After some time in Baghdad she recuperated enough to tackle the last leg to Damascus – just another 600 kilometres through the Syrian deserts. Some camels, gear, and men had been disposed of, and a lighter and quicker party finally arrived back at Damascus in the first days of May, 1914. Gertrude had been six months away.

It had been by far her longest and most difficult journey, and was to be her last major desert trek. In a way, she could see that she had gone for the wrong reasons. Rather than make a journey for the sake of the discoveries it would reveal, she had done it all to escape the frustrations of her love life with Charles. The last leg of the journey should have left her with feelings of triumph, but this was not the case. It only brought her the realisation that the journey was never more than a distraction, and that her situation with Charles was as before.

At this time she heard from Charles. He had received the diary she posted from Baghdad, and several letters. He wrote from Addis Ababa on April 26. Gertrude had joined him in his garden, but April 26 was a more auspicious date than he knew. He had exactly a year to live:

"They came by last mail your letter and your diary. Today is a great feast to which I should have gone, but I sent my wife and Capt. Sanford my No. 2, pleading despatches and business for this afternoon's post, …. But what I did once alone, was to re-read your letter…

I don't want to talk or write, but I want to be with you – you and I all alone for a little, in the locked garden with the high wall where I live and you too now. That is where I have loved my mistress that you hated & have forgiven. Solitude – and great and dear she will always be, for you too are now a worshipper, for now we walk in her garden."

The Royal Geographic Society later awarded Gertrude a gold medal for the journey to Hayyil, and a lot of the knowledge she gained would be useful to Britain in the coming war. This meant little to her as she had gained no personal satisfaction.

She wrote to her mother about the medal and said: *"It was an absurd thing to give me – they must have been hard up for travellers this year."*

Gertrude Bell then made her way back to Britain for more rest, and was there when the War broke out in early August.

Coffee Being Made in the Desert

The making of coffee was a ritual in the desert. When it was being photographed by an English woman it became an event.

Gertrude's photo of her party finally leaving Hayyil

Chapter 12 - Gertrude Bell and Lilian Doughty-Wylie in The Early War Years

When war broke out, Gertrude wasn't the sort of woman to stay at the family home in Rounton, Yorkshire and spend her days knitting socks for the men in France!

The Ottoman Empire stretched from the Dardanelles almost to the vital Suez Canal. The southern lands were controlled by an assortment of Arab sheikhs, kings and bandits, albeit under distant Ottoman rule.

Britain needed to know the mood of these southern tribes if it was to attack the Ottoman Empire, and open up a second front. Would the Arabs support Britain as liberators, or would they stay with Constantinople?

Bell was the best qualified person in the world to answer this. She well understood the politics of the tribes and races involved. As an esteemed foreign visitor she had dined as guest of honour with the most important leaders of these regions.

Her grasp of local tongues had always allowed the dinner conversations to go beyond the polite small talk that would have been expected via interpreters. She was inquisitive enough to pursue what it was that her hosts really thought.

She spent months writing detailed reports for the War Office, and the knowledge in them certainly found its way to the people at the top. Churchill would have considered the opinions of Miss Bell (as he called her) when he was promoting the Gallipoli invasion. These early reports and others later during the war would have also encouraged the British campaign with T.E. Lawrence and the armed Bedouins during the second half of the war. [see note on page 301]

(In April 1927, her old friend David Hogarth had become president of the Royal Geographic Society. At a dinner to honour Gertrude Bell he said: *"Lawrence, relying on her reports, made signal use in the Arab campaigns of 1917 and 1918."*)

Gertrude Bell was an articulate and expressive woman, even when writing in a military vein. Here as example is a brief summary she wrote of the Turkish army, in her book *'The Desert and the Sown'*. It is not the dry and colourless report that would be expected from a regular army man:

> *"Arabic-speaking races are all eager to be at each other's throats, and only prevented from fulfilling their natural desires by the rugged half-fed soldier who draws at rare intervals the Sultan's pay. And this soldier . . . is worth a good deal more than the hire he receives. Other armies may mutiny, but the Turkish army will stay true to the Khalif; other armies may give way before suffering and privation, and untended sickness, but that of the Sultan will go forward as long as it can stand, and fight as long as it has arms, and conquer as long as it has leaders. There is no more wonderful or pitiful sight than a Turkish regiment on the march; grey beards and half-fledged youth, ill clad and often barefoot, pinched and worn – and indomitable. Let such as watch them and salute them as they pass: in the days when war was an art rather than a science, of that stuff the conquerors of the world were made."*[*]

Perhaps Winston Churchill should have given more attention to the content of a report like this, as we now give our attention to its abundance of style. The Gallipoli invasion plan almost relied on the assumption that the Turkish troops would flee at the first sight of the might of Britain.

This was another of the major misjudgements of his career. If nothing else, they were now battle-hardened from the unsuccessful Balkans War, where the Ottomans effectively lost Serbia, Montenegro, Greece and Bulgaria from their Empire. At Gallipoli there were differences. The soldiers were well led by experienced Turkish and German officers. The fighting would now be in familiar territory, and in defence of their true homeland.

---

*The whole description is also quoted in the Marshall Cavendish 'Encyclopaedia of World War One.' It comes in the section dealing with Turkey's entry into the war.

Compare this to the Allied forces. They were essentially young and under-trained volunteers. All were certainly keen, willing and patriotic, but with a certain naivety as they headed off to the horrors of war. Many were expecting it to be an overseas holiday and their great life adventure. Australian and British recruiting posters certainly promoted it this way. The officers were a mixture of the young and inexperienced, with some older regulars. The experience of the older ones was strangely irrelevant here; that of the guerrilla war against the Boers, or colonial service in India. Without a doubt, the best of the officers were already busy in France.

In November 1914 Gertrude volunteered for the Red Cross. She joined the Wounded and Missing Enquiry Department in their Boulogne branch office. Before long she had taken charge, and enlarged Boulogne to be the head office.

The Army of course, had bigger things to do. It allowed the Red Cross an ever-expanding role in dealing with the thousands of enquiries from home about the dead and missing. While the Enquiry Department had started out only providing information about officers (i.e., gentlemen!) it was now covering all ranks. World War One was in fact the first war when the British attempted to keep proper details of the names of ordinary soldiers. Prior to this there had only been officers and ranks of nameless others. [see note on page 302]

In March 1915 the Department moved its European headquarters back to London, with Gertrude in charge. In the early days of the War the wounded had been in hospitals on the Continent. Now they also filled the British hospitals, and the assortment of halls, barracks, and stately homes that had been acquired. The role of the Department got even bigger when the Foreign Office added the task of cataloguing and collating the long lists of Allied POW's in German prison camps.

The scale of these offices of the Red Cross can be appreciated, when you consider that in May 1916, just the branch that followed up Australian servicemen had 60 staff in their London base alone.

When the Great War broke out in 1914, husbands and wives were separated as their country called on them, and things were no different for the Doughty-Wylies. Charles was soon preparing to join Sir Ian Hamilton in Egypt.

Before they left Abyssinia, Charles and Lilian offered to fund a 100 bed hospital in France, almost certainly with Lilian's own money. The British War Office refused the offer, but the French did not.

Lilian thus became the directrice of the Anglo-Ethiopian Red Cross Hospital in France. It was based firstly in Frevent, and later at St. Valery-sur-Somme. The hospital cared primarily for French soldiers.

Lilian (at very front left) with her staff in France

The unusual hospital name came about because the ruler of Ethiopia (ie Abyssinia) made a slightly odd contribution that is explained later in this book.

Here she was close to the fighting, and as always was able to achieve great things under difficult circumstances. Her diaries show that dealing with the patients was incredibly difficult, but added to this were many problems with the French Red Cross, and the assortment of staff she had to work with. She was there until at least October 1915, six months after Charles had been killed.

These were hospitals filled with men who had been felled by machine-gun fire, or had gaping wounds from hot shrapnel. Amputation cases were common, and so was the fatal gangrene that often followed. Many admissions had no chance. They arrived on stretchers, but would leave in coffins. This war was a generation after the Crimean war, and its lessons of hygiene and the treatment of infection had been learnt. Unfortunately for so many, the wonder of the WWII sulphur drugs were still another generation ahead.

On April 22, 1915 the Germans announced a new phase of this terrible war, when they opened the valves on 5700 cylinders of chlorine gas near Ypres. The gas turned a man's skin brown. It reacted with the body's moisture to become hydrochloric acid, and burned the eyes, nose, throat and lungs. Victims couldn't be bandaged or touched without excruciating pain, and had to be set up in the hospital bed with a sheet on a frame like a tent. The worst cases didn't suffer for long, because they drowned as their lungs filled with a yellowish froth.   As it wafted across the battlegrounds, the gas was heavy enough to lie in shell holes and the bottom of trenches, so sometimes the victims were wounded men already on stretchers.

Every ambulance that arrived was full of new horrors, and Lilian and the nurses, doctors and surgeons would never have imagined how bad it could be.

By April 1916 she was far away from the mire of Europe. She had become the matron-in-charge of a British hospital at Mudros, the main town on the island of Lemnos. She had left the Red Cross and the French, and was now caring for British servicemen again.

Lemnos is just over the horizon from Gallipoli, and it was from here that the invasion had been launched a year earlier. Her husband had been in his grave for a year, and now she was living and working nearby.

Information is lacking, and not everything is known about what path Lilian was on at this time, and definite records concerning her whereabouts at the end of 1915 do not seem to exist.

Chapter 13 – The End of the Gallipoli Campaign

After four months of battle the initial optimism was now gone, and various factors changed. People started to seriously question the continuance of the campaign. Bulgaria entered the war as an enemy in September. German guns and ammunition could now come by train directly from Germany to Istanbul.

The Dardanelles Committee in London started to consider all options but the outlook was worsening. Stopford reported to the War Office from Suvla and was critical of Hamilton.

Keith Murdoch* was an Australian journalist who went to Gallipoli and then back to London. He also wrote a report very critical of Hamilton and his underlings, and gave it to Asquith. The Prime Minister passed it on to the Dardanelles Committee. Even though it was seen as having some exaggeration and over-simplification, it found plenty of interested readers.

Ian Hamilton was recalled in the middle of October, and was replaced by General Sir Charles Monro. Monro visited Helles, Anzac and Suvla in a one-day tour on October 30, and recommended evacuation in a report the very next day. Kitchener was now sent out to see what was really going on. Before he left he was all for fighting on and rewarded Monro's speedy evaluation by replacing him with Lt. General Sir William Birdwood.

Kitchener toured Gallipoli for a week in early November. He proposed an assortment of attacks and even new landings to the General Staff, but finally was forced to face the facts. Evacuation was the best way out.

*Father of Rupert Murdoch and grandfather of James Murdoch.

While the War Office wavered, officers on the Gallipoli Peninsula seriously wondered if the increasing storms would even allow a successful evacuation. Finally it was decided in early December to evacuate Suvla and Anzac. Both evacuations were carried out successfully on December 18 and 19.

By late December it was decided that Helles would go the same way, and this happened on January 8 and 9, 1916.

Heavy losses were expected during the evacuations, but there were virtually none. This was primarily because the evacuations were unlike much that went on during 1915. For a change, they were well planned and carried out according to the plans. It may have been also that the Turks were complicit, and allowed the almost seamless night-time operations.

The Gallipoli campaign was over.

Of course the invasion of the Gallipoli Peninsula was never going to be simple. There was nothing easy here. A vivid description of the hardships was published before 1916 was over.

Famous author and poet John Masefield was 36 at the outbreak of war. He volunteered for the Red Cross and was on site as a self-funded nautical ambulance-man. His account of the campaign was published in 1916, and eloquently described how tough it really was. The words spill out and drive us to an understanding of the real horrors:

> *"Those who wish to imagine the scene must think of twenty miles of any rough and steep sea coast known to them, picturing it as roadless, waterless, much broken with gullies, covered with scrub, sandy, loose, and difficult to walk on, and without more than two miles of accessible landing throughout its length.*
>
> *Let them picture this familiar twenty miles dominated by three hills bigger than the hills about them, the north hill a peak, the centre a ridge or plateau, and the south hill a lump. Let them imagine the hills entrenched, the landings mined, the beaches tangled with barbed wire, ranged by howitzers and swept by machine guns, and themselves three thousand miles from home, going out*

before dawn with rifles, packs, and water-bottles, to pass the mines under shell fire, clamber up the hills under the fire of all arms, by the glare of shell bursts, in the withering and crashing tumult of modern war, and then to dig themselves in a waterless and burning hill while more numerous enemy charge them with the bayonet.

And let them imagine themselves enduring this night after night, day after day, without rest or solace, nor respite from the peril of death, seeing their friends killed, and the position imperilled, getting their food, their munitions, even their drink, from the jaws of death, and their breath from the taint of death, and their brief sleep upon the dust of death. Let them imagine themselves driven mad by heat and toil and thirst by day, shaken by frost at midnight, weakened by disease and broken by pestilence, yet rising on the word with a shout and going forward to die in exultation in a cause foredoomed and almost hopeless.

Only then will they begin, even dimly, to understand what our seizing and holding of the landings meant."

Chapter 14 – If Only….

Winston Churchill's early career was marred by some unwise decisions, but there was no denying he had a memorable turn of phrase. He summarised all those nearly successful aspects of the Gallipoli campaign in only four words:

"The terrible 'ifs' accumulate."

Many have looked back and written of the Gallipoli Campaign, its eventual failure, and the myriad reasons why it failed. At so many times it was the campaign that looked like succeeding, and should have succeeded, but never quite did.

Some writers have said Kitchener was at fault during the naval phase. It is said he held the troops in Europe and Egypt, when opportunities occurred to capture forts left reeling after the naval barrage. Instead, the ships withdrew and allowed Turkey the chance to recover and regroup.

It was actually Kitchener who sent all of the Anzac troops from Egypt to Lemnos on February 16, a month before the big naval attack. More likely, we should allocate the Navy-only approach as a legacy of Winston Churchill. He had a low opinion of Turkey and her defenders, and saw the ships alone as more than enough.*

A telling comment is in the diary of Lady Hamilton, (wife of General Sir Ian Hamilton). She notes that Churchill was *"very anxious in case it would come out publicly that Kitchener had wanted troops to go in before the fleet had eliminated surprise."*

---

*Churchill's early career wasn't characterised by the leadership and qualities of wisdom he showed during World War II. One of the references in the bibliography here is 'Gallipoli' by R R James. In 1970 he also wrote about the early career of Winston. The book's title was 'A Study in Failure.'

When you consider the enormous losses of men and ships, March 18 was a disastrous day, yet some who were there certainly thought the Allies were on the cusp of victory, but couldn't see it.

Roger Keyes returned to the scene of the naval battle, late on March 18. He arrived after dark on the destroyer HMS *Jed*. His orders were to look for HMS *Ocean* and HMS *Irresistible*, to sink them if they were still afloat, and pick up any stragglers from the water.

Keyes felt that no matter the level of carnage that the afternoon had brought, victory was close. He wrote:

"I had a most indelible impression that we were in the presence of a beaten foe. I thought he was beaten at 2 pm. I knew he was beaten at 4 pm – and at midnight I knew with still greater clarity that he was absolutely beaten; and it only remained for us to organise a proper sweeping force and devise some means of dealing with drifting mines* to reap the fruits of our efforts."

Some evidence certainly backs up what he said. Few of the forts were seriously damaged, but Turkish guns had fired 2000 rounds that day, and few of the high-explosive armour-piercing shells remained. Fort Hamidieh had only seventeen left, and at Kilit Bahir there were only ten. March 19 might have been the day when the glorious deeds of the previous day bore fruit, but the chance was lost.

If only mine-sweepers had come in that night, with destroyers to cover and destroy the coastal searchlights, the way to the Narrows would have been cleared.

The mighty Allied fleet relied on mine-sweeping being done by converted trawlers with crews of civilian fishermen. They had no urge to be dead heroes. Their slow work in the strong currents caused more lost opportunities to advance up the narrow waterway. When they were eventually given Navy commanders and brought closer to the command structure, the time had passed.

---

*Without knowing of the nocturnal mine-laying deeds of little *Nusrat*, the Allies assumed mines were being sent drifting down the Narrows in the current.

Thus it would be realistic to look at the naval campaign and the mighty allied battleships, and say that it was the smallest ships that let the Allies down. Ironically, it was the smallest Turkish ship that turned the tide on the decisive day. I refer of course to the *Nusrat*.

Any wonder a replica sat on the shore in the naval museum at Canakkale, to be revered by Turks for playing a role way above its proper station.
[In March 2011, the replica on shore was replaced by a real floating replica, which can put to sea on special days to re-enact the heroic deeds.]

The land campaign was seen by most of the older books as similar to the naval campaign, in that it was a string of missed chances and near successes. Most of these opportunities were similar to the 'non-attack' by the fleet on March 19. Speed of advancement should have been seen as the essence of success on shore but a different viewpoint was coming from the top man.

Sir Ian Hamilton's mindset before the landings was that just being ashore was enough. In his diary Hamilton gives himself away when he says:

> "In my mind the crux was to get the army ashore. ... Once ashore, I could hardly think that Great Britain and France would not in the long run defeat Turkey."

The reality was that the Allies started with a vast superiority but didn't know it. Captured prisoners said that originally, the Cape Helles area was defended by only 1000 troops. They weren't believed, and the gist of Hunter-Weston's instructions was that everyone was to hang on and expect the worst.

Churchill's 'ifs' are piled high. If only the Allies had taken their chances! If only Hamilton had accepted that Hunter-Weston was fixated on V and W beaches, and had insisted on sending the later waves of troops to S and Y. (He suggested it, but was essentially ignored.) Turkish forces would have been out-flanked and cut off, and at the mercy of their attackers.

If only more troops were put ashore at X Beach. They could have attacked to the south-east and routed the Turks defending V and W beaches at Cape Helles.

If only Hunter-Weston had more sense of urgency during the first days. If the First Battle of Krithia had been only a day earlier, there might have been success. Turkish documents (only fairly recently released and translated) show that the defences were on the cusp of collapse, and reinforcements had arrived with only hours to spare.

Hunter-Weston was not a successful commander, and left the Peninsula on July 23. The reasons given range from sunstroke to enteric, but Ian Hamilton called it a breakdown. Hunter-Weston certainly lost the confidence of those around him ten days earlier, when a badly planned and disorganised attack caused 500 needless casualties.

As that first day unfolded back at Y beach, Matthews had Krithia and the strategic hill of Achi Baba there for the taking. The Turkish defenders had retreated to avoid the barrage of the ships offshore. Hamilton watched through binoculars from the HMS *Queen Elizabeth* and described Matthews' forces as *"dawdlers by the sea."*

If only they had dawdled unopposed to that low hill, they might have controlled the whole end of the Peninsula. To further elevate this from a blunder to a farce, they evacuated. Hamilton said he did nothing, because he 'assumed' Hunter-Weston had ordered them out! [see note on page 302]

To the north there were soon 4000 Anzacs faced by 700 Turks. If only their headlong initial assault had been over easier ground. If only a larger beach-head had allowed less of the initial chaos and mixing of units.

What of the French at Kum Kale? Here was one landing where the attackers seemed better organised than the defenders, yet ironically they were the first troops evacuated. If they had provided a strong point on the Asian side, it might have permitted the navy to try again. That Hamilton pulled them out is no surprise. Preceding British wars in preceding centuries had been wars of the Army or wars of the Royal Navy. Here it went unrecognised that success could have happened if this had been a war of both together.

As to the failure of Suvla, it was seen as a distilled version of the whole campaign: keen and well-meaning troops were badly led. They could have succeeded but never quite did. Australia's Charles Bean was the war correspondent who saw the whole Gallipoli campaign unfold. His diaries don't hold anything back when it comes to damning the poor leadership he saw. [see note on page 302]

Newer works have seen through the jumbled pile of 'if-onlys.' Their drift is more that the whole concept of the land invasion was folly. One such book is Scott Anderson's 'Lawrence In Arabia.' In about a hundred words he makes it seem clear and obvious that the whole concept of the Gallipoli Peninsula landings was flawed. They were sure to fail:

"the most basic rules of military logic – even more common sense – argued against it. Not only would a landing force there be vulnerable to defenders dug in on the heights above them, but completely exposed to whatever long-range Turkish artillery remained operable in their nearby fortresses. And even if such a force managed to scale the heights and seize those forts, the Turkish defenders could then begin a slow withdrawal up the peninsula, throwing up new trench-lines as they went, neatly replicating the static trench warfare that had so paralysed the armies on the Western Front. Indeed, one would be hard pressed to find a worse landing site most anywhere on the three-thousand-mile-long Mediterranean coast of the Ottoman Empire – yet it was precisely here that the Mediterranean Expeditionary Force was going ashore."

Winston Churchill was First Lord of the Admiralty, and had pushed the whole Gallipoli concept through the War Cabinet. Another rash but memorable quote from him was: *"Let me stand or fall by the Dardanelles."*

So it was. He resigned from the War Cabinet on 11 November 1915, and soon found himself on the Western Front.

Roger Keyes was in the thick of the action during the naval phase in March, and would have argued with modern historians about the chances of success in the Narrows.

It should also be said some of the enemy thought the land campaign was a similarly close thing.

Charles Bean returned to the Gallipoli Peninsula in early 1919 for two reasons. Firstly, to gather up artefacts for his brainchild the Australian War Memorial, and secondly to check details on site of just how far inland the Allied troops had got. He then felt able to write and edit the majority of the official Australian War Histories.

His small party included the multi-talented Hubert Wilkins as a photographer, and an official war artist in George Lambert. Bean was also was lucky to have a Turkish officer appointed to help him in his investigations. Zeki Bey was sent back to the Peninsula where he had spent most of 1915. He joined their camp and was helpful and informative advisor to Charles Bean.

Back on April 25, 1915 Mustafa Kemal had realised before his German masters that the Anzacs were the real threat if allowed to advance across the Peninsula. He ordered Zeki Bey to lead an attack *"without losing a minute,"* and his task was to *"push them back into the sea."* [Zeki Bey's words to Charles Bean.]

He was an officer who stayed close enough to the fighting to be shot in the arm on that first morning, so he knew very well how things looked from the Turkish side.

Zeki Bey told Bean of a near turning point later in the campaign:

"The Lone Pine demonstration cost the Turks very heavily, about 5000 casualties. But not only that: it drew in all the troops in immediate reserve, the 5th Division. It drew reserves from the south, and it prevented troops being on Chunuk Bair when the New Zealanders arrived.

If you had got to the top of Chunuk Bair I don't think we could ever have got there; we would have lost the Peninsula."

MAJOR ZEKI BEY
COMMANDANT OF TURKISH REGIMENT
AT GALLIPOLI.

Charles Lambert was an official War Artist and part of Bean's Gallipoli Mission in 1919.

As well as this sketch he did sketches for several famous paintings that were completed later. Most are in the Australian War Memorial in Canberra.

That history repeats itself is a cliché, but it is so very often true. Military leaders always assume that they are smarter than those who came before.

Adolf Hitler knew that Napoleon had been broken by the Russian winter, but believed his blitzkrieg was quicker and stronger. America saw the French defeated in Vietnam, but thought they could do better. They saw the defeat of the Russians in Afghanistan (dubbed decades earlier by historians the 'Graveyard of Empires') but still followed.

Something similar happened in the Dardanelles, and the British ignored their own history of only a century earlier.

Turkey declared war on Russia in 1806. Russia was already fighting with Britain against Napoleon, and asked Britain to help keep Turkey out of the war. Vice-Admiral Collingwood sent a force of twelve ships under Admiral Sir John Duckworth. They were to force the Dardanelles and shell Constantinople and the Turkish fleet. [Does that sound familiar?]

Duckworth actually made it past the forts of The Narrows (luckily under-manned during Ramadan), with small losses of men and ships. He reached Constantinople but the main Turkish fleet didn't come out to fight. Duckworth loitered, and then had to fight his way back out through the Sea of Marmara and the Dardanelles. When he reached the Mediterranean, he had suffered heavy losses and gained absolutely nothing. The whole operation was seen as a failure.

All these 'if-onlys' are small scenes of history. They help to make up only a localised Gallipoli picture. There is a bigger picture that warrants looking at. It is a much, much bigger picture – a picture that might have changed the modern world.

If the Gallipoli campaign had been successful, a warm water route to Russia via the Black Sea would have opened. It would have allowed the Allies to more directly aid the Russian Empire of Czar Nicholas II.

If this support had been available, Russia may have had success on the Eastern Front against Germany. The Russian Revolution of 1917 may not have occurred. The suppression of communism would have meant that the USSR would never have come into being.

The world today would be a different world, and the preceding ninety five years would have a vastly different history.

Chapter 15 – Both Women Learn of the Death of Charles Doughty-Wylie

On May 1st, 1915 Lilian was busy as usual nursing French soldiers at her hospital in Frevent. She was handed the telegram that every serviceman's wife opens with trembling hands. It wasn't from His Majesty's Government, but from Charles' brother. Captain H. M. Doughty was the commander of HMS *Agincourt,**, and was no doubt told of his brother's death through a network of mutual friends. He sent a telegram to Lilian that broke the news quicker than official channels.

"May God comfort you," the telegram ended.

Lilian has left a series of handwritten diaries from the time. They are a day by day record of everything that happened. Her entries are very frank about staff and what she saw as inept management by the French Army medical services. The diaries suddenly stop at this time, and only resume six months later when she resumed work at St.Valery-sur-Somme.

It would seem that she probably had a breakdown when she heard the news, as you would expect from someone in her stressful position. She returned to the comfort of family in Britain. When she did feel up to a return to nursing, the hospital was in St. Valery. As front lines moved, so did hospitals. They couldn't afford to be too far from the front lines, or too close.

One of her diaries records the day of the dreaded news:

"The shock was terrible, I don't know what I did for the first sixty seconds. Something seemed to tear at the region of my heart. All my life was so much of

---

**'HMS Agincourt'* was one of the two brand new vessels that Britain had built for Turkey. Churchill had seized them on the eve of the war.

his life, all his life mine. I suppose I shall have to pick up the pieces of a spoilt life, too old to start again, just a lonely widow, nothing to look forward to, nothing to work for – a blank."

Lilian wrote that she was too old to start life with a man again, even though she was only in her middle thirties. We might expect the passing of time and the lessening of the pain to change this attitude, but it was not to be.

The last letter that Charles ever wrote shows that a breakdown was almost what he expected of her, in the likely event of his death. Just days before the landing, he wrote to Lilian's mother Jean Coe, at her home in Wales. The letter was naturally all about Lilian, and started with a report of his brief visits on the way back from Abyssinia to London, and while going from London to join Hamilton's staff:

"I wanted to tell you how she was when I saw her in France, both coming and going. She was very full of work, and doing I think rather too much herself, as she is always prone to do, but on the whole well."

After some more small talk, he got around to the true purpose of the letter. He was explaining to Jean that there was a good chance he would die, and that he feared Lilian would struggle to cope. The letter would be received well after the Gallipoli landing, so there was no need to be secretive about the *River Clyde*. He went on:

"Now I want you to do something for me. I am going to embark tomorrow on what is certainly an extremely dangerous job, namely the wreck ship of which you will see in the papers…. If you hear I'm killed go over at once to France with H.H. and seek her out. Telegraph her at once that you are coming and want her to send Frank Wylie and a car to meet you at Boulogne – don't lose any time."

So although he thought his wife *"strong minded,"* he thought seriously that she would be *"intolerably lonely and hopeless"* and urged Jean to go and comfort her, and: *"-don't lose any time."*

Charles didn't think Lilian could handle the extra burden and worry of prior knowledge, and he went on:

> "I haven't told her yet of this wreck ship because I don't want her to know till it's over."

He obviously thought Gertrude was more able to cope, because she knew more than Lilian. Gertrude at one stage wrote knowingly back to him: *"I am very calm about the shell and shot to which you go."*

[This was the same letter when she had implored Charles to leave Lilian and make an honest woman of her: *"let me stand upright and say I never walked by furtive ways."*]

As it panned out, Jean wrote to her daughter about Dick's last letter, and didn't go rushing across the English Channel. Lilian quickly wrote back to her mother on May 13:

> *"My dear Mother, Please send me Dick's letter by registered post. It will be quite safe. I don't want anybody to come out to me, I am doing my work as usual."*

This doesn't read like the letter of a distraught widow, because Lilian's personal beliefs allowed her some comfort. She saw their separation as only a temporary thing.

Gertrude Bell was not a member of Dick's family, and certainly wasn't in contact with Lilian and the Wylies, so the news of his death reached her only by chance.

At a London luncheon or dinner party on May 1st, she was discussing with friends the bad news leaking out about the disaster of the Cape Helles landings. When someone brought up the tragic news of Dick's death, Gertrude was completely stunned. She left the party and went to cry on the shoulder of her younger step-sister Elsa, who lived nearby.

The reason she could run to the arms of Elsa is revealed in Gertrude's letter to Dick that she wrote on April 19. It was a letter that he never received, but is available to us today:

"Do you remember I was on the edge of telling you something I had done, & then hesitated lest you shouldn't like it. I've remembered now & I'll say it. I told Elsa everything. 8 weeks ago – the day after you left. Everything from the very beginning. I even showed her your last Abyssinian letter. You don't know her, but I know her very well, & even I was amazed. When she had heard, she said I had the one true thing which was worth having – which I knew - & that my way was the right way, my chapter of Genesis, no other."

Gertrude's way was for Dick to divorce, and to marry her, instead of the possibly easier and more common way where she would simply become his mistress. Gertrude went on about Elsa and her support:

"She's steel true and blade straight - my dear that's why she wouldn't look at any way but mine. She'll forgive me whatever way I take, but she wouldn't like the other….

That's all the secret; you don't mind really, do you? She'll never speak of it to either of us, but what it is to me to have her tacit backing, now that you are so far away, I can't tell you. I should like you to tell me that you don't mind – give me absolution."

Such absolution would never come, as Dick was dead and buried in his shallow grave when the letter reached Gallipoli.

Not surprisingly, Gertrude's next move was to flee London and return to the security of the family home at Rounton. London was an impossible place for Gertrude. She could never express her anguish and sorrow amongst friends and acquaintances who didn't know of her deep love for another woman's husband.

There is no reason, and no evidence to suggest that she immediately confessed all to Hugh and Florence when she went home. They were both busy people, involved daily in business and war work. If nothing else, the large country home and gardens gave her the space to grieve and think about life. It is possible that Dick's death was a big enough reason for Gertrude (or Elsa) to reveal the truth, but just when it happened is unknown.

An interesting letter survives from Elsa to Gertrude. It is undated, other than being headed 'Friday.' Its tone indicates it was written not long after Gertrude heard the terrible news, and ran to her step-sister:

> *"Darling, Don't regret what didn't happen. The phrase has kept coming into my head ever since you told me about it after he left 'Possession kills desire.' I don't know where I've seen it & like all those things it is only a half truth, but there is some truth in it …. It is only you who have to fear, my poor beloved lonely sister, this agony of longing. Mental and physical. He is spared the misery that was in store for you both, for your happiness could not have been unattended by much bitterness. And he was splendid & gallant & brave, & you have his beautiful image always in your heart. My dearest you have more than many many women. Ever yours, Elsa."*

It seems she was hoping to alleviate some of Gertrude's pain, but the letter also reveals that Elsa couldn't foresee a smooth and happy life for Gertrude and Dick:

> "your happiness could not have been unattended by much bitterness."

Lilian of course, found a way to carry on. She had great inner strength. She never seemed to quite sink to that depth of despair she expected when she foresaw herself as: *"just a lonely old widow."*

The main reason is that she came to see her husband as certainly dead and gone from this life, but definitely carrying on somewhere in an afterlife. She believed that when the time was right, he would call for her to join him in this place.

Her diary entries before Charles was killed were purely about the day to day trials of her role as the person in charge of nursing at a military hospital. Entries concerned the patients, her nurses, and the doctors. They continued in this vein for another few weeks after the news:

"The poor gangrene case has got it on the other leg now. I am afraid there is very little chance for him." (6th March, 1915)

"One of the arm cases started bleeding tonight, of course Dr. Barret's case." (9th March, 1915)

"I was on till 3 a.m. the shoulder amputation case is a handful. He had the cheek to tell me I did not look at his arm often enough to see if it was bleeding. He's the chap who told me he'll report Mrs McAllister to the doctor, because she would not do exactly what he said." (10th March, 1915)

"This evening I find both Miss McAllister and Miss MaCoy seedy so I am doing night duty in Miss McAllister's ward." (10th March, 1915)

By early May, her diary entries are still about daily happenings, but her mind is also occupied with a new issue. Lilian had now settled on the idea that she must make her way out to the Dardanelles, and work in the area where Charles died. Some diary entries now include:

"This afternoon an old gentleman arrived from Madame Carnot to try & put things right for us, he was very surprised to see how fast events had marched. I am afraid there is nothing to be done now but I asked him to speak to Madame Carnot about the Dardanelles." (6th May, 1915)

"Madame Carnot wrote today she could do nothing for the Dardanelles, & I heard from Gwen that Tom is going there. I have written to the Ministry of War on the subject. If they have nothing for me I ask the Red Cross." (23rd May, 1915)

In truth her determination to get out to Turkey was more than just to be near where Dick died. Lilian wanted to be out there so as to be able to join him! When she had written to her mother on May 13 and asked her to forward Dick's last letter, she had continued:

"I am glad Dick was worried over me as he will no doubt do his best to get me permission to join him. We always have done our shows together, & I really don't see why this should be an exception. I have applied for the Dardanelles. I

somehow feel if I am allowed to go there I shall not come back, but shall join Dick. I would be curious; he escaped twice with his life from a bullet in Turkey, the first time in Adana the second at Sehiri when his launch was full of Bulgarian bullets; the third time he didn't. I escaped from Malta fever once cholera the second time. They should get me third shot. I always follow Dick's example.

Of course all this is pretty far off. Still it's just as well that you make up your mind to the possibility. If anything were to happen to me, it would really be a matter for congratulation for it would be ever so much jollier for me to go on doing things with Dick in the next world, than to drag along here by myself."

This tone of letter was never going to calm Lilian's mother, and losing her daughter certainly wasn't going to leave Jean *"ever so much jollier."* Again Jean wrote about sending over some family support, and Lilian wrote back stubbornly on May 20:

"My dear Mother, I particularly do not wish any member of my family to come out here, … I feel it easier to behave with the dignity of my position as the head of an English Hospital by myself. H.H. or anyone else would only upset me. As for the Dardanelles, I shall go if I can. I don't know what Dick has said to you but he said to me if things get too much for my nerves, I could retire with dignity & prepare to join him – I am in every way prepared & look to him for the next move. … He has promised to let me know when I can come, & I am sure he will. There is nothing whatever for you to worry over. If the moment comes I shall go, be it from St. Valery or from Dardanelles or anywhere else. I myself would like Dardanelles for purely sentimental reasons but that's all – I may have to wait, who knows."

Eventually Lilian's letters to French authorities got some response. She heard from none other than the French chief of General Staff, General Joffre. Her diary entry of May 30 said:

> "At dinner Mr Chief came in with a wire for me … It had come last night but he'd been at Abville till this evening. It was condolences from Joffre & said I would be received at the W.O 7th direction (Service de Saute.) the following morning May 31st. Question was how was I to get there."

At short notice and with great difficulty she rushed off to Paris, and soon was waiting to see who she hoped was a new and valuable contact:

> "I had a long wait as my man was out lunching still at 2 pm but he finally came and we had a long talk. As a matter of fact he could have written everything quite easily without bothering me to come to Paris but of course I could not help that. After beating about the bush for a long time I got him to say that sooner or later if the allied armies were successful in the Dardanelles I could count on being sent there in some capacity or other & I was to communicate with him after the fall of Gallipoli or Dardanelles."

This was obviously a fairly meaningless commitment and she left disappointed. The difficult journey back to her hospital involved a train that left her at an isolated station at dawn. The rest of the journey was to be on foot, but the following 36 hours would transform her attitude to life. In a long entry she wrote of being *"profoundly miserable,"* and that *"everything was ended."* By the following day she had progressed to an almost secret renewal of her wedding vows to Dick, in the guise of a farewell toast:

> "June 1st. My wedding day, it was strange to arrive at 2.50 am or so on such a day at a wayside station with a tramp of 4 miles ahead of one on such a day. It was the first wedding day since we were married 11 years ago that Dick & I have not been together. I tramped along in the early dawn thinking of him and feeling profoundly miserable. Watching the sky recede and the herds in the fields get up & stretch & the grey mists rise from the marsh ditches & I thought of the many dawns Dick & I had seen in Abyssinia when trekking early to avoid the heat of day, and I felt now everything was ended.

At 4 a.m. I got in & went to bed & had a strange dream. I suppose it was a dream, because I suppose I was asleep. I was dead tired. Anyway I seemed to get a message from Dick, in which he said that the last words of his last letter to me saying "All my love and kisses till we meet again," were meant to cancel that part of the marriage service which says "til death do us part" & he asked me if I would also renew my marriage vows to him on the same terms. If so, I could no longer consider myself his widow as widowhood meant the conclusion of the contract & I was renewing mine.   Also I was to keep our wedding date as usual.

I kept our wedding; as it happened the Corbetts were leaving us in the afternoon, so at lunch we brought out the champagne, & I gave the toast "till we meet again." & we had strawberries & the spoils I brought from Paris for dinner. Betty & Isobel knew, & were the wedding guests. I was sorry to be saying good bye to the Corbetts, but he wants to serve so there was nothing to be said."

The next day she continued on, and is all but convinced that the dream really was contact from the other side:

"I was thinking of my dream today. It settles all my fears if it really is from Dick. It means that the great transition he has gone through & the wider knowledge he has achieved have not changed his feelings for me, in spite of the fact that he probably knows all my bad points - & that our meeting cannot be at a very distant date....

It is strange too that the vow was to be till we meet again, not for ever, or anything like that; and we are told that in the next world there is no marrying or giving in marriage."

Once Lilian started believing that Dick was making contact from the other side, it was no great stretch to start considering contact via spiritual mediums. Many a widow wanted to contact her loved one, and mediums and clairvoyants were more popular and busy than ever before. Her diary entry of June 3rd says:

> "I got a letter from Mrs. Gillies today sending me some supposed messages from Dick which her daughter had got from a medium friend. There were one or two strange things about it, he mentions his watch & Capt. Deedes letter received 1st says he's sending it to me. He also says tell her to take care of her health, it may not be many years till she comes, but such things are in higher hands than ours, a distinctly Dick remark. Also it's the sort of thing he would say to me if the chances were I might arrive fairly soon & had been warned not to tell."

This seemed fairly promising to Lilian, promising enough for her to write a letter to Mrs. Gillies' daughter, to be taken to the medium. By the 7th she also believed she had heard from him directly:

> "I believe I had some sort of message from Dick last night. Well it seems I was right, my permission for the Dardanelles has come, that is my permission from Dick, he said in his letter to me of April 21st that when they were through with the landing there might be something for me to do out there & he would let me know. He did today – I received a message through Mr. Doughty from Sir Ian Hamilton that Dick was buried in the castle which now bears his name that the burial was hurried & the grave should be seen to."

She went on about poor Dick and the work needed on the grave:

> "That is not the work for me which I had hoped for, however it is something definite to do for Dick. At the same time I heard he had be(en) recommended for the V.C. Poor old Dick I told him that he would get something out of Turkey when he left; if only he had lived to wear it. Nothing in the world would have given him more pleasure. Mr. Doughty wrote & told me what he wanted over the grave, somewhat premature, as I haven't got things arranged yet. However I wrote off

a letter to De Parrizae at the French War Office & asked him if on any terms I could get sent out at once. I also wrote & tried my luck with the Red Cross."

Lilian then had some more supposed contacts from Dick through other people:

"I had a strange letter from Gerty* on the 10th. She tells me she saw Dick two days ago after they had heard of his death. It was 4 a.m. & quite light & she was wide awake. She suddenly saw him sitting on her bed, he was leaning forward & his eyes were wet. Strange to say I heard from Mrs. Gillies medium friend of hers in London whom her daughter went to see (with a letter of mine) saw Dick & described him & also said he had been weeping. A most un-Dick like proceeding, but it's strange to hear it from two such different sources."

In her mind, Lilian was finding the whole business of friends' dreams and medium messages interesting, but gradually less convincing. She finished off her entry of June 12th with:

"Mrs. Gillies has sent me various messages supposed to be from Dick, but nothing which might not be sent from any husband to any wife. However I have a sort of feeling that if he still exists, he will somehow get through to me – he usually does succeed in accomplishing things if he wants to."

Lilian's diary entries thus became a blend of day to day hospital events, mixed in with things about Dick and her quest to get out to the Dardanelles. Dreams and mail sometimes found their way in, and two entries caught my eye. One is almost bizarre, and the other perhaps is merely odd:

"I dreamed last night that Dick was wounded in the lower regions. That I even had the severed part in my hand. It was a strange muddy dream." (5th May, 1915)

*Most definitely not Gerty Bell!

"I had a letter of condolence from two old flames, Basil being one. Philip the other. His was very nice, Basil's was dreadfully sorry for me, as I very nearly married Basil. My reply to him was the reverse of dreadfully sorry for myself. I admitted it was hard luck, but I asked him if he'd seen <u>how</u> Dick died? & said that my 11 years with him had given me everything in the world I'd started out wanting….

I don't think he can flatter himself that I have any regrets that I did not marry him, though he is <u>alive</u> & Dick isn't." (30th May, 1915)

Life and the war went on of course, but Lilian found personal comfort in her belief that Dick was somewhere out there, and would call for her. Some of the peace she found is beautifully expressed in a poem she wrote in the back cover of one of her diaries from 1918:

You are not here – yet you are still here
a gentle prisoner, vague alas, but found
With you beside me I shall cease to fear
My own transmission to the sphere beyond

For in my soul, you fill again your place
I, in my spirit strive to understand
the flitting glimpses of your dreamland face
the ghostly pressure of your vanished hand

For you are here but I could sweep the veil
that hangs between us for a while aside
then I should see you there should my love prevail
Victor over Death and not be dimmed

The Only Woman at Gallipoli

A year later she wrote another poem. It is a completely different composition, but it follows the theme of the call from the other side, and the idea that Dick is just behind some sort of veil or curtain:

I shall see you in the twilight
I shall see you in the dawn
In Golden sun at noontide
In the dew which decks the morn
The wind shall whisper softly
The name I hold so dear
And you perchance may call me
And I perchance may hear

Then death shall lose its horrors
And life its dread of pain
When you come back in spirit
And claim my love again
Our faith shall rise triumphant
Our love shall reign supreme
Our parting & our suffering
Shall fade as fades a dream

Sweet are those days of future
E'en though I wait awhile
Before their consummation
In the glory of your smile
For you I know am waiting
And we'll not be denied
When God has raised the curtain
Which Veils the other side

Chapter 16 - A Book Unopened

Without a doubt the affair between Gertrude and Charles that evolved during the years before his death became emotionally intense. Amazingly, it appears it remained an unconsummated relationship.

Whilst Gertrude was such an achiever in so many ways, and so often in a male-oriented environment, she was naive (to our modern way of thinking) when it came to personal and sexual relationships.

It must also be realised that Charles was a married man, and was regularly moved around the world in the service of His Majesty. Gertrude herself was also a constant traveller. Her visits to England were only ever interludes to plan and prepare for the next journey. This meant opportunities to be together were very rare. The greatest war the world had known only made things even more chaotic.

Some of their letters indicate that the increasingly loving relationship was never consummated in the bedroom. It would seem that during that first country house weekend some years earlier, the gentle knock on the door at Rounton was answered, but that the person drawing the line at this final step – the opening of this new book of life experience – was Gertrude.

Charles was later to write so poignantly to her about this special book:

"if I can't write to you, I shall always think of you telling me things in your room at Rounton...the subtle book eludes, but our hands met on the cover."

By this stage Charles and Lilian had packed again and he had taken up his new posting in Albania. Here he was on the International Boundary Commission. The difficult task of the Commission was to resolve the boundaries of Serbia, Montenegro and Albania by negotiation.

The British had a penchant for attempting such things. T. E. Lawrence says it all in 'Seven Pillars of Wisdom' when he describes a *"vicarious policemanship which was the strongest emotion of Englishmen towards another man's muddle."*
[see note on page 303]

That it was Gertrude who held back in the bedroom is confirmed in a later letter from Charles. Apparently, while quietly drunk one night, he reflected again on those summer nights at Rounton. He wrote from Albania of those things that she didn't allow to happen. It was playing on his mind when he wrote to Gertrude and said of her reluctance:

> *"It was right . . . and the sober part of me does not regret*
> *− the drunk part regrets and remembers as he goes to sleep."*

Late at night must have been the time when Charles could truly write of how he felt. In another letter from Albania he wrote in a noble and philosophic tone. An earlier letter had mentioned the last minute appearance of an imaginary hedge to keep them apart *("What is a hedge that it should divide us?")* This one continued the metaphor of the hedge, but turned it into a fence:

> *"It's late and I'm all alone, and thinking of ... love and life – and an evening at Rounton – and what it all meant. Does it mean that the fence was folly, and that we might have been man and woman as God made us and been happy ... But I myself answer to myself that it is a lie. If I had been your man to you, in the bodies we live in, would it change us, surely not.*
>
> *I have always maintained that this curious, powerful sex attraction is a thing right and natural and to be gratified, and if it is not gratified, what then; are we any worse?"*

Soon after, he may have again left Gertrude confused as to what he thought, or what it was he was really trying to say. In a letter on July 26 he was still accepting that their relationship might never go beyond a pure and noble love when he wrote:

"Shall I love you less because I shall never be your lover, never lie in your arms and forget the world? I think not."

He then continued in a way that implied he still needed more, saying:

"Passion is the best way, the only way – or men like me think whose heart goes with it – the only way to say I love you mixed with it tied to it by the breath we breathe."

Gertrude took all of this in, and soon had a new outlook. She regretted holding back, and wrote to Charles when he had sailed for Turkey. She was trying to explain that her crucial hesitation was a terrible fear of the unknown, and that she needed Charles to lead her onwards:

"Every time it surged up in me and I wanted you to brush it aside. ... But I couldn't say to you, Exorcise it. I couldn't. That last word I can never say. You must say it.

Fear is a horrible thing. ... Only you can free me from it – drive it away from me..."

Her regrets at the lost opportunity of those precious few days together soon distilled itself into anger. She was now writing to her man on his way to a war, when she wrote:

"If I had given more, should I have held you closer, drawn you back more surely? I look back and rage at my reluctance."

Such powerful words! *"I look back and rage at my reluctance."* This was a watershed moment – it should have been a turning point in her life, but she hadn't taken the turn.

She certainly discussed her reluctance with her step-sister Elsa. When Elsa wrote her the comforting letter after the news of Dick's tragic death, Elsa also revealed that

Gertrude had discussed her intact virginity. At the start of the letter Elsa says revealingly:

> "Darling, Don't regret what didn't happen. The phrase has kept coming into my head ever since you told me about it after he left 'Possession kills desire.' I don't know where I've seen it & like all those things it is only a half truth, but there is some truth in it …. "

The whole concept of her giving herself to Charles came to prey on her mind, and be with her in every waking moment. Gertrude couldn't free herself of it. Sleep was difficult, with the racing of her thoughts. She had come to the conclusion that it must happen, or she could hardly go on; she could hardly live or die otherwise! She wrote:

> "After the long & laborious process of going to sleep, I wake again, as usual & turn to you. Listen. You know what those 18 months were like? Yes, you know. The eagle eating my heart & I'm chained, not free to die –"

She saw now that she needed and wanted to take this step in her life, and become the passionate, intimate person that she had never had opportunity to be. It was with a new state of mind when she wrote:

> "I've grown too this last fortnight which hurts me at every point. Let me spread wings and fly into the sun. You said passion would spend itself – you'd sleep. Yes, but between my breasts, one arm around me, your back half turned to me, & my body part sheath to you, part pillow – I've learnt."

[These lines were quoted in an earlier chapter, but they bear repeating. Gertrude changed. She was ready to spread her wings and fly fearlessly into the sun, but knew also that she had been too slow to come to the realisation. The knowledge made her partly angry and partly sad.]

Her new enlightenment brought even more regrets. Gertrude also came to wish that she had overcome her fear of making love when she pondered fully the prospect of pregnancy.

Pregnancy was something that Charles had feared at the time (and Gertrude had "half-feared.") She now decided such an outcome would have been a wonderful thing. She wrote:

"And suppose the other thing had happened, the thing you feared – that I half feared – that must have brought you back. If I had it now, the thing you feared, I would magnify the Lord and fear nothing.

Not only the final greatest gift to give you – a greater gift even than love – but for me, the divine pledge of fulfilment, created in rapture, the handing on of life in fire, to be cherished and worshipped and lived for, with the selfsame ardour that cherishes and worships the creator."

She went on, the words spilling on to the pages, about that moment of consummation when she had baulked at the brink:

"We thought then of the moment – I think of it still, hourly. But inseparably linked to it is the longing for the fruit of it. What woman fears, when that is in the scale? I'm telling you the profoundest secret of life, newly revealed to me, blindingly. Are you, who welcome life, afraid to learn? You who have never failed to understand, understand this too, for it is the deepest strongest instinct of mankind, the most irresistible, the flowing together of the two mightiest desires – to love & to be loved - & thereby to carry on life."

Gertrude was left with so many regrets as Charles sailed for The Dardanelles. No wonder she saw the episode of their recent time together as such a lost opportunity. No wonder she found herself writing that *"I look back and rage at my reluctance."*

In her mind, these regrets were enormous, but they were all to be absolved when next they were together.

How much worse would she have felt if she had known that Charles would never return?

Chapter 17 – The Arab Bureau

Gertrude left her role with the Wounded and Missing in November 1915. She was seconded to Cairo, to the newly-formed Arab Bureau.

The Arab Bureau was officially the Admiralty Intelligence Service for the region, but was unofficially a gathering of pre-war archaeologists. It would have been nothing without the first-hand knowledge provided by Bell (and T. E. Lawrence, David Hogarth and Leonard Woolley). [see note on page 304]

That she was keen to go is not surprising. Every day at the Office of Wounded and Missing she had been confronted by the true scale of the losses in the trenches, which were being withheld from the general public. She wrote to her friend Janet Courtney:

"I've heard from David. He says anyone can trace the missing, but only I can map northern Arabia."

David Hogarth (Janet's brother), was no longer just a peacetime archaeologist and family friend. He was now a British Intelligence officer with the Bureau.

The role of the Bureau was to draw up-to-date and useful maps of the region, along with writing reports and papers on happenings, local opinions, and policy.

If Gertrude's life needed to be sensationalised, it could be said that this period made all her earlier desert journeys and diaries seem like the skilled work of a glamorous spy, although the reality may never be known. Her mind was full of detailed and current information from a region where it was scarce, and she was able to provide it to the Allies. Her last great trek to Hayyil meant that in fact she was the last European visitor to vast areas of that inland territory.

Her knowledge complemented that of Lawrence. His expertise came from all the seasons at pre-war archaeological digs, and he knew much about the north and west of the region. He could write of railways, military bases and their likely troop numbers, and put it all on maps. Bell could do this for regions of the south and east that he hadn't been to, and had more knowledge of the politics and the local leaders. She had sat with the sheikhs and learnt their family alliances. She heard of their internal feuds, and knew of any leanings to London or Constantinople. It would often turn out that many simply sided with whoever was ascendant in their region, but all knowledge was valuable where there had been none.

Her travels also gave her knowledge of Arabia's most precious commodity – fresh water. Desert campaigns relied upon water, and Gertrude's recent knowledge of the location, quality, and quantity of supply was most invaluable.

The Arab Bureau regularly produced a secret 'Arab Bulletin,' with up to date reports and opinion pieces on local policy. Much of it was written by T.E. Lawrence and Gertrude Bell, and after the war Gertrude's despatches were seen as so astute and interesting that they were published as a book.

[The desert campaign of Allenby, with the Anzac Light Horse, and British and Indian forces was dictated by water. The smallest oasis was worth fighting and dying for, if its water was worthwhile. The famous afternoon charge of the Light Horse into Beersheba became a necessity. Failure to capture the wells before they were destroyed would have meant a halt and even reversal of the campaign, with retreat back to decent water the only option.]

For the trip out to Cairo to join the Arab Bureau, Gertrude packed in London, and then travelled across the Channel for a train down to Marseilles. There she boarded the crowded P & O *Arabia*. Amongst the throng was a friend Helen Brassey, so they travelled together. Unlike most on board, the two ladies avoided seasickness and dined nightly at the Captain's table.

They arrived in Port Said late on November 26th, and Gertrude wrote home five days later, mentioning the terrible journey as a voyage of *"almost continuous storm."*

The Only Woman at Gallipoli

T.E. Lawrence, David Hogarth, and Alan Dawnay in the Arab Bureau Days

Lawrence has his uniform as plain and anonymous as possible, as was his way. [Liddell Hart said of him: "*self-depreciation, like his rejection of distinction, was a kind of vanity.*"]

Hogarth is heading in the opposite direction in the uniform of a Lt. Commander RNVR.

Dawnay fought in the desert with Lawrence, and was much more your regular army man. After the war, Lawrence gave Dawnay the massive hand-written manuscript of 'Seven Pillars of Wisdom' to read. On the way home after retrieving it, Lawrence lost it at Reading station. Deriving almost perverse pleasure from self-imposed challenges, he 'took rooms' in Westminster and threw himself into the task of recreating it. In thirty days and nights he claims he re-wrote an astonishing 400,000 words, about five times the length of this book. It may be one of his many exaggerations.

Gertrude was greeted by Leonard Woolley – now Captain Woolley, and soon settled in to the Savoy Hotel as this had become Arab Bureau headquarters. Gertrude had entered a new phase in her life, and left that of the explorer behind.

Neither would be settled in to the Savoy as long as they expected. Gertrude would be given tasks that took her away, and things took a bad turn for Leonard Woolley. On a voyage in the Mediterranean his ship hit a mine. His rescuers were Turkish and he saw out the war as a POW.

Before long the 'think tank' atmosphere of the Bureau brought about the founding of an unofficial organization within. Bell, Lawrence, and others in the Bureau called themselves 'The Intrusives.' They believed so strongly in the cause of Arab independence that their aims were to go against official British policy and intention if necessary, so as to eventually have their way. British policy in the Middle East was dictated from the Viceroy and his bureaucracy in India, but they did their best to intrude from Egypt.

The move to Egypt from war-isolated Britain brought Gertrude Bell to the Arab Bureau. It also brought her much, much closer to Dick's grave.

Chapter 18 - The Means and Opportunity to Visit The Grave

As it happens, there were only two women in the whole world with the realistic means and opportunity to visit the grave of Charles Doughty-Wylie. The two women were Gertrude and Lilian!

Lilian Doughty-Wylie was certainly in the vicinity at the time.

She left twenty-six detailed and numbered diaries of her time during the War, and they are held today by the Imperial War Museum. Diaries eleven to thirteen run from December 1914 to the following September of 1915. During this period she was nursing in France.

Diaries fourteen to sixteen are from April 1916, when she had transferred to nurse at the British hospital at Mudros.

Mudros is the largest town on the Aegean island of Lemnos, and the whole invasion fleet had assembled here in the harbour before sailing for the Gallipoli Peninsula. From Mudros harbour to Cape Helles is less than ten kilometres.

Interestingly, there are no diaries for the months from October 1915 to March 1916, when she no doubt would have mentioned a special visit to her late husband's grave. Why would she keep detailed diaries of every part of every day, but have a six month gap? Perhaps there were more diaries, but some she destroyed or lost. If the IWM allocated the numbers when they first got the diaries, it would explain why the numbers are consecutive, but with a time gap included.

Mudros was the main off-shore base during the campaign. If Lilian was on Mudros before the evacuation of Cape Helles she would have had daily contact with services personnel. Their task would have been the movement of men and supplies in and out of the Allied toeholds on the Peninsula. As matron-in-charge, and the widow of a Victoria Cross winner, she had the contacts and no doubt the sympathy of those in command. *If she was there!*

One aspect that possibly indicates that Lilian was not the November visitor to the grave is that she apparently started at Mudros hospital in April 1916. Why would she go to the region in November, when she wasn't required until the following April? Or, if she was there in November, where did she then disappear to for all those months until the following April? She was after all a 36 year-old dedicated career nurse and hospital manager, and the Army hospitals were desperate for someone like her.

Gertrude Bell was also in a position to make a visit to the grave in the war zone at Gallipoli. She had the convenience of location in Cairo, and the freedom of being one of the newer members of the relatively new Arab Bureau.

Egypt was a permanent British bastion in the eastern Mediterranean, due to the vital importance of the Suez Canal. It gave shipping the access to India and the Empire. It was here on the edge of Cairo that the green and untried Anzacs had set up their tents near the pyramids, under the solemn gaze of the sphinx. They trained in the sands after their sea voyage from Fremantle, and tended the animals and the mascot kangaroo they had managed to bring. They all thought that this was a strange place to train for fighting in the mud of France, on arrival from the Colonies.

After the Gallipoli campaign, later battalions of Anzac troops still trained in Egypt in the shadow of the pyramids, and then really did get transferred to the mud of France.

A constant traffic was also happening between Egypt and the Peninsula. Men and supplies were shipped to Turkey, and the wounded and sick brought out. One of the major failings of the campaign planning was that there weren't nearly enough hospital beds on the nearby island of Lemnos.

The campaign planners had thought that there was insufficient water on the islands for large field hospitals, but there is wisdom in hindsight. It would have been much easier to ship the water in, than it turned out to be to ship so many wounded to Egypt (and then Malta and even England.)

This was soon the way of things, once the small hospitals on Lemnos were overflowing. Extra field hospitals were eventually established all around Mudros harbour, and hospitals that existed nearby were greatly expanded. An Australian official named Methuen reported from one in Malta in November 1916, and it shows the unimagined scale of what was eventually required:

"From 264 beds I have now reached 25,000, and have over 20,000 in Malta now, sick and wounded. The nurses from Australia, New Zealand and Canada are simply splendid."

Proper hospital ships were called White Ships for obvious reasons. With so many wounded to care for, the British started also using troop ships, and even ships that were for the transport of horses and mules! They were typically under-manned and under-equipped. In the haste to get men off the Peninsula, too many of the serious cases were put on board these unsuitable vessels. Many soldiers died on these longer trips on the so-called 'Black Ships,' and they constantly stopped for burials at sea.*

---

*The list of horse transports that were used as hospital ships included *Lutzow, Ionian, Itonus*, and *Mashroba*.

My own grandfather was in the Australian 8th Light Horse at Gallipoli, and was evacuated to Alexandria on the 'white' hospital ship *Glenart Castle* in December 1915. A more famous soldier was carried aboard on October 25. Private Jim Martin died of typhoid only two hours after arriving on board. His fame came not from his military actions, but from his mere presence at Gallipoli. When Jim Martin died he was only fourteen years and nine months old.

My grandfather (William James Howell) survived the war, but the *Glenart Castle* did not. Although white painted with large red crosses it was torpedoed by a German U-boat off Devon in February, 1918.

Cairo was much further from Cape Helles than Mudros (where Lilian may have been in November), but Gertrude had spent her whole adult life travelling. Often her travel was to difficult places, where people thought she shouldn't or couldn't go – but she had found ways and gone anyway. Finding a vessel going that way was easy. It was the getting aboard that would have been the difficulty. Friends and contacts would be required.

Her network of influential friends was stellar, going right up to Winston Churchill, the Viceroy of India, and Sir Edward Grey, who was the Foreign Secretary and an old family friend. On a more local level, friends from her pre-war archaeology digs were now holding powerful positions in Egypt, from where the majority of Gallipoli shipping came and went. They could pull the strings required.

Gertrude's role in the Arab Bureau would also have been advantageous. Here was a small and almost autonomous group, technically part of the Foreign Office. Although the members were in uniform, they were unfettered by the rigid chain of command of the armed forces. Arab Bureau people were Intelligence Officers and kept to themselves. They didn't need to justify their every action with local military authorities, and the Foreign Office in Whitehall was a long, long way away.

An early author came up with November 17 as the date of the visit to the grave (by whichever woman it was). Some later authors repeated this date, to the stage it has almost become accepted – almost.

Gertrude Bell was in England packing her bags for the voyage out to Egypt on the 17th and Lilian's whereabouts are unknown for months either side of the November. I suppose it could be said that this makes Lilian's window of opportunity huge.

Gertrude's window is much smaller, but more realistic. After the *Arabia* docked at Port Said on the 26th, she was met by Leonard Woolley and later dined with him. Her next few days would have been a little flexible, had she wanted to undertake what she called in an earlier letter to Florence: *"any further journey."*

On November 30, Gertrude wrote home from Cairo:
"I telegraphed you the morning after my arrival."

This innocuous sentence was misread by Virginia Howell and quoted in her book *'Daughter of the Desert'* as: *"I telegraphed you <u>this</u> morning after my arrival."*

This implied that Gertrude had really only settled in Egypt on the 30th, and so could have been somewhere else (i.e. Cape Helles) during the three-day window of November 27, 28 and 29. It's interesting how the reading (or misreading) of Gertrude's terrible scrawl can take a story in new directions!

Gertrude had been head-hunted for the Arab Bureau by a Captain Hall of Naval Intelligence in London. His brother was also a Captain Hall, and was high up in the Egyptian Railways. Probably, she would have been told in London how a lady in need could make contact for travel favours to Port Said. From Port Said, things would have been ridiculously easy. Apart from the helpful presence in Cairo of Lawrence and Hogarth, the intelligence chief for the port was none other than Leonard Woolley.

Without doubt, her arrival in Egypt was a fortuitous meeting of means and opportunity.

Chapter 19 – Morphia and Such Things

In an earlier chapter I quoted a portion of a letter that Charles wrote to his mother-in-law, Jean Coe. He made it clear that he was so worried about Lilian, and how she would cope with his death, that he insisted that Jean should rush to France. The letter is repeated below, but this time I have included some crucial lines previously omitted. They show why Charles had such strong fears. The full letter says:

"Now I want you to do something for me. I am going to embark tomorrow on what is certainly an extremely dangerous job, namely the wreck ship of which you will see in the papers. If the thing went wrong, Lily would feel intolerably lonely and hopeless after her long hours of work, which tell surely on anybody's spirits and stability.

She talks about overdoses of morphia and such things. I think that in reality she is too brave and strong minded for such things, but still the saying weighs on my spirits. If you hear I'm killed go over at once to France with H.H. and seek her out. Telegraph her at once that you are coming and want her to send Frank Wylie and a car to meet you at Boulogne – don't lose any time."

So although he thought his wife *"strong minded,"* he couldn't ignore her threats of suicide. He genuinely believed that she saw an overdose of morphia as the speedy ticket to the after-world that Dick would now inhabit.

Thus his insistent tone when he urged Jean *"-don't lose any time."*

So as Dick prepared himself physically and mentally to go once in again into deadly battle, he did so with the distractions of a wife threatening suicide. The suicidal talk didn't end with Lilian either. Piled on top of this he carried similar burdens from Gertrude!

Was suicide seriously on her mind also, from a long time ago? It would seem it was, and it came to Gertrude early in the war when she first pondered a life without Charles. He had left her in London after those fleeting days together and was heading to the dangers of Gallipoli. Two of her letters confirm that suicide was a serious option for her, if Charles was to be killed. The first time was at the end of a long letter where she said it was his task to end his marriage, to be able to marry her. (*"Before all the world, claim me and take me and hold me for ever and ever."*)

The realisation that in fact he might be killed before there was time for any of this must have come to her almost as an afterthought. Tacked on the end of the letter, she wrote what was almost like some sort of postscript:

"If you die, wait for me – I am not afraid of that other crossing.
I will come to you."

She was never a religious person, but had continued thinking about an afterlife *"beyond the border"* when she wrote again only a few days later:

"I am very calm about the shot and shell to which you go. What takes you takes me out to look for you. If there's search and finding beyond the border I shall find you. If there's nothingness, as with my reason I think, why then there's nothingness … but I'm not afraid. Life would be gone, how could the fire burn?"

As Gertrude saw it, her best option was to seek death, so as to search for her beloved in another place. If that place was non-existent, she didn't care. For her there was no life without Charles.

Charles was naturally horrified. He had spoken with Gertrude about Lilian's threats and the ampoules of *"morphia and such things"* and now Gertrude was of the same mind! He wrote one of his last letters to her about this talk of suicide, but he couldn't even bring himself to use the actual word:

"My dear don't do what you talked of – it's horrible to me to think of it – that's why I told you about my wife – how much more for you? – don't do anything so unworthy of so free and brave a spirit. One must walk along the road to the end of it. When I asked for this ship, my joy in it was half strangled by that thing you said, I can't even name it or talk about it. Don't do it. Time is nothing, we join up again, but to hurry the pace is unworthy of us all."

On March 7th, Gertrude had written of the mental anguish of her intense feelings of love, and that she was swimming in a sea, and being swept over by *"desolating waves of loneliness."* Only on occasions did she sight the *"headland of Paradise"* which was their future life together. Death was what she saw as the only option if she was unable to reach the headland. If she failed in her efforts to reach it, the only option was to:

"fall back into the flood from which I came, but this time under it, full fathom five – too deep to see the light of the seas or hear the sound of tempests, to a calm resting place, a profound eternal peace – an end, the fire quenched. That's not so bad indeed."

So death for her was a double-barrelled option. It was a way to meet up again with Dick, but it was also *"not so bad indeed"* if they couldn't be together.

As Gertrude pondered death as a way to rejoin her beloved, or a way to ease the pain of being alone, she mused on the concept of suicide. She viewed it as a right. As a last resort, it was something that couldn't be taken from her. She explained this to Dick, as part of a long letter on March 7, 1915:

"Yes, about cheating life; what I was saying before, on all those pages before, it's not cheating life. It's outwitting sentient death. That's a human right – the only door of escape to which the almighty builder gave us the key. It's in our hands, the key; once we may turn it, once only, & escape for ever. I told you I was not afraid – afraid! It's the one salvation knowing that there is a door which I can open. I am freed from anxiety – I never think of shot & shell, nor of the

plunge back from the headland which you may ask of me; I never think of them – they can't touch me; I shall be beyond their reach."

Exactly a month before the Gallipoli landings Gertrude had written another letter that would have stunned Charles. She was back in London to run the Office of Wounded and Missing from the new headquarters, and was back in her room where she had spent some of those fateful four days on Dick's last visit there. She wrote:

"My dear. I have just got back to England & it's late. I have had a very rushing time these last few days. But I must write to you, if only because this room is so full of you - & my heart & my thoughts, which are yours and always yours…. I'm anxious about the near East, & therefore dreadfully anxious about you & longing to hear what is the state of things & if possible where you are.

There are no letters – I ache for them. None since Malta."

She then went on to drop a bombshell:

"My dear, my dear, what can I write to you in this room? I can scarcely bear it – only bear it by turning my thoughts as bravely to the uncertain future, about which I will admit no uncertainty – your safe return & then? – That's all I think of. For against any other alternative I have made myself secure. Do you remember that my doctor made me take morphine with me on my last journey? I never used it & now I've sent for it from home & have it always by me, two full tubes, enough, I think, to cut a thread even as strong as mine. That's why I feel safe. …..when my heart quails I remember the morphine tubes & know there's a way out, smooth & easy, a sleep – to wake where? If I can't sleep in your arms, I'll sleep this way."

This was no attention-seeking ploy. She knew that Dick was in no position to rush to her side. She genuinely saw those two glass tubes as: *"a way out, smooth & easy."*

Charles was alarmed by the state of mind of both the women in his life, and how they would deal with his possible death. They both saw a sensible path as suicide via a morphine overdose.

I think the irony of the coincidence would have been entirely lost on him.

Some serious consideration must also be given by us to Dick Doughty-Wylie's own state of mind, as he was faced with the realistic scenario of being killed at Gallipoli.

He possibly saw being killed as one way out of his personal dilemma. He was an Intelligence Officer, on Hamilton's staff to provide experience and expert opinion about Turkey. This was best done from HMS *Queen* or one of the larger ships lying off-shore.

Was it a death-wish that drove him to request a posting on the *River Clyde*, and a death-wish that eventually saw him charge the enemy unarmed? Was the invitation from Colonel Williams seen as a possible way out of what to Dick was an increasingly impossible love triangle?

In that last letter he wrote to his mother-in-law it seems he was ensuring that Lilian's parents be ready to comfort her after her suicidal talk of *"morphia and such things."*

His description of the landing was a clear warning that he saw that his own chances of coming through it were slim. The whole letter could even be taken as his will, as regards Lilian. He wrote:

"I am going to embark tomorrow on what is certainly an extremely dangerous job, namely the wreck ship of which you will see in the papers. If things went wrong, ..."

Another of his final acts was to bundle up Gertrude's letters that were in his kit, and post them back to her. This also seems to be the act of a man who was expecting to die, and who envisaged a comrade going through his personal effects. It was Colonel Weir DeLancy Williams who was first on the scene after Charles fell down dead, and removed his *"watch, money and a few things."* Charles certainly couldn't allow his effects to include a packet of love letters. Everything could have ended up with Lilian, his widow.

A month after his fellow officer's death, Williams wrote more of Doughty-Wylie and his behaviour on the last days. His assessment of Dick's state of mind is interesting:

"... the Clyde was fired on throughout the day and Doughty-Wylie seemed positively to enjoy it. ... He was rather a fatalist ... I am firmly of the opinion that poor Doughty-Wylie realized he would be killed in this war."

This fatalistic attitude makes us look further into the demeanour of Charles when he first went ashore. Most of his actions could have been construed to mean he was seeking his own death. Soon after landing he had had his cap shot off his head. Lieutenant Nightingale was surprised by his reaction when he wrote:

"I ... remember being struck by the calm way in which he treated the incident."

Between the incident with the cap, and the final and fatal charge up to Hill 141, Doughty-Wylie led Nightingale and others through the village. It was dangerous work, as around any corner there could be an enemy soldier. Nightingale says of this time:

"I saw him on several occasions that morning walk into houses, which might or might not contain a Turk ready to fire on the first person who came in, as unconcernedly as if he were walking into a shop."

Was his mood calm because this was how he saw his way ahead, and his escape from his situation? He may have been surprised to survive that morning in the village. He may have seen the final crazy unarmed charge up the hill as the way to achieve the result he had come to desire.

Chapter 20 - A Visitor to the Grave on Hill 141

So which of the two women in Dick Doughty-Wylie's heart placed the wreath on his grave?

If Lilian could do anything to cement her place in history as the visitor, she most surely would have. Humiliation would have been certain with the knowledge that the only visitor to her husband's grave was another woman. This would have been an unbearable burden.

On the other hand, Gertrude Bell still had to deal with the fact that the man she had loved was married. Their whole affair (and a visit to his grave) would naturally be seen in hindsight by her family and the conservative Edwardian society as most indiscreet. Those who didn't know of the affair would be shocked, and the few who did know would have thought it all best forgotten.

Thus it would seem that both women would want history to say that the visitor was Lilian!

It was ten months after his death, and nearly two months after the evacuation of Cape Helles when a picture of Doughty-Wylie's grave was published in 'The Illustrated War News.' The full page photo shows a French officer reading the inscription on the wooden cross of the lonely grave. There is already some permanence to the site, with a rough enclosure and some cannon balls that are the debris of an earlier era.

The caption is almost a waste of space, as most of it continues the story that he was killed fighting with the Australians. It finishes by saying that the wreath was:

"placed there by Lady Doughty-Wylie herself, the only lady allowed to land on Gallipoli Peninsula."

It is no surprise that the officer who appears in the photo is a Frenchman.

The French had originally landed on the other side of the Dardanelles to act as a diversion to the main landings on the Peninsula, and to stop the Turks from transferring troops across the straits to the Peninsula. They were successful in some very heavy fighting against troops not as well led or organised as those at Gallipoli, but Kitchener's grand plan was always for it to be no more than a diversion.

They were withdrawn at night on April 26th after only 36 hours ashore. For the rest of the campaign they fought with the British at Cape Helles. By the time of the November visitor, Hill 141 and the grave were definitely in the French domain.

The Only Woman at Gallipoli

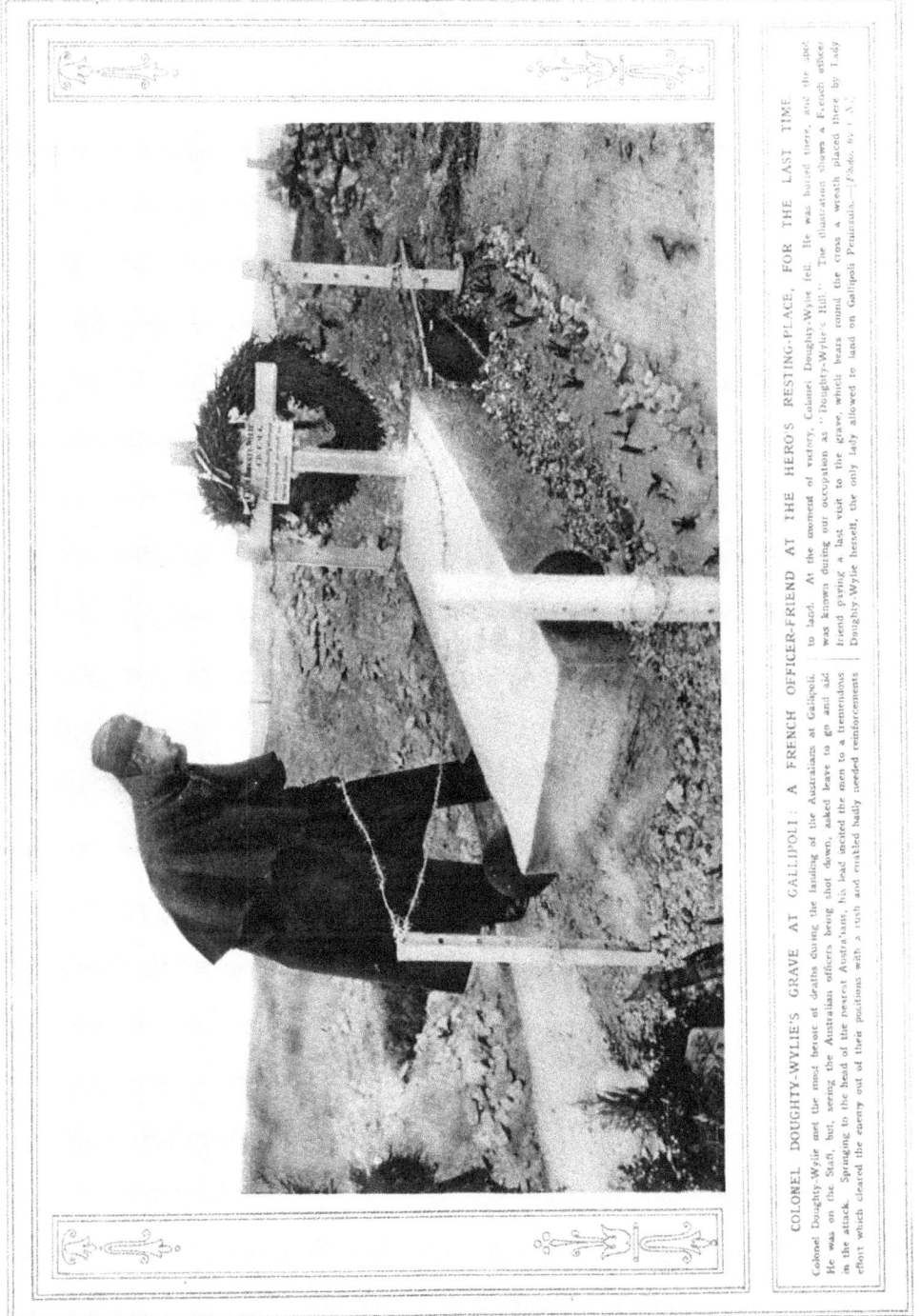

COLONEL DOUGHTY-WYLIE'S GRAVE AT GALLIPOLI: A FRENCH OFFICER-FRIEND AT THE HERO'S RESTING-PLACE, FOR THE LAST TIME.

Colonel Doughty-Wylie met the most heroic of deaths during the landing of the Australians at Gallipoli. He was on the Staff, but, seeing the Australian officers being shot down, asked leave to go and aid in the attack. Springing to the head of the nearest Australians, his lead incited the men to a tremendous effort which cleared the enemy out of their positions with a rush and enabled badly needed reinforcements to land. At the moment of victory, Colonel Doughty-Wylie fell. He was buried there, and the spot was known during our occupation as "Doughty-Wylie's Hill". The illustration shows a French officer friend paying a last visit to the grave, which bears round the cross a wreath placed there by Lady Doughty-Wylie herself, the only lady allowed to land on Gallipoli Peninsula.—Photo. by C.N.

A version of the photo is also in the archives of the Imperial War Museum. It has been cropped at the top, but actually shows a little more at the bottom.

The brief caption hand-written under the photo says:

"A French officer paying a last visit to the grave of his friend, Col. Doughty-Wylie, V.C. The wreath seen at the head of the grave was placed there by Lady Doughty-Wylie herself. Lady Doughty-Wylie was the only lady to land on the Peninsula during the war."

This is a simple repetition of the caption in 'The Illustrated War News', with only the misinformation about the Australians omitted. The date 19/11/17 is also pencilled on (below 'Dar' for Dardanelles) but the caption is in pen and seems to be in a different hand. The date is apparently when the photo was accepted and catalogued at the

Imperial War Museum, nearly two years after the evacuation. When the caption was written is long forgotten, and what it says is quite likely an assumption.

I note also that 'The Illustrated War News' caption claims the Frenchman to be his *"Officer-Friend"* and the IWM caption subtly alters the wording so that the French officer is at *"the grave of his friend."*

Charles was killed on only the second day, before the French arrived at Cape Helles, following their hasty withdrawal from Kum Kale. Is it likely that a sub-editor at 'The News' recognised the Frenchman months later, and actually knew that this officer was a friend of Doughty-Wylie? Surely not! If the identity of the supposed friend was known, why is he merely an un-named French officer?

Is it likely that Charles met a French Officer in India, or the Sudan, or anywhere else where he served in the British Army? Possibly, but who would know this?

All of this caused me to doubt everything written by 'The News' (and repeated by the IWM) in relation to the photograph. The photo itself is a great shot, but I see little of any solid merit in the caption applied many months later by 'The News', and recycled more than a year later by the IWM.

During later research, I came across the photo for a third time. It had appeared in a newspaper, with the addition of a small inset picture of Lilian. The caption mentions yet again the French friend, and yet again that Lilian was the visitor, but the repetition of mistakes does not ever turn them into facts.

The trouble is, nearly everything written in the papers at the time is seen in hindsight to be not quite right. Stories were essentially conjured from tips and rumours, and as the war rolled on they became facts.

When I first received the IWM photo and caption, another handwritten note was attached. This note is from the IWM to me personally, and answered an earlier query I put to them.

I had simply asked them how sure they were of the captions, which were nearly a hundred years old. The note to me says: 'We have no reason to doubt the original caption stating that Lady Doughty-Wylie placed the wreath.'

Dear Mr Howell,
Enclosed is a photocopy of Q 13704 + order form/price list. We have no reason to doubt the original caption stating that Lady Doughty-Wylie placed the wreath.

Yours sincerely,
Laura Clouting

How much store can we really put in any of these original captions, or in the note from the IWM to me? If any photographer was at the graveside when the victims loved one made a visit, would he forgo the opportunity to capture this rare and special visit by a woman to the battlefield? Surely not!

That a widow could make such a visit is extraordinary. The grave was near the front line of a war zone, on an isolated peninsula in Turkey. The only approach was by boat, and the boat would be under enemy fire.

That it could be another woman is even more extraordinary, in these very proper and (outwardly) moralistic times.

What of the wreath? It wasn't produced by the Frenchman or the photographer. They didn't scour the devastated locale for suitable foliage, and pull some appropriate ribbon from their pockets. This is a wreath brought from off-shore by a visitor intending to pay homage to a loved one. If nothing else, the wreath confirms that there was a visitor from off shore.

As to the timing of the photograph, it was taken soon after the visit of the mystery woman. A wreath of green foliage wouldn't have lasted a long time.

The French Officer must have been included by the photographer, to make it more than just another photo of another grave. It is also certainly late in the campaign, and the cold that arrived with the storms of November is reflected in the officer's heavy clothing. We get a hint of who this French Officer may have been, from the unlikely source of Dick's own brother.

The Only Woman at Gallipoli

French friend's farewell to the grave of Col. Doughty-Wyllie, V.C.—(Inset) Mrs. Doughty-Wyllie, the only Englishwoman who landed in Gallipoli during the war, and who herself placed the wreath on the simple headstone.

A Newspaper's Version (from during the war) of the Photograph of the Grave

The newspaper touched up the barbed wire for dramatic effect and superimposed on it the face of a young Lilian.

Hugh Doughty visited his brother's grave three or four months after the time of the landing, and took his own photograph. The wooden cross is all there is at this time, but the name plate can be clearly read. What strikes the eye is what goes across the top of the cross. The grave was near the French Headquarters, and the cross has been used as a telegraph pole! Telephone lines are strung across, emphasizing that although a grave is a respected thing, this is a grave in the middle of a battleground. [When the later photo with the French officer was taken, the lines are in the background.]

Hugh kindly sent a small print of his photograph to Gertrude, in September 1915. The covering letter starts: *"Dear Miss Bell"* and finishes with:

"I enclose a photograph that I took of his grave as it is at Sedd el Bahr. It is in the French lines by their Head Quarters & artillery observation.

A French major kindly promised to look after it while he was there.

Yours sincerely H.M.Doughty"

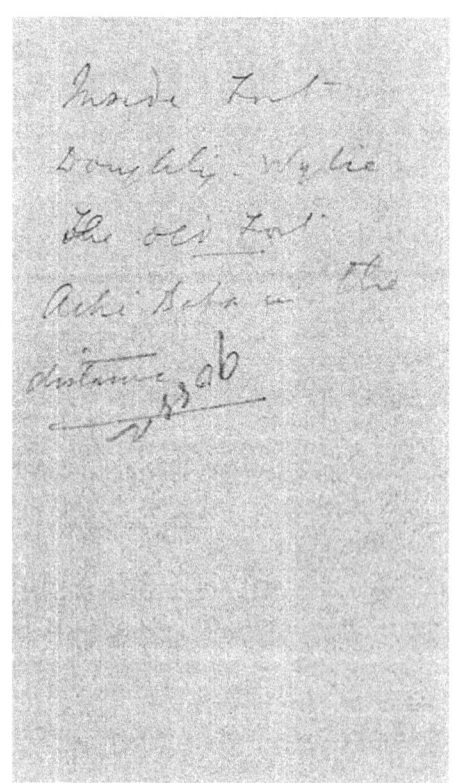

So the French major was simply someone stationed nearby, who promised a visiting British naval officer that he would keep an eye on a grave near his headquarters.

Of course there is one last possibility to consider for the trio of photographs. It is that the original including the French officer was taken while the mystery female visitor was still there, but that she declined or refused to be photographed.

I see no reason why Lilian would have feared to be acknowledged as being at the grave of her husband – she would have been pleased and proud to be there.

None of this reasoning applies to Gertrude. I see a string of reasons why Gertrude Bell would not want to pose at the graveside.

The cemeteries of Gallipoli contain many (too many) thousands of graves. This is one of the few that weren't moved after the war. As an example, Captain Garth Walford was killed nearby only hours before Doughty-Wylie, and was also buried where he fell. Walford's and Doughty-Wylie's Victoria Crosses were announced together, so their cases are very comparable. Captain Walford's grave was moved, and is now among the many in the V Beach cemetery you can see in the picture on page 28.

Because of the special and singular nature of the Doughty-Wylie grave, we have an individual report of its rebuilding in 1923, to the grave that is there today. [see note on page 305]

The engineer's name was Cooke, and he was working for the Imperial War Graves Commission. It is easy to see from his writings that the original internment on April 26 was done hurriedly by tired men:

"The grave was located on a small knoll just outside the village. I was requested by the IWGC to make the site more permanent as his widow had in view building a monument over it. We went to the spot and I instructed my men to make a trench down to solid ground around it, then to pour concrete in it and cap the whole grave with a 6 inch slab of concrete. Within a few inches his body became visible – enveloped in a ragged uniform with belt, huddled in a crouched

position. I hurried to get the foundations around the bones and waited to put the concrete slab over him. I hope he now rests in peace."

Engineer Cooke mentions Lilian, so she must have had some contact with the IWGC, and her wishes were passed on to him. Effectively, they came as instructions to consolidate the grave rather than exhume. She certainly had involvement with the IWGC for a few years before Cooke's 1923 works, so the credit for the retention of the unique single grave must go to Lilian.

His account of the state of the body also gives us some insight into the harrowing nature of the post-war task to create the cemeteries we see on battlefields today.

To write a book about Charles, Lilian and Gertrude meant seeking information from many original sources. With a mystery to be solved, it also meant reading what others had thought.

It turned out that various authors have offered all combinations of opinion, of both the visit and the visitor. They disagree on when it was, or if it happened at all, and just who it might have actually been.

Les Carlyon, in his 2001 *'Gallipoli'* says that most likely the woman who came ashore at the *River Clyde* was Lilian - but that it just may have been Gertrude. His splendid suggestion is for a film to be made. Only in the last reel will the mystery-woman's veil be lifted to reveal her true identity.

It was Les Carlyon's few pages about Charles, Lilian and Gertrude that first caught my eye and started my search for the flesh to put on the bones of this tale.

An earlier *'Gallipoli'* is the 1956 book by Alan Moorehead. He was an Australian living in London when he wrote the book, and it was perhaps the first popular book by an Australian to criticise the British command in respect of Anzac Cove. For many decades it became the oversimplified truth for all those in Australia and New Zealand, that everything done by High Command was not quite right, and that everything they should have done was now obvious. Moorehead doesn't mention Doughty-Wylie's grave but quotes from a 1936 book *'Letters from Helles'* by a Colonel Darlington.

Darlington's book doesn't claim that a woman came ashore at all, but that a group in a launch come in close. He quotes from Darlington that:

"Sure enough there was a party of Australian nurses being shown around the shore to see how the wild soldier lives and sleeps. I got my glasses to see the unusual sight and much to all our Tommies' annoyance a young nut of a staff officer with much ostentation put his arm around one of the nurses' waists, struck an attitude and waved his hand to us. We all shook our fists at him, which caused great amusement on the launch."

This story comes in a part where Moorehead is making *his* point that any woman on the Peninsula would be an extraordinary thing. I include his story because *my* point is that he (and Darlington) obviously heard no talk of any woman being ashore.

On the same theme of the absolute novelty of a woman ashore, there are tales around that some of the feared Turkish snipers were women. The claims are unsubstantiated, and published mentions usually bring a flood of rebuttals. They seem to be the military version of an urban myth.

Aubrey Herbert was the officer who supervised the burials in no-man's land during the May ceasefire. He had landed with the New Zealanders and said that after a few days *"spy mania"* started. Wild and ridiculous rumours were on every soldier's lips, but he was not taken in.

He wrote sarcastically of a female sniper:

"The first convincing proof of treachery which we had was the story of a Turkish girl who had painted her face green in order to look like a tree, and had shot several people at Helles from the boughs of an oak."

Eric Bush in his 1975 book, again simply called *'Gallipoli,'* sees it quite differently to Les Carlyon. He is not sure either woman could have made the journey in 1915, but says that Lilian was a visitor in 1919. There is some more on his puzzling pieces a few pages on.

Michael Hickey, in his 1995 *'Gallipoli'* also uses the term *"most likely"* for a visit to the grave by Lilian, and calls talk of Gertrude *"a persistent story."* He leaves the door open a little bit by acknowledging that she was *"also in the area at the time."* He then goes on to say that Gertrude Bell *"certainly visited the grave in 1919."*

All that is *certain* is that this is the complete opposite of Eric Bush's version of 1919! Michael Hickey also says that the reason the grave is the only single grave on the peninsula is that it was the wish of Turkey - the hero's grave should be left at the site of his triumph. It is a noble thought, but doesn't seem to fit with Engineer Cooke's report.

Harvey Broadbent in his book *'Gallipoli - The Fatal Shore'* makes no call. He accepts that Lilian was probably the visitor, but covers his options by adding that Doughty-Wylie: *"had also been the lover of the English writer and explorer Gertrude Bell."*

Georgina Howell (no relation of mine, to the best of my knowledge) in her 2006 book *'Daughter of the Desert,'* presents some evidence for both sides, but firmly believes that the visitor to the grave was Gertrude Bell. This is no surprise, as she is unashamedly a Gertrude Bell supporter and so by inference, a Lilian Doughty-Wylie detractor.

Richard Stowers in his 2005 book *'Bloody Gallipoli. The New Zealanders Story'* is unable to say whether the woman was Lilian or Gertrude. He does however; say that the visit was on November 17, when Lilian *"was nursing with the French Hospital Service in France."*

Surely this leaves Gertrude as his only option?

He goes on to say that the woman landed alongside the *River Clyde*, and walked to the grave. Her clothing was black. These days we would interpret the black clothing to be appropriate for a widow. It isn't that simple. In those days all women (especially of the upper classes) would have worn black mourning clothes to a graveside. If it was Gertrude Bell, she was going to V Beach with only one purpose. She would have dressed appropriately for the man she loved.

The Only Woman at Gallipoli

I am unsure where the particular date of November 17 comes from. It is in quite a number of the publications, quite possibly because later authors read it in some early work and took it on face value.

Stephen Snelling, in his detailed 1995 book *'VCs of the First World War - Gallipoli'*, writes the facts and details as if set in stone. The visit was on November 17, and the visitor was Lilian.

The official Australian website about Gallipoli agrees with Stephen Snelling. www.anzacsite.gov.au mentions also Lilian visiting the grave on November 17. They apparently based their notes on Snelling's well-respected book.

Huw and Jill Rodge in their 2003 *'Gallipoli: The Landing at Helles'* make no call on which of the two women it might have been, but do have a slant on the visit not mentioned by others. They point out that at the time of the visit, V Beach was a zone under French control. Permission to visit was possibly granted by them due to: *"the romantic streak in their personae"* – In other words, the British would have said "No!"

French control in the area would better explain the presence of the officer in the photograph. He is thus much more likely to have been an escort for the visiting photographer, rather than a friend of our dead hero.

For maybe three years during writing, the title of this book was *'The Only Woman at Gallipoli.'* In April of 2013 I was forced to rethink that exclusiveness. The bookshops now had *'Australian Heroines of World War One'* by Susanna de Vries. The book follows the almost untold story of some nurses, and the heroic work they did under appalling conditions in Europe and the Middle East.

One of the nurses featured is a woman called Hilda Samsing, and she was on a hospital ship near Gallipoli called *Gascon*. The part of Hilda's story that caught my eye was during the dreadful weather of late November 1915. It culminated in snow and blizzards, and too many soldiers were ill-equipped to deal with these extremes. Many died and were found frozen at their posts, and thousands more had frostbite.

The story was that *Gascon* went to Salonika (in Greece) and loaded almost to capacity with suffering men. They then sailed to Suvla Bay, as they had room to squeeze in 300 more.

In the first days of December 1915, Hilda became the second woman to set foot on the shore. She went with a Doctor Hugo, and their task was to pick those 300 lucky men from the vast numbers with frost-bite. By December 5, her diary records that they had been taken aboard, and the *Gascon* sailed from Suvla to Egypt.

This came like a lightning bolt from a blue sky to me. I reluctantly shortened the working title to: *'The Woman at Gallipoli.'* Hilda's story fascinated me nonetheless, so I obtained some copies of her diary from the Australian War Memorial.

To my great surprise I found that Susanna de Vries had misread Hilda's poor handwriting, or had mistaken her own notes. *Gascon* hadn't loaded men in Salonika and then squeezed in 300 more from Suvla Bay. They had simply loaded 300 men in Salonika and sailed directly to Alexandria and the hospitals there. Hilda Samsing went ashore in neutral Salonika with Dr. Hugo to choose the lucky 300.

I contacted Susanna de Vries, and she accepted my version and thanked me for discovering the error. She was gracious enough to not want to 'shoot the messenger,' and three months later I reverted to my original title.

Writing a book about events that happened a hundred years ago is a journey. It is a physical journey through libraries and their books and journals, and it has taken me around Australia and to Britain and Turkey.

For me, it has also been a journey along emotional paths, with sudden changes of direction. For the first year, the path zig-zagged and took me to many places. I simply accumulated pieces of an interesting jigsaw puzzle as I came across them.

Early in the second year the pieces were being assembled, and new pieces to fill old gaps came to light. I could see an overall picture starting to appear. At about this time I wrote the following page:

The most tantalising pieces I leave to last.

Whilst neither woman was plain about a visit in her own hand, two interesting letters remain from Gertrude Bell. She plainly hints that she had plans.

Gertrude had been summoned to Cairo to join the Arab Bureau in early November, and actually embarked from Marseilles on the 20th. On the 16th she wrote to her step-mother Florence:

"I think it likely that when I reach Egypt I shall find they have no job that will occupy me more than a fortnight, and I may be back before Christmas. It's all vaguer than words can say. <u>As to any further journey nothing definite is said and I think the chances are strongly against it.</u>"

Her next letter to Florence was written from Cairo, but mentions the day of arrival in Port Said. Between being greeted by Capt. Woolley and dining that night, he took her to see a Colonel Elgood. He was the governor of Port Said, and we must assume that it was Gertrude's idea to get straight off the dock and go to his office. She was manoeuvring for this *"further journey,"* and wrote to her mother that she: *"had an interesting talk with him."*

While researching this project, I have at times thought that the 1915 visitor to the grave was Lilian, and at times thought it was Gertrude. More often than not I had been unable to decide.

At the end of the day I decided I should make a decision, and that my searching had qualified me to make one – be it right or wrong.

I truly believe now, that the visitor to the Doughty-Wylie grave in 1915 was Gertrude Bell.

At the end of the second year of writing, a pathway was long enough to take me to the Imperial War Museum in London. They had been posting information to me in Australia, but it was never new knowledge. I had to know the gist of what they would send me. Without prior knowledge I didn't know what was worth requesting.

In May 2011, I stood outside the IWM under the shadows of the pair of 15 inch guns (identical to those of the *Queen Elizabeth*) and waited for the doors to open. I hoped doors would open for me also, and that I would make new discoveries. I hoped for exciting new pieces of my puzzle, that previous researchers had missed or not appreciated.

Boxes of archived material were waiting for me in the Research Room, as my visit had been booked a month before. For five hours I delighted in going through the first-hand information. Interesting titbits abounded, and were transcribed or put aside for copying. In the middle of the afternoon came that special moment I had hoped for.

It was a short letter - just a note, really. A note that I had heard existed, and that had received brief mentions in only some writings about Charles, Lilian and Gertrude. Quite possibly it had been also read by some writers who then chose to ignore it. Acceptance of what it said may have blown years of their work out of the window.

As I read it out to my wife that night I realised that it was a piece of puzzle that wasn't going to drop conveniently into any of my gaps. A shuffle of pieces was now required, with the shifting of some that had seemed quite settled until this day.

My single page conclusion was put on hold.

The note had been written by Lilian from the Greek island of Thasos, to Lord Granville. At the time he was the British Ambassador to Greece.

Here for the first time in full is Lilian's note. The underlining of the last paragraph is mine:

March 21st, 1918 BMGS Hospital, Limenaria, Thasos:

Dear Lord Granville

I wonder if you could persuade the Greek Government to do something for the people of Thasos.

Conditions here are very bad indeed; one of the French officers from Limenaria, the chief town on the island, tells me that there were 150 deaths from privation last month.

The flour ration which comes to the island is very scanty & what is worse very irregular, & there seem to be no other cereals to fall back upon. When we go out we are followed by women and children asking for bread, & altogether the situation is very sad.

I tried to get 50 pounds worth of flour from Mudros for the most destitute families in the village, but the export is not allowed and as we in the Hospital are on service rations we have nothing to give away.

I do not know what the conditions are in other parts of Greece, and it may be quite impossible to do anything but I could not help writing to you on the off chance & I do hope you don't mind.

<u>*I have been out here since November 1915. I took your advice and was somewhat importunate at the French War Office, with the result that they sent me out here in time to visit Sedd. El. Bahr before the evacuation, a success I owe in some measure to you.*</u>

Believe me
Yours very truly
       Lily Doughty-Wylie

Lilian's 1918 note to Lord Granville

So here it was, spelt out in unusually legible black and white. A definitive statement, that brought my search and a great mystery to a close.

Or did it? Was it the truth?

Chapter 21 - With Gertrude For The Duration

Gertrude Bell had arrived in Egypt in late November of 1915 and had surmised that she may be going all that way for *"no job that will occupy me more than a fortnight."* In fact she was a valuable asset to the Arab Bureau, and in January 1916 was given a new task.

British administration in the Empire was such that those in Cairo had responsibility for only Egypt and the Sudan. Arabia, Persia, Jordan and Mesopotamia were administered by Viceroy Lord Charles Hardinge and the government in India.

The two groups saw most things differently, and whereas a war should have brought about more cooperation, the opposite was the case. Those in Cairo had a long term view of the founding of some new Arab nations, and a short term view of promoting an Arab uprising against Constantinople. The Indian colonial administration was far removed, in more ways than one. Soldiers and money were needed from India to support and fight alongside the Arabs if any uprising was to avoid being crushed by the Turks.

When Gertrude was a young woman staying with her uncle and aunt in Bucharest, she had got to know Charles Hardinge as a lesser diplomat. Cairo saw her as the ideal person to go and try to gain support for what they saw as the way ahead.

She wrote to her father on the 16/1/1916 about correspondence she was having with another old and influential family friend in India, and the problems between the two administrations:

"I rather hope I may hear this week from Domnul in reply to a cable I sent him saying I might come out to India at the end of the month. My chief here is warmly in favour of the idea and if Domnul gives me any further encouragement

I think I shall go. There's not much time to be lost if I am to catch Lord H. And not much point in going if I can't. "

She went on to comment about the awkward communications between the British administrations in Egypt and India:

"There is no kind of touch between us except rather bad tempered telegrams! And it would be a great advantage if we could establish more direct and friendly relations, so that each side may cease to regard the other as composed mostly of knaves. It's too silly."

Her visit to India was soon confirmed, and by January 28 she wrote of rushing to catch the *Euripides:*

"I'm off at a moment's notice to catch a troopship at Suez. I really do the oddest things. I learnt at 3pm that I could catch it if I left at 6pm. ... I'm charged with much negotiation – I hope I may be well inspired."

When she arrived in Delhi she was picked up by Domnul Chirol*, who took her to her lodgings. The same day she dined with the Viceroy and discussions began.

Hardinge was agreeable and positive, and the next weeks were spent building bridges between Egypt and India, and exchanging information and intelligence. He also came to see that the girl he had known in Bucharest was now grown up, and was knowledgeable and useful.

On 18/2/1916 she wrote again to her father, and her next move was about to happen: *"The V. is anxious that I should stay at Basra and lend a hand with the Intelligence Department there."*

---

* Domnul was in fact Valentine Chirol. He was an old family friend of the Bells, and was a life-long confidante of Gertrude. Domnul is Rumanian for 'gentlemen,' and this was a nickname he was given in Rumania. He was in Bucharest as a correspondent for the 'Times', when Gertrude stayed with her Aunt Mary and Uncle Frank Lascelles as a young adult. By 1916 he was in India, and was now Sir Valentine Chirol.

She went on to express her surprise at the reception she had got from Hardinge and his officials: *"They have been curiously eager to talk – much more than I expected – and I think I have pulled things straight a little as between Delhi and Cairo."*

She ended up as an Intelligence Officer in Basra until December, 1916. She was now officially a Major! Gertrude certainly found plenty to do in Basra, and it seems she felt the Intelligence Department here was optimistically named. She wrote to Hugh on 14/5/1916:

"Dearest Father ... I might be recalled to Egypt where they are fussing to have me back, but I am persuaded that for the moment I am much more useful here. ... None of these people from India know Arabic and what that means in an Intelligence Dept. I leave you to guess."

Six weeks earlier she wrote to Florence about the passing visit of another friend she had left behind at the Arab Bureau in Cairo:

"This week has been greatly enlivened by the appearance of Mr. Lawrence sent out as liaison officer from Egypt. We have had great talks and made vast schemes for the government of the universe. ... He goes up river tomorrow, where the battle is raging these days. With what anxiety we watch for news it would be difficult to tell you."

Mr. Lawrence met up in Basra with Aubrey Herbert, and the two stayed at Gertrude's house. Herbert was the officer in no-man's-land during the Gallipoli ceasefire mentioned earlier. By now he was a British MP and was also with the Arab Bureau. He too was an old acquaintance of Gertrude, and she had met him and stayed with him many years earlier in Japan. T. E. Lawrence and Herbert were to go *"up river"* together, with a Lt. Col. Beach.

Their destination further up the Tigris River was the town of Kut, and the three men were sent on a mission that can have few parallels in the histories of wars past and present. A large British force was besieged there, and the situation was increasingly hopeless. Lawrence, Herbert and Beach were to offer the Turks a fortune in British pounds; a desperate bribe to buy freedom for the besieged force, and avoid an annihilation!

Mesopotamia is the region to the north west of the Persian Gulf. It includes the valleys of the Tigris and the Euphrates, and the lands between the two mighty rivers. Military control during the War came from British government in India. According to London, India was the East. Beyond India was Asia, so this became the Far East. This left Mesopotamia and Arabia to become the Middle East. [See map on p.188]

Whitehall's only desire for this Middle East was the security of the oilfields and the refinery in the south. Those in India accepted this, but had their own grander visions. The capture of Baghdad would essentially eliminate the southern half of the Ottoman Empire. It would enable the British to control the whole of the Arabian Peninsula, from the Persian Gulf to the Red Sea. Baghdad was 500 kilometres from the mouth of the Tigris, and several times this amount when you travelled by boat around the countless meandering bends. Even so, river travel was the only practical way to move troops and supplies. Gunboats were the local equivalents of armoured cars, and hospitals were on paddle steamers.

British forces secured the southern oil fields, but then started continual advances up both the Tigris and the Euphrates. It was justified by claiming that the occupation of the next town upstream was always 'strategic' to the holding of the town just captured. By October, 1916 the British were at Ctesiphon. They were only 40 kilometres from Baghdad, but were very strung out from their southern starting point.

Reinforced Turkish forces now attacked the British, forcing them into a chaotic retreat for eight days and nights. Every day the temperature reached 115 F (46 C) and there was seemingly endless fighting with little water. The retreat was said to be the most arduous ever made by the British Army.

On December 1 they fell back to the town of Kut. Here they would stop and defend. Reports from Kut continued the use of superlatives. The town was seen as the most unsanitary town ever occupied, and was simply described in a war encyclopaedia as *"filthy beyond description."*

Kut was a small town surrounded on three sides by the Tigris. 12,000 British troops (of which 2,000 were sick or had been wounded during the retreat) added to 3500 Indian non-combatants, and all were besieged in a town only big enough for its 6000 Arab residents.

In command was Major-General Sir Charles Townshend, who said, *"I mean to defend Kut as I did Chitral!"* - for this was the very same Townshend that had been with Dick Doughty-Wylie back in 1895.

By April 16 they had been besieged for over four months, and Gertrude wrote to her father Hugh: *"How Kut holds out still I can barely guess, but it does hold out and we may yet get through in time."*

Townshend could see the hopelessness of their plight, and realised that even if they surrendered then most would die. He suggested that the ransom be offered for their freedom. Lord Kitchener showed more concern for the Empire than the garrison, and cabled to a General Lake:

"I sincerely hope that it is fully realized by you and all general officers under your command that it would be ever a disgrace to our country if Townshend should surrender. Our prestige in the East would be greatly prejudiced by such a disaster."

When Kitchener was convinced that the death of 15,000 soldiers was also a disaster, he relented and negotiators were sent in.

Lawrence, Herbert and Beach arrived at Kut late in April and tried to negotiate some terms with an offer of a million pounds! By this time, the siege had been going for five months, and it had started with a food supply adequate for only two months. In a world first, some food had been dropped in by air, and thousands of horses and mules had been killed and eaten. Cats and dogs were next to go, except of course Townshend's pampered hounds. Many of the Indian soldiers in Kut refused to eat the animals, so their condition was the worst.

By April 27, Gertrude was writing to Florence: *"Nothing happens and nothing seems likely to happen at Kut – it's a desperate business. Heaven knows how it will all end."*

General Pasha Khalil (the Turkish commander) thought the offer of a million pounds was a joke, when the three men were brought to him under a white flag. He thought exactly the same when the offer was promptly doubled by Lawrence and Herbert! They had no authorisation to do so, and while it raised no Turkish eyebrows, it would have certainly raised a few British ones.

Two million pounds then was of the order of 100 million pounds today. Negotiations in French and Turkish (which Herbert could speak) went on until late, so the three were invited to dine with Khalil and stay the night. The next day, with the money of no interest, found the British officers with little new to offer. Meanwhile hundreds more within Kut were dead and dying from starvation, exhaustion and disease. Negotiations eventually focussed on the wounded and possible prisoner exchanges, as nothing would buy the garrison a free passage. Having achieved no result, Lawrence, Herbert and Beach were sent back through the Turkish lines.

Townshend sent a last radio signal and surrendered on April 29. The siege had cost 1,000 dead and 2,500 wounded through the fighting, with more than 700 extra deaths from disease.

The Turks showed little urgency in the first week after the surrender, and a further 300 died. The shattered remnants of Townshend's force were then sent on a death march to distant prison camps, and a further 4,000 were to eventually die, including 70% of the British rank and file.

On top of these numbers, thousands more were killed and wounded trying to fight their way to relieve Kut. All available forces had been sent north, but without success.

Townshend was criticised after the war for not trying to break out during General Nixon's several attempts to relieve the siege. Making the Turks fight at Kut as well as against Nixon might have brought results. As Kitchener had feared, the whole episode was a blow to British military prestige, and no-one could ignore the terrible mistakes that were made.

As the sorry columns of men from Kut were marched north to prison and work camps, the weak and injured were left to die. Stragglers were stripped and killed by local Arabs. Any onlooker could see that these soldiers of the British Empire were far from invincible.

Kut and its sorry aftermath thus became one of the starting points for a phase that some call the End Of Empire.

The Turks had honoured the white flag of truce and allowed the negotiators to depart. They returned to Basra where Lawrence and Herbert stayed again with Gertrude Bell, and told her the sorry tale. Lawrence wrote a report to the Arab Bureau from Basra, and told Cairo he had been on a mission to *"Blunderland."*

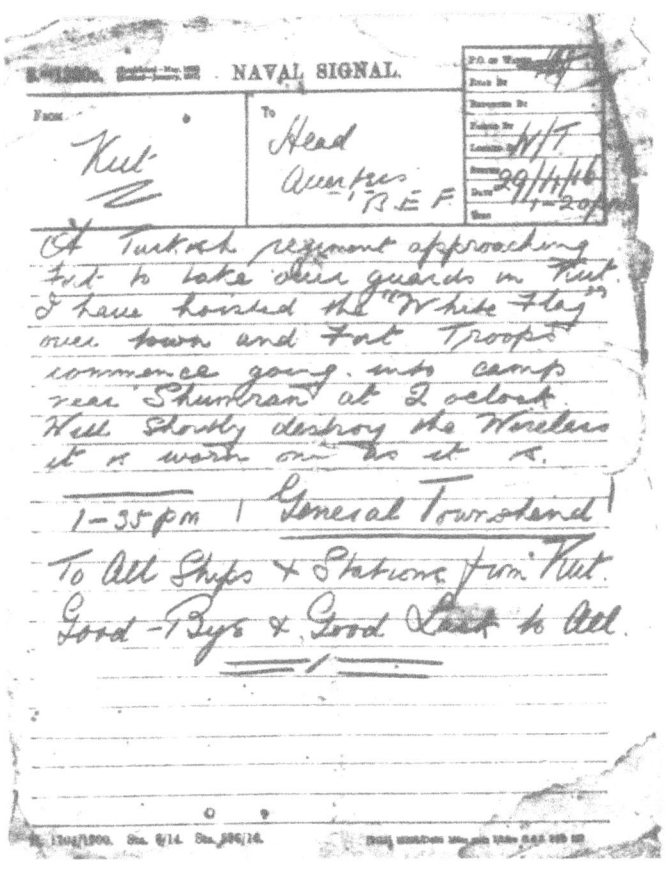

The transcript of Townshend's last message from Kut.
"To all Ships & Stations from Kut."
"Good-Bye & Good Luck to All."

1917 found Gertrude still in Basra, but with a new title. The local civil administration was now based in Basra under Sir Percy Cox, and Gertrude held the title of Oriental

Secretary. One biographer saw her title as a simple euphemism for 'spy,' and today we might call her a special advisor.

In May, Gertrude Bell had moved to live in Baghdad, and still worked for Sir Percy Cox. In July he was made the Civil Commissioner of Mesopotamia, and it could be seen that Baghdad would become the capital of any new Iraq.

On November 12, 1918, Australian Papers Headlined with Germany's Surrender.

On page 5, General Townsend was still seen as the hero of Kut.
His star does not shine as brightly in modern times.

By the end of the year the Turks were in full flight and the British had occupied Jerusalem. Throughout 1918 they continued to retreat, at times in chaos. Damascus fell on October 1st, and Turkey was essentially beaten.

By the middle of October 1918, Turkish emissaries were approaching British diplomats in various countries, and both sides were moving for a settlement. The Turkish Cabinet then did a surprising thing. They released a prisoner of war to negotiate on their behalf.

They chose none other Major-General Sir Charles Townshend, who had been a prisoner since the siege of Kut. No-one was impressed with Townshend's negotiating skills back in April, 1916 when he was joined by Lawrence and Herbert in Kut. He must have been chosen, not on merit, but as the most senior British officer in their captivity.

He was brought to HMS *Agamemnon*, which was the flagship of Vice-Admiral Sir Somerset Gough-Calthorpe, Commander in Chief of the Mediterranean. Talks led to the arrival of Colonel Sadullah Bey from the Turkish General Staff.

On October 30, 1918 an armistice agreement was signed on board *Agamemnon* and Turkey's war was over.

Chapter 22 - Lilian Sees Out The War Years

Charles Doughty-Wylie died a hero's death and received Britain's highest military honour after his death. His heroism was front page news.

Gertrude Bell was famous in life and would also be famous after death, with a large obituary and photograph in 'The Times'. Glowing and public tributes came from many, including King George V.

Lilian's later life and eventual death were far more humble. Her whole life was as a dedicated nurse. She didn't win a Victoria Cross, and books are not dedicated to her, but hers was a career of serving that would last for over half a century. She was never in the public eye, but never stopped working for the good of others. Her contribution should really be seen as more than the other two combined, when taking into account the incredible length of her almost unsung working life.

After leaving France in 1915, Lilian had come back to familiar territory – a military hospital in the Middle East. Her diaries in the Imperial War Museum in London record the period from April 1916 to July of 1917. This whole period was after the evacuations of the Allies from Gallipoli, but a military hospital must remain operational until all its patients are healed or transferrable. The role of the Mudros hospital evolved to where they cared only for the personnel of the Royal Naval Division. The Division was transferred to France in May, 1916 leaving the hospital the lesser role of caring for the much reduced garrison of Lemnos.

In July, 1917 Lilian was still on the Greek island of Thasos. As can be seen from the earlier part of her letter to Lord Granville, it was a difficult time there for both service personnel and the locals. The island is not far from the Greek coast, and had a base and airstrip of the Royal Naval Air Service. (They had an assortment of other bases in the Aegean, including at Mudros where she had also been, and Imbros.) Thasos was the home of RNAS 'A' Squadron, who flew DeHavilland DH4 bombers and Sopwith Camel fighter planes. [see note on page 306]

Lilian established, and was the matron of the Limenaria Hospital on Thasos; something she had done well at previous locations. Her diaries from Thasos finish in December, 1918. They probably ceased when the majority of the personnel were repatriated home.

The hospital carried on for some months after the Armistice, because when she was presented with her MBE in January of 1919, she was still officially described as the matron of the Limenaria Hospital, Thasos. She was also decorated by the government of Greece for her service on the island, when in December 1918 Greece awarded Lilian and a Surgeon L.B.Stringer their Cross of Military Merit.

The end of the Great War also brought a temporary pause to her life of nursing. Within a few months she changed her role from looking after sick and wounded soldiers, to looking for the graves of those that had died.

She joined the Imperial War Graves Commission and went back to Turkey.

Chapter 23 - The Arab Uprising

When Sharif Hussain fired a shot into the air on June 2, 1916 it was the first symbolic shot of the Arab Uprising. He fired the shot from the balcony of a palace in Mecca, because he was Sharif Hussain, Amir of Mecca, and therefore a direct descendant of Mohammed. This made him the most powerful leader in Arabia.

The next two most powerful men were Ibn Rashid (whose base was Hayyil, where Gertrude had journeyed in 1913 and 1914), and Ibn Saud. The power of these two men was somewhat lessened as they were continually pre-occupied with fighting each other.

It was one thing for Gertrude Bell and the other Egypt-based British 'Intrusives' to be whispering in senior ears about Arab independence. It became much more when the Arabs themselves started to believe, and had the courage to fight their Ottoman masters.

Understanding the power and prestige of Hussain, Lord Kitchener had held discussions even before World War One broke out. Various official talks continued over the years, to ensure that Hussain had the courage and backing to revolt. Kitchener himself died only three days after the first symbolic shot. On June 5 he was on the cruiser HMS *Hampshire* going to see Tsar Nicholas II. The ship hit a mine off the Orkney coast and sank in a gale with nearly all on board.

By this time Sharif Hussain was having discussions with Henry McMahon, the High Commissioner of Egypt. He arranged a payment of £20,000 to Hussain, and armed the new allies with some surplus and out-dated British armaments. Lawrence described the weapons early on in the uprising, including two old fifteen-pounder field guns:

"Rasim, ... was fighting these two guns; and he made a great demonstration with them. They had been sent down as a gift from Egypt, anyhow, old rubbish

thought serviceable for the wild Arabs, just as the sixty thousand rifles supplied the Sharif were condemned weapons, relics of the Gallipoli campaign."

At this time, Lawrence left the security of the Arab Bureau and the comfortable base at the Savoy Hotel. He was sent (against his will, he later said) to be a temporary liaison officer with some unruly tribesmen led by Faisal (one of Hussain's sons).

Lawrence was only to stay until the arrival of the real appointee, a Captain Stewart Newcombe. His orders were to try and turn the Arabs into a fighting force, but after Newcombe arrived, Faisal saw that Lawrence would better promote the Arab cause. Faisal went over both their heads and insisted Lawrence should stay.

Lawrence himself carried and used one of the rifles that were relics of the Gallipoli campaign. It is in the Imperial War Museum, with its own fascinating provenance.

Whatever the age and conditions of the arms, they were a lot better than nothing, and gave the Arabs confidence. When they chose the field of battle, they felt they could now be a match for the Ottoman forces.

The skill of British diplomacy was that they had reached this stage without making concrete promises about any later Arab independence. This enabled them to postpone solving the issue of the French claim to Syria, and their own need to control the oil fields.

Back in November 1914, the Indian Expeditionary Force had captured Basra. Holding Basra in southern Mesopotamia meant also holding the new oil fields. Whitehall was satisfied with this. Hardinge, Viceroy of India had accomplished what was necessary, but had bigger plans to push the Turks northward. While he was all for the Allies continuing to advance, he saw great dangers if it was in conjunction with an Arab uprising.

In Delhi he was amongst so many Sunni Muslims that they made the British Empire the world's largest Muslim empire. The religious head of all these Sunnis was technically the deposed Sultan of Turkey. Would the Indians' nationalism override their religion? More relevantly, if Sunni Arabs were seen to rise up, might thousands of Sunni Indian troops revolt also?

The Only Woman at Gallipoli

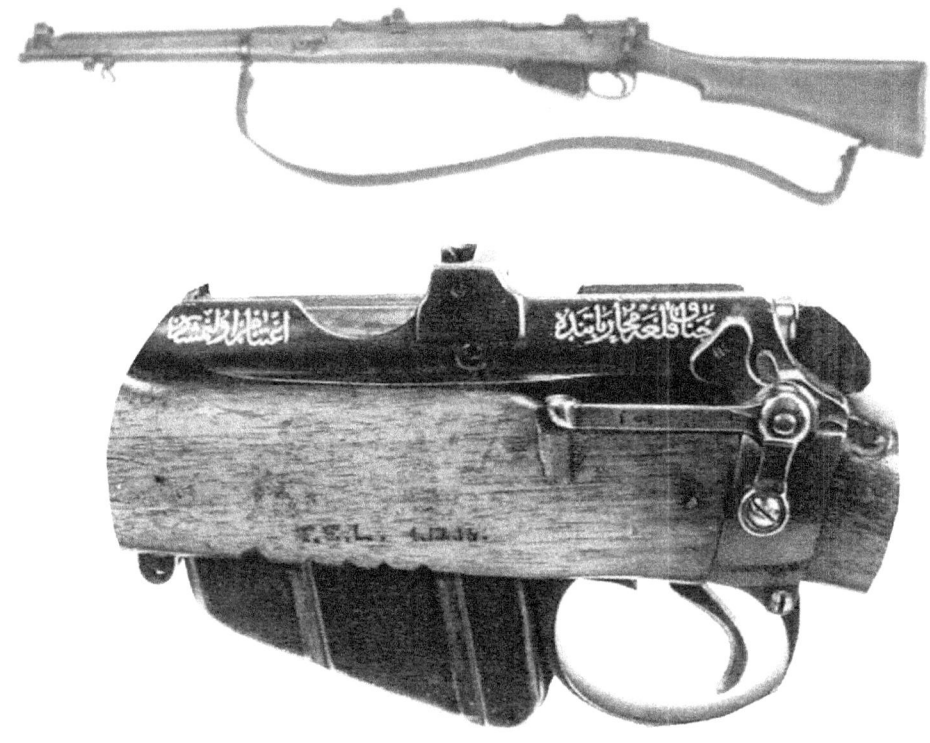

T.E. Lawrence's Own Lee Enfield .303 Rifle

The rifle has had an amazing journey. It was carried ashore and used at Gallipoli by an Allied soldier, and was part of the large amount of equipment gathered by the Turks after the withdrawal.

The Turkish leader Enver Pasha then presented it to Prince Faisal early in 1916 (and well before the Arab Uprising made the two of them enemies.)

Faisal then gave the rifle to T.E.Lawrence, and he carried it throughout the desert campaign. After the War, Lawrence had it sent back from Aqaba and presented it to King George V. He was the last owner, and the King presented it to the Imperial War Museum.

The Arabic script says: 'Part of our booty in the battles for the Dardanelles.' Below that Lawrence has written: 'T. E. L. 4.12.16' Below that are four notches, apparently carved by Lawrence for the first four men he killed with it.

Before the Arab Uprising started, the Sultan wanted the war against the British to be declared a Holy War – a Jihad. This was to test the loyalty of the thousands of Indian troops of Hardinge. The announcement of the Jihad was supposed to be made by Hussain, as Amir of Mecca, but he refused.

His outward reason was that their German allies were Christian, and he could not call a Jihad on his supposed allies. His private reasons were different. Independence from Turkey was his goal, and he realised that only British support would provide the means. A Jihad was announced, but from Constantinople. It didn't have the effect the Turks had hoped for.

Hussain had four sons. They were Ali, Abdullah, Faisal and Zaid. If you viewed the Arabs as an army, the sons were Hussain's generals, and below them was a level of 'officers' who were sheikhs leading their own tribes. This is a rough approximation, as the tribes were united by the common cause, but still maintained a certain independence of mind. At times this led them to diverge from the normal chain of military command.

There were skirmishes when things went against Arab forces, and complete tribes would flee the site of the battle. These sheikhs didn't see this as desertion, but more as preserving the forces of their own tribe until a more suitable occasion.

Lawrence claimed he was with Faisal one night early during the uprising. An episode happened that illustrates this different attitude to duty and the chain of command. The Arabs had attacked some Turks that day, but a whole section of Arab troops had disappeared at a decisive moment. A likely victory became more an episode of self-preservation for those left behind. The leader of the section that 'deserted' was Abd el Kerim. That night he presented himself to Faisal, who said:

"And why did you retire to the camp-ground behind us during the battle?"

"Only to make ourselves a cup of coffee," was the reply. *"We had fought from sunrise and it was dusk. We were very tired and thirsty."*

Lawrence says that he and Faisal lay back and laughed! This was obviously not the British Army, and the reaction of Lawrence shows that he was not quite a career soldier. Events like this coloured Lawrence's thinking, and he saw that the value of the Arabs was more to act as a guerrilla force. They could conduct raids, harassment of supply lines, and sabotage. They would never be reliable enough to stand beside the British in a conventional battle.*

Hussain was more optimistic than Lawrence. His opening moves were to have Faisal and Ali attack a vastly superior Turkish force occupying Medina. Abdullah and Zaid were to similarly liberate Taif and Jidda, and so consolidate Mecca. At this time it was all about the rescuing of Medina and the protection of Mecca.   [see note on page 306]

The attacks on Medina were unsuccessful at this time. The Turks were able to use the Hejaz railway to bring in supplies and ammunition, and easily repelled the Arab forces.

The Turkish retaliation for these early attacks was to massacre everyone at another town called Awali, where the Ben Ali tribes had tried to negotiate their own surrender. Lawrence described what followed:

"Hundreds of the inhabitants were raped and butchered, the houses fired, and living and dead alike thrown back into the flames. Fakhri and his men had served together and had learned the arts of both the slow and fast kill upon the Armenians in the north."

The massacre at Awali didn't turn the Arabs into a disciplined fighting force, but it certainly united many more tribes and factions, and gave them the determination for the two years of fighting ahead.

In January 1917, Faisal finally assembled a united force of the western Arabian tribes. His strong personality and wisdom inspired loyalty and confidence in the Agail, Ateiba, Billi and Juheina. They stood side by side for the first time.

They marched northwards up the Red Sea coast to Wejh, and arrived fortuitously as the Royal Navy blasted the Turkish base from the sea. Whoever really caused the garrison to capitulate, this became the first great Arab victory.

*It is also possible this whole story of the coffee was made up by Lawrence as a cover for the incompetence of the Arabs as a fighting force. He once said of his stories to a biographer: "History is not made up of truth."

Inland, the Turks had a major force at Medina, and the great fear of the Arabs was that they would move south and take Mecca. Lawrence thought any Arab designs on Medina were optimistic, due to numbers, training and armaments. He was proven correct, and Medina was never taken. Guerrilla tactics along the railway line to the north did isolate it however, and tied up many battalions of Ottoman forces.

The realisation also came to Lawrence that the Arabs didn't have to take Medina to save Mecca. Once Medina was isolated from the coastal ports and the lifeline of the railway from the north, a Turkish force would never be strong enough to march on Mecca.

Lawrence, Faisal, and followers now left Wejh and marched north and west through the desert to attack Aqaba. This was a Turkish coastal fortress, and their last port on the Red Sea. The master stroke was to attack the defences from the rear. For centuries, whoever held Aqaba had seen the desert and dry hills inland as like some defensive moat of sand. All the artillery and defences faced the sea.*

Aqaba was strategically important, because it was a northern port, and the essentially north-south Hejaz rail line 'bulged' westward at Maan. Between Maan and Aqaba there was only 60 miles of desert.

The British were as surprised as the Turks when Lawrence and the Arabs captured the fortress at the Red Sea port of Aqaba, because it wasn't an Arab plan or a British plan – more something that Lawrence and Faisal saw as a possibility when they were joined by Auda abu Tayi and his strong force of fighters.

In fact, the British didn't really want it as an Arab success and an Arab possession. In the long term they saw it as their own, as a future part of the defensive strategy for British Egypt and shipping using the Suez Canal.

The port had possibly been in Lawrence's mind since he did a preliminary survey of the back-door entry to Aqaba just before the war. Gertrude Bell also played a small part in the eventual achievement.

*Move ahead to WW2 and consider what happened at Aqaba and the British with their 'impregnable' fortress of Singapore. Camels were traded for bicycles as the Japanese came through the jungles inland. Large guns facing seaward were again found to be useless.

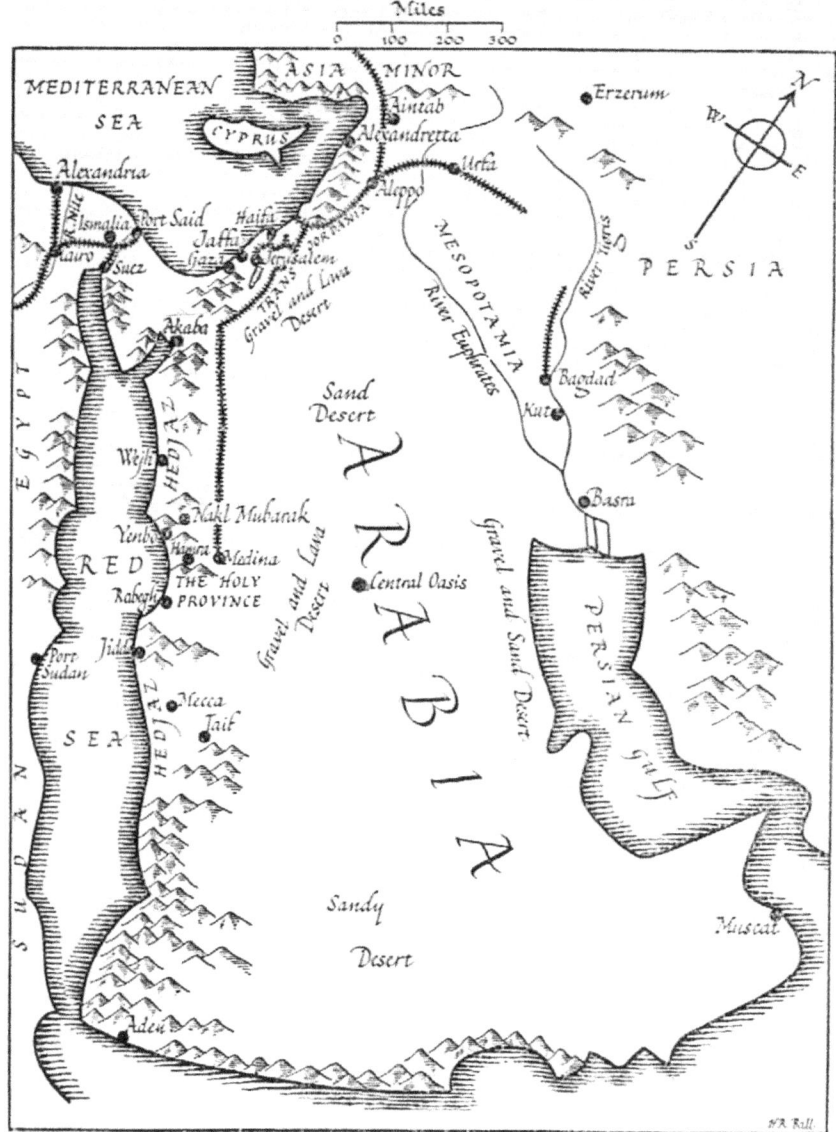

A 1934 Map of Arabia

Hayyil is shown as Central Oasis. The Nefud and Nejd deserts that Gertrude Bell crossed are shown as the Sand Desert, and the Gravel and Lava Desert. Akaba is at the top of the Red Sea, and its capture by T.E. Lawrence clearly threatened the Haj railway to Medina, and allowed him to isolate the Turkish garrison there. Flowing into the Persian Gulf is the Tigris River, and Kut is shown between Baghdad and Basra.

With war imminent, Lawrence and Woolley had become part of the 'Palestine Exploration Fund.' They left their desert dig early in 1914, to come home via a circuitous route. That route allowed a brazen scouting foray into Aqaba.   [see note on page 306]

The two men then arrived back in Oxford only weeks before the assassination in Sarajevo, and this is when Gertrude got involved. She was an early dinner guest, and filled Lawrence in on the who's who of the local Howeitat tribes near Aqaba. She had drunk coffee in their tents on her recent journey to Hayyil, and photographed these tough men. After being entertained by Muhammad abu Tayi (brother of leader Auda) she wrote that he was:

"A magnificent person. He carries the Howeitat reputation for dare-devilry written on his face – I should not like to meet him in anger."

Local support was a crucial part in the taking of Aqaba less than three years after the Oxford dinner. Only when Auda abu Tayi and his fierce Howeitats joined Faisal's forces, did they have the numbers and strength to succeed at Aqaba.

The taking of Aqaba had several other effects. The Arabs now had even more self-belief in what they might achieve, and Turkey now could see that their safest option was to prepare an inevitable retreat northward. On top of this the British started to see that Faisal's growing forces (with the addition of British guns and gold, and Lawrence's clever counsel) could really play a useful role.

The Arabs practised this role of a mobile force, able to attack Turkish troops from almost anywhere. Their campaign nicely complemented the more traditional ways of Allenby and the Allied armies, as Lawrence continually chose targets suited to a guerrilla-style harassment and sabotage.   [see note on page 306]

From the first serious march on Wejh to when Turkey signed the armistice, there were twenty one months of fighting. It left Hussain, Faisal and the many Arab tribes with the belief that they not only deserved independence, but they had earned it as well.

Hussain declared himself King of Syria. He had local support, but not that of Britain or France.

T.E. Lawrence in his full Arab finery
In the thirties he wrote of selling an antique dagger that he had owned for a long time, to pay for the repairs to the roof of a cottage. This may be the dagger tucked into his belt

Chapter 24 – The Paris Peace Conference of 1919

On November 11, 1918, Germany and the Allies signed a document in a railway carriage to end the fighting in Europe. This was a document of armistice to cease hostilities. It was not a document of unconditional surrender – many conditions were still to be resolved.

Very early in this book I stated that this is the true story of a man, two women, and world events in time of war. I went on to say: *"The lives of all three are inseparable from what we call The Great War, and the opposite is also true. Each of the three left their own imprint on the war history."*

This is especially true of Gertrude Bell, and the second half of her life. From her time in the Arab Bureau onwards, she evolved from an archaeologist and explorer into a specialist political adviser cum lobbyist.

The Paris Peace Conference of 1919 was the first time that national politicians really believed that they could get together and think and plan with international vision. They optimistically sought to solve all of the world's ills that had accumulated by the time the fighting had ceased.

National leaders, their conference delegates, and their teams of advisors and sub-committee members added up to thousands of people. Gertrude Bell was the single woman among these thousands of men.

The Conference started early in 1919 as delegates from 32 nations gathered. Germany was not one of those 32, but was absolutely the main item on everyone's agenda.

Beyond Germany were lists of smaller issues, with many other nations and interests. The world powers also saw an opportunity to re-shape Europe and the Middle East, and for this they needed people like Gertrude Bell. Politicians and other delegates sought her knowledge and advice. Most questions would have been asked of her by people seeking to flesh out and support their own pre-conceived notions. Without a doubt these opportunities also enabled Gertrude to colour and steer her responses. Eventual outcomes could be massaged according to her own agenda.

A speedy conference was required. Germany was still blockaded to ensure immediate compliance, but millions there and in neighbouring countries were starving. A new disease had been identified and named. Mangel-Wurzel disease was caused by a diet consisting of beets only. Things were beyond very bad, they were dreadful. Vienna had been a gracious and civilised city for centuries. Now the power went on and off and the electric trams were stopped. Many local coal mines had been left idle during the War and were now flooded. Infant mortality in the struggling city was 50%. Australia, New Zealand, Canada and the United States were keen to export food to hungry Europe, but who could pay? Germany still had some gold reserves, but France had ear-marked them for war reparations.

Communist revolution had also spread from Russia to Hungary, and it was feared it would happen in Germany. The Ottoman Empire had collapsed, as had the Austro-Hungarian Empire, and a deadly influenza epidemic was sweeping the world like nothing ever seen before. A senior member of the British delegation died of the 'Spanish Flu' in his Paris hotel, and became one of an estimated 50 million people to die during the epidemic. [Compare this to the 19 million death toll of The Great War.]

Delegates gathered from all over the world. Britain allowed one or two delegates from all of its many dominions. By the time you added all their officials, expert advisors and clerical staffs, the delegation of the British Empire alone was over 400 strong. France and America feared Britain would get its own way through weight of numbers, but many from the colonies saw the Peace Conference as a chance to be seen as independent on the world stage. British jaws dropped when the Australian P.M. Billy Hughes announced that Australia might not follow the 'Mother Country' into its next world war. [see note on page 307]

France ensured that every ally could attend and have a say, and the list of nations eventually included minnows like Liberia and Siam.

U.S. President Woodrow Wilson seemed to be the man around which everything revolved. He appointed Georges Clemenceau to be President of the Peace Conference, as the French rightly felt the most aggrieved by the ravages of the long war. Indeed their six million dead and wounded totalled more than all the Allies combined, and their lands had borne the brunt of the fighting. Despite Clemenceau's appointment, Wilson still maintained his central position by refusing to change his stance on most issues.

Lloyd George arrived to head the British delegation. He still carried the glow of an election victory at home where he had popularly promised to *"squeeze the German lemon until the pips squeaked."*

Clemenceau liked this talk, but in truth only France wanted to completely dismantle Germany in revenge. The other nations still saw a place for Germany in the European economy. In the middle of all this, Clemenceau was shot in the back while travelling in his car, Theodore Roosevelt died back in America, and Woodrow Wilson's own health was fading. (Wilson never regained his full health. He died in early 1924.)

Obviously, the cumbersome Conference could never really be expected to be both speedy and successful. There were months and months of negotiations, with the major players naturally pre-occupied with the fate of Germany. Sub-committees were set up to tackle the side-issues, as Arabs, Ukranians, Koreans, Armenians, Indians and Asians sought to present their own special situations. Middle East 'arrangements' were further complicated as the major powers tried to appease the increasingly important Zionists. Could a homeland for the Jews be created while somehow not upsetting the Arabs of Syria and the lands beside the Jordan? [History says no!]

Gertrude would have had something to say about the Jews, as well as the Arabs. The homeland had been a subject of discussion in Britain for years, perhaps more so there than anywhere else. There was a great range of opinion. Back in 1915 she had written to her mother about discussions with an un-named peer:

"I had a long and characteristic letter from the Lord. Incidentally he concurred in my view that the Jewish kingdom of Palestine was all moonshine. So Herbert Samuel needn't begin to stitch at his robes yet, nor rub up on his Hebrew."

Count Aldrovandi — Italian Secretary
Sir Maurice Hankey — British Secretary
Professor Mantoux — French Secretary

SIGNOR ORLANDO   MR. LLOYD GEORGE   M. CLEMENCEAU   MR. WILSON

The Council of Four in Paris, 1919

Vittorio Orlando, Lloyd George, Georges Clemenceau and Woodrow Wilson are seated in front of some senior aides. The four men were the centre of everything that happened.

Some international border issues were actually resolved in Paris. Poland was re-created, and Yugoslavia and Czechoslovakia were born. Finland and some Baltic states were nudged nearer to independence.

So many other causes and issues arose, but most were abandoned or just ignored. Suffragettes met and demanded that women should be represented and able to vote.

They got nowhere. An Asian kitchen hand from the Ritz Hotel presented a petition for the independence of Vietnam. The young Ho Chi Minh never got an official reply.

Every nation that got an invitation had its own concerns. These limited their response to every other nation's problems. Canada is a good example. They were concerned about the strong bonds between Britain and its ally Japan. They could foresee that America might go to War with Japan over issues in the Pacific. Canada would then find itself at war with its southern neighbour! Japan arrived expecting that they would turn the Council of Four into one of five, but they never got the acceptance they felt they deserved.

Prime Minister Orlando and his Italian delegation went home, as Italy was in upheaval with the rise of Fascism. (Mussolini became the Prime Minister within two years.) Japan, Belgium and China were set to walk away, as developments fell short of their wishes. (China never did sign the eventual agreements.) Poland had been re-created, but was not alone in being unhappy with nearly everything that was decided. Despite all this a document to deal with Germany was somehow produced.

The penalties and reparation demands insisted on by France shocked even the U.S. and Britain, but the conditions stood. Woodrow Wilson told his press chief:

"If I were a German, I think I should never sign it."

The German delegation was now summoned, and came in two specially arranged trains. They were expecting the worst. This was confirmed as the trains deliberately crawled along for them all to see the devastation of France. There would be revenge, and the 200 page Document of Treaty was presented to them on May 7.

The German delegation was led by a Herr Ulrich Brockdorff-Rantzau. Without having read the document, (their single copy wasn't in German!) he rose and spoke defiantly. The whole delegation then left the Conference, returned to Germany, and resigned.

During these days of waiting, the German government collapsed and left President Ebert as a solo figurehead. Defiant German sailors then scuttled their own fleet, which was impounded at Scapa Flow in Scotland. The Allies began to seriously plan to attack Germany again!

In the face of all this, Germany sent some new officials back to Paris, and in the Hall of Mirrors they eventually signed the Treaty of Versailles on June 28.

Under the terms, Germany lost all of her overseas colonies, and 13% of her homeland, with all of those people. In the west they lost the Alsace-Lorraine, and the rich mining area of the Saar Basin. In the east, an area of land as big as Holland and Belgium became part of Poland.

Germany's army was also to be very small (by European standards) and have no tanks. The navy was also to be more a token force, with no submarines. No air force at all was allowed.

Reparations were to be assessed by an Inter-Allied Reparations Commission, with an immediate payment of 20,000 million gold Marks!

Germany was thus to be pushed to her knees, and be made defenceless, penniless, and in debt. The ability to generate the wealth required to pay reparations was lost without the riches of her colonies and best mines. [see note on page 307]

Gertrude Bell's official role at the Peace Conference was assistant and advisor to A. T. Wilson, who was the Acting Civil Commissioner of Mesopotamia. To say that Arnold Wilson was an enigmatic and unusual character is an understatement, but he and Gertrude got on – most of the time. [see note on page 308]

Advisors and map-makers drew options for boundaries in the Middle East, and sub-committees mulled them over. Much was considered, but nothing in the region was settled. It would have to be done soon, just not in Paris.

With such a massive and ambitious agenda, the Conference went on for six months, and Gertrude was able to come and go at times. London brought bad memories of Charles, so this was not where she went for respite. For the first time in years she was able to spend time with her father Hugh. They travelled nearby, through Belgium and France, with an excursion to Algiers.

At the time of the Conference, Turkey was militarily defeated but (like Germany) had signed no peace treaties. There was no end of manoeuvring by Arab peoples, who were suddenly relieved of their Ottoman rule.

Faisal also attended Paris. At first there was to be no-one to speak for the Arabs, and his attendance was unofficial. France thought their split-up of the region was no business of the inhabitants, and they didn't need Faisal to be building an international profile. Britain changed this, and the conference seating plan eventually allowed two places for the non-existent nation of 'Hedjaz.' Faisal and Rustem Haidar had their chairs in between delegates from Ecuador and Liberia. A deputation of Kurds also attended, but they remained in an unofficial capacity only.

Lawrence attended with Faisal, partly as his mentor, and partly as his minder. Knightly and Simpson summarise his contradictory role well:

> "So while Faisal believed that through Lawrence he could get what he wanted <u>for</u> the Arabs, Curzon* and others believed that through Lawrence the British could get what they wanted <u>from</u> the Arabs."

Photographs of Lawrence from Paris seem to show that even his dress was a classic illustration of his contradictory sympathies. He wears his British uniform, topped by an Arab headdress. Perhaps this is an over-simplification. In *'With Lawrence in Arabia'* Lowell Thomas explains that Lawrence wore the headdress because he didn't want to look too British. Presenting Faisal as having overt British support would antagonise the French, as his presence was seen as threatening their right to Syria. Thomas says a British Major named Marshall had the headdress with him when he arrived with Faisal, and Lawrence borrowed it and wore it - almost on the spur of the moment.

The French were unimpressed. The instructions to a French Colonel Bremond concerning Lawrence were that:

> *"You must be quite candid with Lawrence, and point out that he is in a false position. If he is in France as a British colonel in British uniform, we welcome him. But we don't accept him as an Arab, and if he remains in fancy dress, he is not wanted here."*

*George Nathaniel Curzon had been the Viceroy of India before the Great War, but was now in Paris assisting Prime Minister Lloyd George.

Faisal and the Arab Delegation in Paris
Lawrence was his right hand man, but here is over his left shoulder. Rustem Haidar is on the left and behind them all is Faisal's man-servant.

The full conference of 32 parties was naturally unwieldy, and only met eight times. February 6 was one of these, and Faisal addressed the whole assembly. He spoke in Arabic and Lawrence translated.

Faisal said that the Arabs wanted, needed, and deserved self-determination. Diplomatically, he said he could accept the French in Lebanon and Palestine, but Clemenceau still thought his claims extravagant.

Lloyd George was more supportive, and asked easy questions about the Arab support of Allenby in the defeat of Turkey. He knew the answers, but asked anyway to curry favour for Faisal's claims with the other delegates.

Around this time, Faisal left us a few pearls to show that the man from the Hejaz was not overawed on the world stage. When asked what he thought of the huge assembly of world statesmen in Paris he replied:

"They are like modern paintings. They should be hung in a gallery and viewed from a distance!"

On another occasion at a London banquet, he was asked by Lord Balfour what he thought of the British government. He held back very little when you consider that this was the government that was supporting and promoting him. He replied:

"It reminds me of a caravan in the desert. If you see a caravan from afar off, when you are approaching it from the rear, it looks like one camel. But riding on you see that camel tied to the tail of the next, and that one to the tail of the next, and so on until you come to the head of the caravan, where you find a little donkey leading the whole string of camels."

Lawrence's role at the Conference was more or less a continuation of the relationship between himself and Faisal during the war years. The two-faced nature of it was still hard for Lawrence to bear.

In 1916 the British and French had signed a secret agreement, called the Sykes-Picot agreement. Sir Mark Sykes and Georges Picot led talks that essentially carved up the post-war Middle East between Britain and France. The whole time that Lawrence was with Faisal and the Arabs, he was in personal turmoil. To the Arabs he was assisting on a path to self-government after victory, and this was where his heart took him. In his head he knew all along that the Sykes-Picot agreement ordained otherwise. As the deception went on, his life was increasingly one of self-loathing. [see note on page 309]

He was further demoralised when in the midst of promoting the Arabs and their abilities to rule themselves, fighting broke out in Arabia. Ibn Saud had long sought to challenge Hussein and the Hashemites. In May of 1919, Abdullah (the son of Hussein and brother of Faisal) made a pre-emptive strike to put him back in his place, but failed so badly that only British threats stopped Ibn Saud from rolling on to occupy Mecca.

Little was achieved at Paris by anyone from the Arab world, including the deputation of Kurds. We are a century on, and the Kurds still await their chance of self-rule.

The powerful nations had eyes only for their own interests and the punishment of Germany. Bell, Lawrence and others were keen to see some sensible agreements also reached for Arab independence and nationhood, but they left disappointed. They were a handful of voices among thousands of officials. While those at the Conference were paying lip service to the Arabs, higher British authorities saw more need to keep in with France, and ensure long-term control of the oil fields.

Unbeknown to most there, Georges Clemenceau and Lloyd George had private discussions before the conference. They were along the lines that the British expected to come away with Iraq and Palestine, and so would let the French have Syria. Thus neither man was whole heartedly behind Woodrow Wilson's more idealistic plans for self-determination in the Middle East.

One thing in the region on which the delegates did settle was to give what is today the west of Turkey to Greece. An area from the Dardanelles down the Mediterranean coast to the large town of Smyrna (today Izmir) became Greek. Once more they controlled the Hellespont, where Jason and the Argonauts had sailed in quest of the Golden Fleece. Once more they ruled in Troy, Pergamum and Ephesus.

Lawrence's frustration in Paris could be seen on his face. By now he started to feel the unsaid attitude of the British around him. He had been useful during the war – far more than anyone expected – but now his time of usefulness was over. It is ironic that just as he was becoming famous to the man in the street, his pro-Arab stance was clearly not desired or required by his colleagues in Paris.

He temporarily abandoned his noble cause for Arab independence, and started to focus on what he might achieve for himself. Hearing of the death of his real father (Sir Thomas Chapman) he decided to return to Britain for the funeral, and to then immerse himself in writing 'Seven Pillars of Wisdom.'

His return would be via Cairo, where he would retrieve his personal papers. He hitched a ride from Paris on a Handley-Page bomber, but even this became a personal ordeal. The plane got lost in Rome and crashed into a quarry. The pilot and co-pilot were killed. Lawrence was sitting in the gun pit in the nose, and was luckier. He broke his shoulder, a collarbone and some ribs.

Virginia Howell summarises Paris and 1919 Peace Conference well, in respect of the Arab lands:

"The Paris Peace Conference proved for once and all that the ignorance of the West about the Middle East was equalled only by its lack of interest."

Chapter 25 - Faisal, Oil and Iraq

Faisal had arrived in Paris in 1919 with high hopes, but had left with nothing concrete. He went back to Damascus where his father had become the self-styled King of Syria. His father's position would only ever be temporary, without support from France and Britain. France wouldn't relinquish the control of Syria that it had gained under the Sykes-Picot agreement, and Britain couldn't let France see that it wasn't going to honour the documents it had signed.

Arab nationalists now talked 'Prince' Faisal into succeeding his father to become King of Syria. The son would have no better hold on the position than his father.

In April 1920 there was another conference with high ideals. Germany was now dealt with, and the Arabs and the Middle East now moved up to top of the world agenda. The San Remo conference in Italy was attended by leaders of Britain, France, Italy and Japan.

Lloyd George spoke for Britain (and so for the Arabs) and said that British promises for Arab independence should be made good.

The French would have none of it. They pushed through their proposal that Arabs could rule Syria under a French mandate. The arrangement was to be confirmed by the fledgling League of Nations (the forerunner to the United Nations) but the scene changed before the mandate could be ratified.

The French General Gourard arrived in Damascus to be High Commissioner. Not surprisingly, there was an atmosphere of unrest and open rebellion. He gave a list of demands to Faisal that seemed reasonable from the French side of the table. The list included the unconditional acceptance of the French mandate.

Some Arabs then attacked a French outpost in late July, and the French had an excuse to do more than talk. Soldiers occupied Damascus and Faisal was told to leave Syria. His brief rule was over, and he was more or less an exile in Europe. He was a King looking for a kingdom.

Britain meanwhile was struggling with its own plans for Mesopotamia. It had been captured from the Ottoman Turks and they now found themselves attempting to control a vast territory, peopled by an assortment of restless tribes. In truth, the only thing that interested most British in the region was the oil under their feet.

Britain's concern for the region was now being driven by her thirst for oil. That simple statement summarises her recent realisations that oil had spurted to the top of any wish-list. After many centuries coal was starting to be displaced.

The 1920s saw the twilight of the steamship era with coal bunkers full of blackened stokers. Official policy was that the Royal Navy (still the world's biggest and best) would switch to a future of oil-fired boilers. HMS *Queen Elizabeth* was Britain's newest and best battleship at Gallipoli, and was their first oil-fired capital ship. Its 15 inch guns had pounded the Dardanelles forts during the naval phase, and it was stationed off Gallipoli during the early days of the landings of April 1915.   [see note on page 309]

Traditional oil supplies had been from America and the Russian Caucus, but the recent exciting discoveries were in the Middle East. An Australian named William Knox D'Arcy suspected that oil could be found in Arabia. He got a concession to drill from the Shah of Iran, and in 1908 discovered oil after seven years of drilling. D'Arcy built a pipeline from the oil fields to a refinery at Abadan on the Persian Gulf. These became the immensely valuable assets of the Anglo-Persian Oil Company.

Government money had bought Britain a 51% share in this, the world's biggest oil refinery at Abadan. Churchill himself had driven the purchase, in the months before the Great War erupted. The transaction had only been finalised in June, 1914. The refinery of the APOC, the oil fields to the north-east, and the connecting pipelines were assets that were protected at all costs. Thousands of the Empire's soldiers had died to safeguard it all during the War, and none of this could be jeopardised by an unfriendly emerging nation.

Britain needed to find a way to extricate herself from this vast land with which they had become stuck as a spoil of war. At the same time they needed to retain the oil rights. The Arab Bureau talk of post-war independence was the way out, and with Faisal they had a pro-British leader under their noses.

Chapter 26 – The Cairo Conference of 1921

Regardless of the achievements at San Remo and the Paris Peace Conference, there was still a need to sort out the various national and tribal claims from the Middle East. Empires had crumbled and powerful countries no longer saw the need to colonise and exploit the weak.

Britain quite simply wanted to offload the responsibility and expenses of its civil administrations in the East. Since the end of the War, they had also to deal with unrest in Egypt, India, and Afghanistan. The constant trouble in their new acquisition of Mesopotamia was more than Britain needed on top of all this, and this caused Britain to call what came to be known as the Cairo Conference.   [see note on page 309]

Gertrude Bell was back on the world stage, taking part in talks in Cairo that would further shape the modern world. I wrote earlier that the Arab Bureau was a meeting of Oxford archaeologists, and it could also be said that the group in Cairo was a re-convening of the Arab Bureau.

Winston Churchill's peacetime portfolio was now Secretary of State for the Colonies. Leading the world to accept the creation of an independent Iraq was something he saw as saving millions of British pounds. Lawrence was now his official advisor on Arabian affairs, and he and Gertrude Bell were both still Britain's experts on the region. They also remained dedicated believers in the creation of Iraq.

Their motives were quite different to that of Churchill. Instead of creating Iraq to save Britain money, they saw the more noble reasons for self-rule – the philosophy of The Intrusives. These differences could be ignored. All three were willing to look ahead, and work towards the same result.

Churchill called for a conference of only ten days, to resolve policy and hear opinions, and to establish sensible future directions. Other attendees included Air

Marshall Hugh Trenchard, and Kinahan Cornwallis, who had been the recent chief of the now disbanded Arab Bureau. A. T. Wilson also attended. He had effectively been Gertrude's boss at the Paris Conference when part of the British delegation. He was now the head of Britain's Anglo-Persian Oil Company on hand to protect their interests.

Iraq was first on the Cairo Conference agenda, followed by Syria and the whole issue of the Jews in Palestine. In November 1917, Britain's Foreign Secretary was Lord Balfour. His famous declaration then had been:

"His Majesty's Government view with favour the establishment in Palestine of a national home for the Jewish people... it being clearly understood that nothing shall be done which may prejudice the civil and religious rights of existing non-Jewish communities in Palestine."

Looking back on these words, all that is clearly understood today, is that it was always impossible to create Israel without upsetting the native Palestinians. Gertrude Bell could foresee the trouble that would brew, and wrote:

"The next episode in Arab history is going to be the fury raised by the confirmation of the Palestine mandate by the League of Nations.

[see note on page 309]

Few of us can say we have had a direct say in the creation of new nations and the formation of national borders. Yet here was Gertrude Bell being again involved with lands and peoples of the Middle East, ironically just as Charles Doughty-Wylie had been involved with the Balkan countries when he was in Albania a year before his death.

The principal outcome of Cairo was that Iraq would be 'created' from Mesopotamia. Arab nationalists were causing a constant string of uprisings that were being put down by the Army and the RAF. Britain needed to find a quick way out. Independence would be granted, as long as a leader friendly to Britain could be found.

Gertrude Bell, Lawrence and like-minded others now pushed Faisal's name to the top of a very short list. They 'sold' him to Winston Churchill.

Throughout the ten days of talk, Churchill was able to keep his concentration on doing all of this to save money. This focus was clear in one of his final cables back to

London. He was brief and to the point when he sent: *"Sharif's son Faisal offers hope of best and cheapest solution."*

Gertrude Bell admired Churchill for his skill in managing the delegates, and coming away with some practical solutions, but she didn't necessarily like him. Some years later she wrote from Baghdad of a Mr. Amery. He was a visiting British Secretary of State, and she assessed both men when she said: *"Though I like him infinitely better than Winston Churchill, for instance, I haven't the same sense of swift power."*

Before long Faisal was the new King of new Iraq. He was 'popularly chosen' by a virtually rigged British selection process. It included the removal of one of the other main candidates, a Sayyid Talib. He was invited to tea with Gertrude Bell and Lady Cox, but was then kidnapped for a long 'holiday' in Ceylon.

To the Christian British, Faisal became the Muslim King of a Muslim country, but there was a general ignorance of the sects within the religion.

A few people were less naive. In a biography of T. E. Lawrence by Harold Orlans, he quotes a diary entry summarising the events. Lawrence wrote: *"The Sunni Faisal was imported to a heavily Shia country by force, diplomacy, manipulation and deception."*

Nearly a hundred years on we still see several Middle Eastern countries tearing themselves apart because of the endless struggle between Sunni and Shia Muslims.

[see note on page 310]

Another national creation of the Conference was Transjordan. This was to avoid inflaming the French, and yet still go some way to fulfil British promises to the Arabs. With the Wisdom of Solomon, Palestine was divided down the middle at the Jordan River. The deserts inland became Transjordan and the coastal land between the river and the Mediterranean became the Mandate of Palestine. Faisal's brother Abdullah became the emir of Transjordan, with British moral and financial support. Transjordan is Jordan today, and continues to be the best long term result from Cairo. The restless Mandate is Israel, Lebanon, and the disputed Left Bank.

'The Intrusives,' that small and like-minded group thus changed this part of the world. That they did it without full support from London and India, and under the restrictive ties of the Sykes-Picot agreement, is a credit to them. Their persuasive whisperings in important ears had a huge result.

At the Cairo Conference of 1921

From left: Gertrude Bell, a Major Welsh (pilot of the plane), T.E. Lawrence, Sir Herbert Samuel and Emir Abdullah, brother of Faisal and about to become Emir of Transjordan. Over the years he became simply the King of Jordan.

As a ruler Abdullah was more successful than most British bureaucrats expected, but his long reign ended in 1951 when he was assassinated.

The Only Woman at Gallipoli

An Iconic Publicity Shot From the Cairo Conference in 1921

The first six people under the gaze of The Sphinx are: Clementine and Winston Churchill, Gertrude Bell (side-saddle with fur coat!) T.E. Lawrence, Churchill's ever-present bodyguard, and Sir Herbert Samuel. Bell and Lawrence were comfortable on a camel, but Churchill was certainly not. The shot was taken and he slipped off, landing in a heap on the ground.

Chapter 27 - Creating Modern Turkey and Becoming Ataturk

When Italy entered the war in 1915 they signed the Treaty of London. Lloyd George and Georges Clemenceau were signatories, and certain promises were made to Italy to bring them to the Allied side. If and when the war was won and the Ottoman Empire was carved up, then Italy would get 'a just share.'

During the Paris Peace Conference in 1919, Italy cashed in some of these promises and occupied various Turkish coastal cities and their surrounds, including Smyrna. Today it is the large coastal city of Izmir.

The Sykes-Picot agreement had also allocated France a large area, including Adana (where Doughty-Wylie had saved the Christian Armenians.)

Greece also had eyes on a piece of the Ottoman pie, including the Gallipoli Peninsula, the Dardanelles, and the rest of western Turkey. They also wanted back 'Italian' Smyrna.

In early May 1919, Clemenceau and Woodrow Wilson thought Italy had overstepped the mark by occupying Smyrna. For centuries it had had a large Greek population. They 'authorised' the Greek Prime Minister Eleutherios Venizelos to take over Smyrna before the Italians were too entrenched.

On May 15 the Greek forces arrived, but fighting soon broke out, fuelled by mobs of Greek and Turkish locals. By nightfall there were 500 dead, and the Italians were ousted.

Much of the rest of the country was under British occupation. They now insisted the Turks send in a government official to maintain law and order in the fragile Turkish interior. Mustafa Kemal got himself appointed, and was granted sweeping powers.

Unbeknown to the occupying Allies, Kemal spent the summer marshalling troops and their nationalistic officers, and anyone else able-bodied, to create a force of national resistance. Delegates back in Paris were still squabbling over Ottoman spoils, yet deciding nothing, when the British realised what Mustafa Kemal was up to. They ordered him recalled to Constantinople on June 23, but he resigned and called the country to arms.

Soon he controlled at least a quarter of the countryside. In March of 1920 the Allies took over completely in Constantinople, and imprisoned some nationalists. Kemal responded by arresting every British officer he could lay his hands on, and moved his forces to Ankara. He declared it to be the new capital of a new Turkey, and so it remains to this day.

Britain had endured long and hard years of war and hadn't the stomach to start anew. They had been pulling troops out of Turkey for nearly a year, and continued to do so. Their biggest regret was abandoning Armenia. The Armenians had declared their independence in the spring of 1918, but were now being swallowed up by Turkey from the south and the Bolsheviks from the north.

Kemal found his first ally in the Bolsheviks, and they even sent him some much needed gold and arms. As the Italians and British went home, the Turks found themselves needing only to deal with the occupying forces of Greece and France.

Greece was still prepared to fight for what they wanted, and prepared to march out of Smyrna to face Kemal and his forces.

In August 1920, the Allies finally signed a peace treaty with the remnants of the Sultan's Ottoman government. Optimistic western bureaucrats thought it meant peace! Kemal completely ignored this 'Treaty of Sevres'. In the north-east he took part of Armenia, and signed the balance to the Bolsheviks in a treaty. He then turned his gaze back to the west of Turkey.

By October the French had signed a treaty with Ataturk, as he was now being called. They were glad to leave Turkey, and the nasty guerrilla war which had developed around those few parts of the coast they still occupied. Ataturk means the father of

Turkey, and this is what Mustafa Kemal was now seen as from within and from outside Turkey. [see note on page 310]

Now only the Greeks around Smyrna were left to be dealt with.

It was August 1922 before the Greek forces were pushed back into Smyrna, and an all-out attack could be launched on the city. The Turks were victorious by September 10, and full revenge was now taken. The city had ended up packed with its Greek residents, and all the stragglers from villages inland who had fled to the port. Looting and killing began, and fires broke out all over. As toothless Allies looked on from ships in the harbour, Smyrna was completely destroyed.

Turkish forces now turned north toward the Dardanelles and the Sea of Marmara, sweeping everyone of Greek heritage before them. Soon a million people were on the move, with Greece as their only safe destination. Most had never been there before. They were of Greek heritage, but were Muslims born in Turkey and spoke not a word of Greek.

Ernest Hemingway was a young reporter in Greece at the time, and said of the tired, hungry and dishevelled arrivals:

"They are the last of the glory that was Greece.
This is the end of their second siege of Troy."

The Greek disaster saw the Venizelos government fall, as did the British government of Lloyd George. The new British government of Bonar Law sent Lord Curzon to Lausanne to make peace with Ataturk. A treaty was signed in July 1923, and the Turkey we know today came into being.

Chapter 28 – Lilian's Later Life

Lilian Doughty-Wylie was the matron of the hospital on the island of Thasos in January 1919, but changed her scene and career quickly. She joined the Imperial War Graves Commission (nowadays the Commonwealth War Graves Commission) and became part of the Graves Registration Unit in Turkey.

An official toured Turkey and reported on the various tasks the Graves Registration Unit was undertaking. He couldn't spell her name, but in his report of 2/4/1919 he wrote:

"I am informed that a Mrs. Doughty Wyllie is touring Anatolia in a motorcar doing G.R. work, and was last heard of at Eskie Shire."

Her role with the Commission was to record the names and locations of the graves of the Empire's soldiers. Many had died and been buried in Turkish prisoner of war camps. The lists she compiled were long, as some camps had very low survival rates. This was not because of deliberate neglect or starvation of Allied prisoners by the Turks. It was more that conditions at all Turkish prisons and camps were appalling. The graves of the thousands of men were spread all over Turkey, and this was an unworkable situation for the IWGC.

The back pages of some of her diaries of this time show her practising some Turkish script and learning some necessary vocabulary. Someone fluent in Turkish has also translated some crucial clauses for her to learn including: 'I wish to find the graves of English Prisoners of War,' and 'Are many buried far from the camp?'

The IWGC brief was to set up cemeteries that could be maintained in the long term. Firstly they had to let the Graves Registration Unit establish just who was buried where. The phase after Registration was called Concentration. Many pockets of scattered graves would be concentrated into a small number of large cemeteries.

This is when Lilian used the influence and opportunity her position created to put some focus on the grave of Charles. It is certain that it would have lost its exclusivity as the only single grave on the Peninsula if she hadn't been nearby. Scattered Allied graves were exhumed in hundreds of locations all over the battlegrounds and prison camps, and were gathered together in new locations. Only then could they be managed and maintained by the War Graves Commission, as they still are today. Interestingly, the Turkish authorities saw their own dead differently. They settled on building memorials that were for all of their dead. The concept of graveyards full of single burials was generally not their approach, and there survive gruesome photos of large pyramids of Turkish skulls. They were piled up while the battlegrounds were being cleaned up during those early post-war years. [for an example see the AWM website and photo H11907]

The small cement cap on the single grave was undoubtedly an extra factor in its survival of those years after the evacuation. Many other graves marked only by a wooden cross seemed to have disappeared. When Lilian was there in early 1919 she wrote in her diary:

"I saw one British subaltern wandering about, he belongs to the Graves Commission & told me Dick's grave was the only one left on the peninsula. Every cross had been moved [i.e., by the Turks] *and it was impossible to locate anybody."*

Lilian's plans were actually to build a grand memorial – almost a temple. A lavish plan was drawn that never came to fruition. She revealed some of her thoughts when she first saw what had survived the war, writing that:

"I am rather afraid that to make a decent tomb we shall have to disinter as one can't do much with a grave on a slope.
If so we won't touch it now, but till the memorial is building & bury him under the altar."

By 1923 Lilian had been in Turkey for over four years. All the graves on the Asian side of the Bosphorus were to be exhumed and moved to a cemetery near Constantinople. They would go to Haidar Pasha (now called Haydarpasa). It is on the Asian shore of the Bosphorus in Istanbul, and can easily be seen looking across the water from the Topkapi Palace in the old part of Istanbul on the European side. Lilian was to have a permanent role here, and a report by the Registrar of the IWGC says bureaucratically:

"With reference to Colonel Durham's 21/H23/304/W, dated 21.8.23, and Major Dowse Brenan's note of the same date. I find on examining the WG. File that the Commission resolved at the 54th Meeting to concentrate all possible located graves in Asia Minor to a selected cemetery near Constantinople, and I gather that negotiations are still in progress with Mrs. Doughty-Wylie as to the acceptance by her of a position as Registration Officer. In the P.A.S.'s notes on the interview with the lady he makes it clear that graves in Cilicia will be included, and that the scope of her duties will not necessarily be confined to Cemeteries and Graves Sites which she has already visited. Haidar Pasha British Crimean Cemetery would probably be the most suitable Cemetery."

[see note on page 310]

A long term job as Registration Officer it was not to be!

Cyril Emerson Hughes was a civil engineer from Tasmania, who enlisted in the Light Horse during World War 1. Post-war he joined the IWGC and was the Chief Administrative Officer, and therefore Lilian's boss. He was based on the Peninsula when Charles Bean visited with his Gallipoli Mission in 1919. When construction of the cemeteries commenced he became the Director of Works and Cemeteries. He was still in this role in January 1926 when he wrote a report while on a ship going from Constantinople to Haifa. The report finished off with:

"By the way Mrs. Doughty Wylie is in Roumania* having been given 4 hours to leave her house at Pendickey and reside in C'nople. She has badly queered her case and is I believe reconsidering her opinion of the Turks. I hope to be in Cairo on Feb 23rd. and shall be glad to come to rest again.

With all regards Sir and be assured everything will work out alright here.

Yours very faithfully, C. E. HUGHES

*Hughes spells it Roumania, but Lilian spelt it Rumania. Today it is called Romania. So be it!

What Lilian did to badly queer her case (i.e., to make it impossible to continue in her role) is not known. She obviously upset Turkish officials enough for her to be told to move from Pendickey* to Constantinople. Perhaps she then chose to leave the country entirely, and so went to Romania. The evidence of her life and career would indicate that her opinion of the Turks was high - up until this time.

In the later years between World War I and World War II Lilian also spent some time in London. I have seen some patent application documents describing her as Lilian Doughty-Wylie, a widow of Charing Cross.

Her five year stint with the IWM in Turkey was also broken up by at least one visit to London, because she personally accepted Dick's Victoria Cross from King George V in March, 1921.

A family recollection is that she also set up and ran a mission for the poor of Calcutta in India "*at the end of the War.*" This seems impossible, even for a woman as capable as Lilian. Even she couldn't handle so many overlapping commitments. Her obituary in *'The Times'*, mentions a refugee relief centre in Bombay in 1899, and there was also the Adams Wylie hospital mentioned much earlier. This is when she had time to be of service to India.

The war mentioned might have been the Sudan war, or wars on the Indian frontier. The Empire had no shortage of wars at that time.

So in 1926, Lilian suddenly moved from Turkey to Romania. The first version of this book had a large time gap as regards these 14 years in Romania, but by very good fortune some gaps in the tale were filled. It also became clear that the Romanian perception of her was soon far better than the one she had just left behind in Turkey.

---

*'Pendickey' seemed a very British piece of spelling to me. I converted it to Pendikoy, as the 'dikoy' is more a typical Turkish word ending. I then realised that just near Haydarpasa is Kadikoy, so this may be the place Mr. Hughes was referring to. A typist probably misread his handwriting.

I have also learnt that there is a Pendik Koyu in eastern Istanbul.

The Only Woman at Gallipoli

During World War II, Lilian became life-long friends while nursing in Egypt with a Marguerite Maund. Marguerite married there, and Lilian would have been at the wedding. Marguerite became a Mrs. Hill, and in 1923 a daughter was born and named after her mother. Mother and daughter always called Lilian 'Judith.'

This younger Marguerite is still alive today and Lilian was her godmother*. I have been lucky enough to get some information via her daughter Patricia. Some time ago Marguerite (now over 90) wrote of her mother:

"I met many of the lifelong friends she made. Judith D-W being the most important to her and me, as she was my godmother and a truly remarkable woman –all four foot eight, thin, and strong-minded to a fault."

I knew that in her new country Lilian had soon set up the grandly titled 'Anglo-Rumanian Dispensary for Women and Children' in Bucharest. No doubt she had done this using some of her own money. Patricia also forwarded me two cards that Lilian had given to her goddaughter. They show that by 1931 Lilian was close to Romanian royalty – close enough that she would send flowers to a princess, who would write back calling her 'Tataka' as a term of endearment.

The hyphenated title of the 'Anglo-Rumanian Dispensary for Women and Children' implies a partnership, and information about Elisabeta says that she also used her money for a home and hospital for Romanian children. Most likely Lilian and Elisabeta were co-founders. [see note on page 311]

---

*Lilian in fact was godmother to two young girls and two boys. The second lady is also still alive, and is a high-profile woman in the United Kingdom. I know little of the two boys, other than one was in the army and changed his surname to Doughty-Wylie. Colonel Brian P Doughty-Wylie did eventually inherit what money wasn't eaten up in Cyprus or in death duties.

> 1 Jan 1932
>
> Dear Tatara
> Thank you with all my heart for your lovely flowers. I am so touched at your kind thought and wish you all luck and happiness for 1932 —
>
> Elizabeta
> 1932.

Ileana
1931

Postcards from Romanian royalty sent to Lilian.
They were given later to her goddaughter Marguerite. Elizabeta was born a Romanian Princess, but by 1932 was also the exiled Queen of Greece. Princess Ileana was her younger sister.

I have found little else from this period in relation to Lilian, other than a 1935 letter to the editor of *'The Times.'*

This was about the time when Mussolini's fascists were fighting a colonial war in Abyssinia (Ethiopia). There were appeals in Britain for financial and moral support for the inhabitants. Lilian's letter pointed out that when she had left Abyssinia for France at the outbreak of the World War, she had received great support. Her point was that now it should be repaid.

Her story was that back in 1914, Lij Yasu was the King of Ethiopia. He donated 400 bulls to be taken to France to feed her patients. Sensibly, the bulls were instead sold, and she took only the money to France. In honour of the generous gift, the hospital had been named the Anglo-Ethiopian Hospital.

She signed the letter: Judith Doughty-Wylie of 8 Boulevard Pache, Bucharest.

ANGLO-ETHIOPIAN HOSPITAL IN THE GREAT WAR

TO THE EDITOR OF THE TIMES

Sir,—At a moment when there are so many appeals in the Press for help for Abyssinia, it might interest your readers to know that during the Great War that country gave her mite towards Red Cross work in Europe.

My husband and I were at the British Legation, Addis Ababa, when war broke out, and an offer by us of a 100 bed hospital, not having been accepted by the War Office, the French Minister asked us if we would give it to the French Army. This was arranged, and the day before I left for Europe to collect staff and equipment, Lij Yasu, the then ruler of Abyssinia, came to say goodbye. He also said that he would like to be associated with me in my work, and presented me with 400 bulls, " for soup for my patients."

This somewhat cumbersome gift was taken off my hands by one of the Prince's entourage, who bought the whole herd, and I used the resulting dollars for the hospital's commissariat in France.

We called it the " Anglo-Ethiopian Hospital " in compliment to the Prince, and flew the Abyssinian flag alongside our own.

Yours faithfully,
JUDITH DOUGHTY-WYLIE.
8, Boulevard Pache, Bucharest, Rumania.

Lilian's Letter to 'The Times' From Around 1935

The Only Woman at Gallipoli

In the middle of this period in Rumania came the Great Depression. Lilian was staying in Wales at Holyhead in 1934. She was holidaying with friends when she heard of the needs of the Holyhead Unemployed Association. She obviously had a place in her heart for Wales, and had stayed there with her mother on many occasions before World War 1.

Lilian now donated £650 for the building of a small hall for the Association. There was a proviso that it included two memorial plaques. One was to be to her second husband, and the other to remember a Captain John Fox Russell. Russell was a local, born in Holyhead. He went to the Middle East as an Army Medical Officer. We must assume that Lilian knew him, either from Wales or from some hospital where she nursed. He also was a posthumous Victoria Cross winner, and had been killed in Palestine in 1917. His body is buried in the cemetery at Beersheba.

The little hall was restored in 1996, and the plaques and photographs of both men are on display.

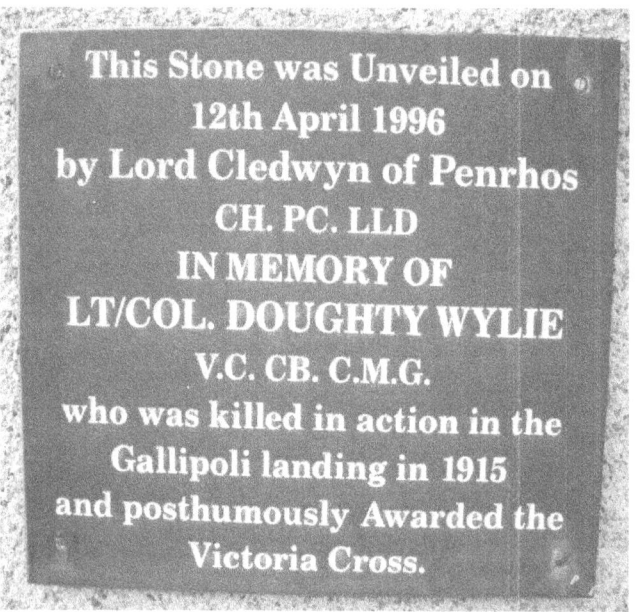

The Memorial Stone to Doughty-Wylie in the Holyhead Hall in Wales
Lilian Doughty-Wylie donated the money for the hall in 1934, and this replacement stone was installed when the hall was renovated in 1996. The original stone was illegible by then.

With the outbreak of World War II, Lilian left Bucharest in 1940 to go to Beirut, in what was then French Syria. Here she set up a convalescent home, no doubt for wounded servicemen. The French medical authorities had some people who remembered her capabilities. Her work in France back in 1915 was not forgotten. She was now 62 years old, but still an active and capable woman.

As in the first war, she then went from looking after French soldiers to looking after British ones. She moved to Cairo, and the care of Allied wounded was how she saw out 1941 and the rest of World War 2. In 1944 she was officially Mentioned in Despatches for distinguished services, and the Secretary of State for War had a notice published in the London Gazette on April 6. A Miles Lampson was High Commissioner for Egypt and the Sudan from 1933 until 1946. Under his wife's patronage, Lilian paid for and managed a convalescent home and club for weary and wounded officers in Cairo.

The place came to be called the Lady Lampson Club.

The Lady Lampson Club from a postcard in the 1960s when it became the YWCA

With the mess of the Suez crisis, the British left Egypt in the fifties. The club, with Lilian in charge (and financing everything to the tune of 20,000 pounds) transferred to the RAF base at Akrotiri, Cyprus.

Akrotiri is on a peninsula overlooking a bay in southern Cyprus, and is still an important and strategic RAF base today. It was created as a Sovereign Base Area by the UK in 1960, when Cyprus changed from a crown colony to an independent sovereign state. In the documentation for the creation of Cyprus (and the exclusion of Akrotiri), it is specified that the Lady Lampson Club should continue as an Authorised Service Organisation, and be a member of the Council for Voluntary Welfare Work.

It's a wonder Lilian didn't get a special mention in the documentation. She was still paying the bills and running the club in her eighties! She still had some of that feisty spirit into her old age too, as indicated in a 1959 letter from Akrotiri to the Air Ministry in London:

"Mrs Doughty-Wylie, at the age of 81, is not the easiest of persons to deal with; the club is not run by the book but will go on as long as she does, as the old lady has financed the whole show. (We) let her have her own way as much as possible."

And so it was that Lilian never married again. Apart from the years with the IWGC, her whole adult life had been dedicated to nursing, and caring for service men and women. Her diary entry on hearing of Dick's death was where she had foreseen her future as:

"Too old to start again, just a lonely widow."

This turned out to be correct for 46 years. A widow she remained. The support of the Armed Services, and the family atmosphere created by the fraternity of nursing became her substitute for a family of her own. Although twice married, she was childless.

The Only Woman at Gallipoli

Two Photos of Lilian between the Wars

The first shows her formally dressed and wearing her medals (and apparently the jewel-encrusted gold Red Cross watch mentioned in Chapter 2)

She was awarded medals by Britain, Greece, France, Turkey and Abyssinia and was deserving of them all. In June 2013, her OBE and Queens South Africa 1899-1902 medals were sold at a London auction.

The second photograph was taken in a London studio.

By the late sixties the building in Akrotiri had become the YWCA, but was still called the Lady Lampson Club. In 2007 it was operating as the *'Lady Lampson Café,'* and in 2015 it is simply *'Lady L's.'* It would be more appropriate perhaps, if it commemorated Lilian's name and life-long dedication. She gave her money and of herself for two decades yet the place is remembered for the wife of a bureaucrat.

Lilian died in Cyprus in April, 1961, at the ripe old age of 83. She never retired. A memorial service was held in London, but she was buried in a military cemetery in Cyprus.

A detailed obituary of Lilian appeared in *'The Times'* on April 27.

The obituary prompted a letter to 'The Times' from a W. D. F. Vanstone that was published on May 1. He paid glowing tribute to her final years in Akrotiri:

"During the Cyprus emergency, when facilities were few, the Lady Lampson Club did much to combat frustration and keep morale high. Although not of dominating appearance, Mrs. Doughty-Wylie would deal every night, with long queues of ever hungry, often brash Service men. She was affectionately accorded the respect which discipline would have commanded for senior ranks.

Throughout the history of the fighting services there have been those who have given up their lives to make the lot of Service men easier. Mrs. Doughty-Wylie, the ministering angel of Akrotiri, was one of those. Her memory will linger long."

These sentiments could be applied to much of her life.

Lilian Doughty-Wylie's grave in the Dhekelia Cemetery, Cyprus

Several times during the writing of this book I put out feelers to RAF and ex-RAF people in Cyprus to try and get a photo of Lilian's grave. The typical response was that due to the high levels of modern day security, any access was very difficult. Naturally access with a camera was on another level again!

It was out of the blue when Ray Burrow (an ex-RAF man living in Cyprus) sent me some photos, including this one of Lilian's grave. It turns out that it is in Dhekelia which is in the Eastern Area Sovereign Base. Akrotiri is 100 kilometres away in the Western Sovereign Area.

I was pleased to receive Ray's photo, but disappointed to actually see it. It is the standard headstone of that cemetery, but its similarity to its neighbours is not the problem for me – it is the inscription! Lilian gave her wealth and a large part of her life to the care of service personnel, but it seems she outlived anyone who knew her as anything more than that funny old lady from the club. To be merely Mrs Charles Doughty-Wylie is not even close to doing her justice.

My suspicions were confirmed later when another meaningful snippet was passed to me. It was after her death and details were being sought from London by someone in Cyprus. They referred vaguely to:

"her second husband, believed to be English."

So sadly, by the early sixties, they didn't really know any more who Lilian Doughty-Wylie MBE was. Nor did they seem to know of her even more-decorated husband.

Chapter 29 - Did Lilian Imagine a Gallipoli Visit?

Such a statement immediately puts focus on her state of mind, and even her sanity. This is the direction that Eric Bush took in his 1975 book *'Gallipoli,'* and he certainly has modern support in the book by Georgina Howell. Before transcribing Lilian's note from Thasos, I said that I had read references to it. It was given a brief mention by Bush, and his work was partly included by Virginia Howell.

Unfortunately, he presented many pieces of a puzzle for us, but his pieces now don't seem to fit very well together. This is a minor point in a book written by a man in his seventies. It should also be said, that unlike any of us, he could speak on Gallipoli from first-hand experience.   [see note on page 311]

His 1975 book stated that wild gales at Gallipoli meant that *"Boatwork was impossible"* around the supposed date of November 17 – so that there can have been no visit by Lilian?

Forgetting for a moment about both women, consider the issue of the weather.

November was remembered by all as a month of nearly constant wild weather, and all reports of the last stages of the campaign find the weather an unavoidable issue. Charles Bean was the official War Correspondent for Australia at Gallipoli. In his diary, he recorded that on November 17 :

"Seas were breaking over the whole length of the Milo, our breakwatership."

This doesn't sound like ideal conditions to be ferrying a woman ashore in a small boat. His entry for the next day continued in this vein, and was all about the overnight smashing of the Anzac piers.

Gertrude Bell embarked for Egypt on November 20, and couldn't avoid commenting on the foul weather. Soon after reaching Egypt, she wrote home about a voyage of several days in *"almost continuous storm."* At least the timing of her letter means she wasn't at Cape Helles on the *"impossible"* day of the 17th. She arrived at Port Said on the 26th, so the bad weather had been continuous for ten days when she gratefully stepped ashore.

Robert Rhodes James also deals with Gallipoli weather.   [see note on page 311]

He makes no mention of any woman visiting any grave, but quotes a Scottish chaplain saying of the balmy weather of early October:

"The days were bright, and the skies unclouded. The heat was tempered by cool breezes, now from the south and again from the east."

Storms lash Watson's Pier, Anzac Cove on November 17, 1915

Above: HMS *Louis* broken in half and sinking after a wild storm.
It became the last naval victim of the campaign. A tug named *Gaby* also sank at North Beach during the storm of November 17. It had been tied up in the lee of the scuttled *Milo* but broke free and was swamped. On board was the Christmas mail for the Anzacs.

Below: A south-west gale in November causes mayhem in Suvla Bay.
Boat landings on open parts of the coast were obviously out of the question.

The Only Woman at Gallipoli

But storms soon became the norm. On October 31 a storm was strong enough to drive HMS *Louis* ashore, where she broke in half. The biggest storm during the whole Gallipoli campaign was still to come. On November 27, 28 and 29, Watson's Pier in Anzac Cove was nearly demolished by the tempest. The final blizzard of that storm brought snow when the wind veered around to the north.

All this weather talk might cast doubt that either woman made a visit, but the wreath on the grave is plain to see. The wildest on-shore weather at Gallipoli came from the west or south-west. Photographs of the storms smashing the Anzac piers show the wind and waves from this sector.

W Beach was quite unprotected from this side, and had the greatest damage of any of the landing beaches around Cape Helles.

Luckily for this story and a certain grieving woman, there was still a place to land in wild weather at Gallipoli. It was at V Beach. A fairly sheltered wharf had been built alongside the hulk of the *River Clyde*. Photographs taken from shore and above show that other vessels were also scuttled, to further increase the sheltered water provided by the headland.

V Beach had soon become the domain of the French, and they scuttled an old passenger steamer called *Saghalien** and an old battleship *Massena*. They can be seen in the later photographs (as on page 232). The two vessels end to end almost filled the open side of a small harbour, leaving an entry near the stern of the *River Clyde*.

So the weather was bad - as bad as it gets in these parts. Boat work really was impossible, except maybe at V Beach.

After establishing the dreadful weather to justify that all landings would be impossible, Eric Bush gives us two names. These are Lieutenant Corbett Williamson of the Royal Marines, and an F. L. Hilton of the Royal Naval Detachment.

---

*In December 1899, Gertrude Bell had travelled to Jerusalem to study Arabic and Hebrew. As part of the journey she sailed from Marseilles to Athens – on the *Saghalien!*

The Only Woman at Gallipoli

These two are the men who confirmed the visit of a woman! They are said to have given eye-witness accounts *"... of a woman seen on Cape Helles at that time."*
I have not yet found either account, but I can't see Eric Bush conjuring up some naval types and putting words in their mouths.   [see note on page 312]

So whilst admiring Eric Bush the man, and his fine book 'Gallipoli,' he has made a minor stumble here. A brief summary of this part of his book could be that the visit of a woman was impossible, and that these are the two men who saw it happen!

> **V Beach** Hubert Wilkins went to Gallipoli with Charles Bean and others in 1919. His serene photo shows how sheltered the enclosed water at V Beach could be, especially with the protection of the headland his tripod was set upon.
>
> The *River Clyde* looks fairly intact, while the stern of the *Saghalien* seems to have been demolished by the scuttling charges. The old warship *Massena* (far right) was stripped to a hulk in Toulouse, and then towed to Cape Helles.
>
> The village to the left of the fort had been pounded by 1919, and certainly looks different to the modern village seen in my photo in Chapter 4.

He finishes off the mention of the woman's visit, by telling us what he *has* found to be the definite part of the legend. He says that with local British help, Lilian did *really* visit the grave in 1919.

Her 1915 visit, he says: *"may only have occurred in her dreams."*

Thus did I give this chapter its fairly controversial name.

To leave us completely mystified about Lilian's 'definite' visit that followed the 'imaginary' 1915 visit, Bush says her comment about the appearance of the grave in 1919 is supposedly that it had fallen into disrepair: *"... since the last time I saw it."*

Virginia Howell agrees completely with the Bush version, and reinforces it quite well with Dick's *"misgivings about his wife's stability."* It seems a real possibility that Lilian's note from Thasos that I quoted in full, had as its only purpose the laying of a false trail. Bush claims the note was written with this in mind, and deliberately never posted.

This I find interesting - even plausible. If the note was posted to Lord Granville, how did it end up in Lilian's files at the IWM? Was there some indication that it was never posted in the original envelope, when Bush first came across it? I have held that particular piece of paper in my hands. It had plainly been folded into eight at some stage. It would fit into the small square envelopes that Lilian was using at that time, that are loose and with some other correspondence in her IWM file.

I can't believe that Lord Granville would have ever considered this note as important, or worth preserving for posterity. If he had received it, I could see it going next into the fire, whether or not he bothered to reply.

There's more that intrigues me.

The letter was written in 1918. Lilian certainly had no suspicions about Dick and Gertrude in 1915, but I cannot imagine that she heard nothing in the following years. Why not try something simple to tilt the historical view as she wanted it to be? Also, her 1915 visit (if there was one) was surely a huge event at that stage of Lilian's life. If the ambassador had really pulled strings to make a visit possible, why wait three years to thank him? Why tack it on to a request for a bag of flour?

That Lilian could take such a long term view of history, and try to 'groom' her story is not fanciful. Some important letters between Charles and Gertrude were held by the two families to be too private to publish, and not opened up to scholars and researchers until Lilian's death in 1961. Several more in this book are published for the very first time. They are now a century old, and I was honoured to get permission to use them.

"V" BEACH, OLD FORT AT SIDD UL-BAHR, AND *RIVER CLYDE*.

This small photo was published in 1917 but would have been taken from a similar position before the evacuation in early 1916. The stern of the *Saghalien* and the rock walls are in good condition.

As mentioned previously, any thought that another woman had visited Charles' grave would have been an impossible thing for Lilian to live with. I read her note (here on pages 169 and 170) many times, and was always fixated by that last paragraph that I have underlined.

One day I suddenly looked at the next words with new eyes: *"Believe me."*

"Believe me" - What a strange way to end her writing! This is an ending that isn't seen in any of her other correspondences. Is it somehow more important to believe what she fears may be viewed as unbelievable? We will never really know.

I do know that at the start of the paragraph I have underlined, she claims to *"have been out here"* in Thasos since November 1915. This was certainly not true, when she wrote it in March 1918. The IWM archive boxes contain diaries from Mudros about her nursing the men of the Royal Naval Division, and the dates start in April, 1916.

She was there for over a year, and wrote to her mother regarding their respective wills from Mudros in June, 1917. That letter is also in the IWM.

Lilian's *"out here"* can't have meant the general area either, as she had been almost continually in the region since going with Charles to Adana in 1907.

Perhaps her diaries from Thasos would have been able to provide a confirmation, but unfortunately the otherwise perfectly full and continuous set of diaries has a critical gap at the end of 1915.

Eric Bush pondered Lilian and the diaries as well, and made some interesting comments in a letter from 1970. (The letter may well have arrived at the IWM with Lilian's diaries, all sent together by the donor). The letter thanked a lady in Kent who gave him a lot of information about Lilian. He was possibly wondering to himself whether this Mrs M. might have had a little more to reveal when he wrote to thank her after his visit. I feel sure he hoped this one last prompt would encourage her to reveal a secret kept by many for more than half a century. He wrote:

"Lily D-W's is indeed a sad but beautiful story of devotion and faith. One can only hope that she was not too unhappy in later years waiting for the call from her husband which never came. ... I keep on thinking of the missing diary with the account of her visit to the grave at Sedd-ul-Bahr Cape Helles, on November 17th, 1915. I have a feeling that she would like her story to be told. Could someone have borrowed it and forgotten to return it? It almost seems mysterious, the vital part - in a sense."

The letter really dangled a proverbial carrot in front of Mrs M. and then he jiggled it some more. A little postscript is written across the top, where he says:

> *"I have just opened this envelope with this thought: Could the missing diary have been buried with Lily D-W by her wish, do you think?"*

It's an interesting thought, and I could imagine that it could possibly be true. True or not, the question was certainly his final prompt for Mrs M. to hand over the crucial missing diary – if there was one.

I wondered about Lilian and all those wonderful surviving diaries. I couldn't see her moving between hospitals in France, and various islands near Turkey with a suitcase full of them. In reading the diaries of Australian nurses you learn that they were quite plainly instructed that diaries weren't to be too detailed, or cover too long a time. This was a common-sense security requirement, as nurses at the Casualty Clearing stations were always close to the front. That they might be captured, or have to flee and abandon their diaries was a real possibility.   Lilian's solution was to post them to her mother Jean, as she revealed in a letter on May 13, 1915 when her whole hospital was moving site:

> *"It's rather a wonder we arrived here alive, the staff between them managed to have three motor accidents on the way down. It's all in my diary which I have gone on keeping. So you will know all about everything. It will be ready to send in about ten days."*

Thus if any diary was to be removed from the set, it could have been done by her mother Jean, or far more likely by Lilian herself after the war. It would have been a major step in leaving history the way she wanted to leave it.

Eric Bush could keep secrets too!   When his 'Gallipoli' came out in 1975, he had obviously seen the whole of Lilian's letter from Thasos. What is hard to fathom is why he chose to only offer up a single cryptic line. Lily states plainly that she visited the grave, yet by omission he implies that she only hinted at a visit. I think he simply didn't believe her.   His book offers us only a single and vague phrase. He tells us only that she thanks the ambassador for an unspecified: *"success I owe in some measure to you."*

Eric Bush called Lilian's visit to Dick's grave in 1919 the definite one. No other authors seem quite so sure, but through good fortune I had someone else verify that her post-war visit was definite. Timothy Daunt is a fellow member of the Gallipoli Association, and a fellow researcher and historian. He read through Lilian's diaries, without doubt more thoroughly than earlier authors had done. He sent me some important entries from January, 1919 when Lilian left Thasos. A year later I was able to see them myself in the Imperial War Museum. Lilian wrote of packing to leave Thasos permanently. She was heading not to Cape Helles, but to what she called 'Chanak.' [Now Canakkale.] Here there was a British presence including a hospital. It was also her chance to seek an appointment with the Imperial War Graves Commission, as they were already active on the Gallipoli Peninsula. She wrote in her diary:

"7 January. Good bye Liminaria!
I told my staff they have to start packing up my gear at 7am, but at half past seven if you please Gareth appeared on the scene to ask if there was any change in the orders. I made a few remarks!
On board met a Monitor Captain who said he had to take his monitor 16 to Helles either the same night or on the morrow – no objection to taking me if I could arrange it."

On the 8th she was in Canakkale where she met a Brigadier Hare. She wrote in her diary how it all occurred that day and the next:

"8 January. He & Captain Rice arranged that the latter should take me down to Helles the following day."

"9 January 1919. We went right up to the River Clyde and landed by scrambling through a hole in her side. We walked down a gangway on to the shore & then straight on up to the fort. Things were much changed since my last visit. Everything is in ruins. The gate of the old fort is demolished & we got over the remains of the wall at the back. Dick's grave has sunk very much at one end, which accounts for the breaking up of the cement."

It seems to me that when Eric Bush wrote that Lilian thought things were changed *"since last I saw it"* he took her to mean the grave. I think the fuller transcript shows that she meant the fort and village of Seddul Bahir.

Also, if Lilian had visited Seddul Bahir during the Gallipoli campaign, it wouldn't have been *"much changed"* in January 1919. The fort had been a wreck since November, 1914, when it was heavily shelled by the British fleet and a lucky shot caused a massive explosion in a magazine. Gunfire from the ships caused even more damage on April 25 and 26.

That her 'real' visit was during her post-war stint with the IWGC was further confirmed, and from a completely unrelated direction. The previous chapter had some recollections of Lilian's now-elderly goddaughter, and some postcards from Romanian princesses. Marguerite is elderly, but still has an alert mind and a good memory. After her daughter Patricia sat and chatted to her on my behalf, Patricia wrote to me saying:

"Mum remembers she always knew that 'Tataka' did go to Gallipoli to her late husband's grave and that she knew about Gertrude, and her relationship with her husband. In the way of people in those days it was 'not mentioned' and while the marriage may not have been very happy, they remained married. Mum also commented that in her opinion, nothing would have stopped her going to Gallipoli and as she was working for the War Graves Commission, she had more chance to get there than many others."

When Lilian died in 1962, her goddaughter Marguerite was nearly 40. What she knows of this whole story - of the visit to the grave and Dick's relationship with Gertrude - is only what Lilian told her over the years. There was certainly talk about a visit to that single grave on the Peninsula, but it was always coupled with her post-war role with the IWGC.

So there is all the evidence about the visit to the grave.

Part way through the writing I was convinced that the woman who placed the wreath in 1915 was Gertrude Bell. I was then taken aback by Lilian's letter that claimed otherwise. Who was to be believed? What is the truth?

The passing of time means that new and decisive information is less and less likely to emerge. How many more things like 92 year-old Marguerite's precious memories are to be discovered?

I find myself back to where I was while half way through this piece of work.

The visitor to the grave that day in November 1915 – The Only Woman at Gallipoli - was Gertrude Bell.

Chapter 30 – Evidence Emerges

The publication of a new book can cause new things to emerge. It was exciting for me when this book started have that effect. Some people with knowledge of the story read the book, and made contact with me. My jigsaw puzzle had a few missing pieces, and they had some knowledge to fill those gaps. A friend tells me these things are called serendipitous events, and October 2014 brought two of them to my notice. They would cause some changes and re-writing, and some inclusions that include this new chapter.

Firstly I mentioned the book to people in North Wales. They are involved with the Doughty-Wylie archives, which are within the records of the Royal Welch Fusiliers. The first printings of this book had a large gap in time for Lilian, from June 1915 when she was in France, until April 1916 when she was on the island of Mudros. No evidence was available for her whereabouts in the intervening period.

Where had she really been in this ten month gap? The November visit to the grave and the complete evacuation of the Gallipoli Peninsula had occurred in this crucial time.

Anne Pedley is a historian and archivist with the Fusiliers' museum in Caernarfon Castle. She has an interest in Lilian and her story, and bought and read my book.

She told me of a book that would reveal where Lilian really was for some of this missing time. It brought Lilian out of the dark, but not necessarily into the spotlight. The 1928 book was by a Scottish woman doctor by the name of Isabel Emslie Hutton, and it was a World War I memoir entitled: 'With a Woman's Unit in Serbia, Salonika and Sebastopol.'

Anne Pedley heard of this book, and knew that the story had something to say about Lilian Doughty-Wylie, but had been unable to actually read a copy. I was luckier, and soon found that it was right here in Melbourne in our State Library. I was able to read it and even scan some interesting pages for my helper in Wales.

A beautiful photo of Isabel Emslie Hutton in uniform.

Isabel wrote of leaving France in 1915 for Salonika and Serbia, writing:

"It was on the lovely sunny afternoon of October 20th that we and all our equipment and cars embarked on the ... steamer Mossoul."

Her diary entry for the next day, as they sailed from Marseilles included that:

"Mrs Doughty-Wylie and her seven nurses crowded with many others in the steerage. ... Her husband was killed a short time ago in the Dardanelles, and she is on her way to equip and run a hospital on one of the Aegean Islands."

So here is confirmation that from June until October 20, 1915 Lilian was still nursing in France. This single diary entry by a fellow traveller had instantly shortened by five months her time among the missing.

Lilian had been manoeuvring to get closer to Dick's grave since early May, and she was finally on her way. Was the un-named Aegean Island Thasos or Lemnos or somewhere else? The Royal Navy controlled the northern Aegean, so Thasos was a convenient and safe haven close to the fighting north of Salonika. Lemnos is where she would have wanted to be, almost within sight of Cape Helles.   (see Map on p.243)

By October 25 the *Mossoul* was in Malta, and by October 30 they were in Piraeus, near Athens. On November 1st, 1915 Doctor Hutton's diary says:

"Arrived in Mudros Harbour about 10 a.m." She went on that there was:

"not a scrap of green anywhere, and not a drop of water at all. Some of the people who travelled in the ship with us are engineers, and have come to sink wells as quickly as possible."

It was then a full six months since the Gallipoli landings. She described the hopeless inadequacy of the medical arrangements on Lemnos, yet none of her nurses (or Lilian and her troupe) were going to disembark:

"what a fearful sight it was, black with flies and the sun blazing overhead … and wounded and seriously ill men, mainly with dysentery, are pouring in from the Dardanelles .. gaunt pale wrecks of men, and the death rate is very high … flies, flies everywhere. Nursing sisters are to arrive shortly, but at present there are none, and the whole thing is a tragedy."

Much of Isabel's comments are correct. There was a severe shortage of water, and there were thousands of men arriving in Mudros harbour, and many had dysentery. The whole thing was a tragedy that in hindsight should have been avoided, but there were certainly some nursing sisters already working on Lemnos.

Australian nurses were definitely there, and reading their diaries reveals the appalling conditions, partly by what they say and partly by things they choose to omit. They wrote of having 'Lemnitis' (dysentery) and being 'chatty with livestock' (infested with lice) because the severe water shortage meant that proper sanitation was impossible for anyone in the hospitals – staff included. Spreading away from the harbour were growing numbers of British, Australian and Canadian hospitals. Some were called General Hospitals, and some were called Stationary Hospitals. It was an odd term for the latter, as they were supposedly capable of packing up and moving within 24 hours. On Lemnos there were also a few that had all-male staffs, because their Commanding Officers were so old-school that they resisted the benefits the nursing sisters would bring. A recent book captured it by saying:

"the question of why the nurses are needed but not wanted boils down to contemporary beliefs about a woman's place."

Isabel Emslie Hutton's reports from the ship are best seen as an almost-correct version of what was happening ashore. She would have distilled it from rumours that would have spread around the ship soon after it dropped anchor in the crowded harbour. It is her story of what was happening aboard that we should be happier to accept. This was first-hand knowledge.

The Mossoul was only a 3000 ton freighter, so would have been capable of carrying hundreds not thousands of people. Two years after this trip it was torpedoed by a U-boat while steaming from Egypt to Marseilles, and there were only 112 people aboard. It is likely that Lilian Doughty-Wylie took air on deck and probably dined with Isabel Emslie Hutton as a fellow Scottish woman. If Lilian or any of them were to disembark in Mudros she would have said so. She certainly wouldn't have said that nursing sisters would *"arrive shortly."*

The Mossoul soon left Lemnos and arrived in Salonika harbour on November 3, and was still awaiting a berth at the limited wharf space on November 5. It seems that around this time Lilian and her seven nurses, and whatever luggage and equipment they had, were then put on another probably smaller vessel and taken east to Thasos.

In Lilian's 1918 letter from Thasos (at the end of Chapter 20) she wrote to Lord Granville that: *"I have been out here since November 1915."*

When there wasn't any hard evidence as to her whereabouts in 1915, I seriously doubted that this phrase was anything more than an attempt to re-write history. The emergence of Dr. Hutton's book has cleared that up at last. Lilian had bypassed Lemnos and was in Salonika – just a stop short of Thasos.

What I can't seriously entertain still, is that after November 5, even a woman as capable as Lilian was able to get herself and seven nurses and all their equipment and luggage on to a vessel to travel to Thasos. There they unloaded everything and managed to establish, equip and open a much-needed hospital from nothing. Somehow, only a week later she was able to abandon everything and everyone for an excursion across to Cape Helles on November 17!

Anne Pedley and I have had interesting discussions about this time, and what this new information would or wouldn't mean. She certainly steered me to Dr. Hutton's book because she saw it as likely new evidence that would swing the pointer towards Lilian as the visitor who laid a wreath at Doughty-Wylie's grave. From my point of view on the other side of the planet it does completely the opposite.

A 1923 map of the Aegean. It shows the Gallipoli Peninsula, and to the west is Lemnos, Thasos, and Salonika.

So the discovery of 'With a Woman's Unit in Serbia, Salonika and Sebastopol' was the first serendipitous event. The second came when I did an 'Author's Talk' at a library not far from my home. After the talk a woman named Elizabeth came up. She confidently said she would resolve any remaining doubts as to who really was the subject of this book.

That she heard my talk at all that day and was now standing in front of me was a wonder in itself. She had lived her life 4000 kilometres away in Western Australia, but had recently moved near this library to be near a daughter. On this ordinary Thursday afternoon she had come into the library not to hear my sparkling delivery, but to simply return an overdue book. She had no idea that there was even a talk on that day, or that she had some exciting information to offer the author.

Elizabeth explained that her grandfather was named William Thyne Liddell, and he was an officer in the Territorial Services of the Royal Army Medical Corps. One day he was with two others in France. All three were on horseback when a shell exploded amongst them. The other two men were killed, as were all three horses. William Liddell survived but both eyes were badly damaged by the blast. It must have occurred away from the RAMC facility that he was part of, because the system took hold and he was soon at a hospital in the care of Lilian Doughty-Wylie!

Liddell was a Glasgow man, and had a prosperous textile business there before the War. Either through business connections (or through his wife Elizabeth) he knew the Wylie family, including Lilian. Suddenly into her care came a friend – a friend in need of recuperation with both eyes bandaged.

As he sat in bed and slowly recovered there was plenty of time for the two to talk, and it was here that Lilian confided a lot to poor William. She spoke of knowing about her husband's affair with Gertrude. Of even bigger significance to me is that she revealed to her friend and patient that it was Gertrude who visited the grave in 1915, and laid that wreath that is in the first photo of this book.

The family feeling is that Gertrude did it as a 'nose-thumbing' exercise to prove a point to Lilian. They also felt that Gertrude was unhappy, as she expected Lilian to make moves to disinter her husband's body and bring him back for burial in 'Old Blighty.' They felt that Lilian made no such moves, primarily to deny Gertrude easy access to his graveside.

The war was not kind to William Liddell. The family recall that later they:
" went from from being upper middle class to dirt poor in a very short space of time."
While William was in France he appointed a manager to run the textile business. That manager spent his time:
"fleecing the business dry and running it into the ground while Grandad was overseas."

Things went from bad to worse when he returned. He went blind as a result of his injuries, but in the hard-nosed attitude of the day he received no pension. The naturally bitter recollection is that he was ruled ineligible as:

"it could not be proven that he would not have gone blind anyway."

It was little compensation, but in 1920 William Liddell was awarded the highest level of the Medal of Honour by France. If nothing else it strengthens his connection with the French and their medical system which was also the domain of Lilian at that time.

In a wry twist to finish this tale, Elizabeth said that when she was only little and was naughty for her grandparents, her grandfather would say to her:

"Don't you be like Gerty, now!"

Chapter 31 - Gertrude Bell and T. E. Lawrence

This story of Dick Doughty-Wylie, Gertrude and Lilian, and the massive changes they saw to the world, led me back to T. E. Lawrence to round off the tale. Without a doubt, Gertrude Bell and Thomas Edward Lawrence interacted with each other to the extent that each achieved things by connecting with the thoughts and ideas of the other. They were two meteors that shot further in the fire from each other's tail.

That a woman should live her life and be unmarried and childless, is no great cause for speculation. When the woman is as famous and high-profile as Gertrude Bell, things are a little different. When friends and family keep the secret of the love of her life for fifty years, these differences are accentuated.

People have wondered what sort of a relationship Gertrude Bell had with T. E. Lawrence. Perhaps this is more a case of trying to *create* an interesting story, rather than report on true happenings. These are two fascinating and outstanding characters in modern history. It is a symptom of the modern thirst for sensationalism and marketing edge that draws us toward unnecessary entwining.

What a combination they would have made, the virgin spinster and the younger man of such complex sexuality! Scholars have been forever torn between lauding his achievements and analysing his psyche. I have skimmed off some highlights of the former, but have completely avoided delving into the latter*.

Someone quoted Lawrence as saying that he thought Gertrude's appearance pleasant enough, but not beautiful *"except with a veil on perhaps."*

---

*Lawrence's younger brother Arnold certainly thought his sibling had died a virgin. This is not hard to accept when you realise that Lawrence hated all physical contact – either touching or being touched. It is said that the only two women he loved were his mother, and Charlotte Shaw (the wife of George Bernard Shaw) who later in his life became a substitute mother.

While today we baulk at the bluntness of this, she was probably wearing her pale blue veil when Lawrence first saw Gertrude Bell. This is how she travelled the desert, and it was in the desert that they first met. At the time Gertrude Bell was 44, and Lawrence was only 24.

They were certainly close friends, and corresponded over many years. They were together at momentous times, and shared common beliefs. Both were at Oxford and both graduated with an Honours Degree in Modern History. They shared a love of archaeology, and the desire to shape the history of the desert lands they loved. This is enough for me. I see their relationship as an entertaining meeting of two keen minds, and visualise the stimulating discussions that would have ensued.

Lawrence wrote a letter to Sir Hugh Bell after Gertrude's death. It shows some of the real affection between the two, and gives us an idea of the spirited banter between them:

"Her letters are exactly herself, eager, interested, almost always excited about her company and the day's events. ... I don't think I ever met anyone more entirely civilised; in the width of her intellectual sympathy. And she was exciting too, for you never knew how far she would leap out in any direction under the stimulus of some powerful expert who had engaged her mind in his direction. She and I used to have a private laugh over that:- because I kept two of her letters, one describing me as an angel, and the other accusing me of being possessed by the devil, and I'd show her one and then the other, begging her to be charitable towards her present objects of dislike."

Lawrence and Bell first met at the archaeological site of Carchemish in 1911, when Lawrence was a young archaeologist working there under Charles Woolley. In her usual brusque manner, she launched into an immediate criticism of their methods on site, and the two men were taken aback. Lawrence then spent a good deal of time illustrating that their methods and notes were better thought out and more detailed than Gertrude's hastily formed first impression. Her views then mellowed even to the point of appreciation, and from then the three got on very, very well. At nights they ate and drank together under the brilliant stars, using the excavated plates and bowls that were over two thousand years old.

During her stay at the dig, some others on site were imagining a wedding for the two, but it was more a comical misunderstanding than anything else.

[see note on page 312]

Gertrude wrote her first impressions of him to home:

"An interesting boy, he will make a traveller."

Lawrence wrote his own opinion to senior archaeologist David Hogarth, after Gertrude's unexpected emergence from the desert at the lonely site:

"Gerty has gone back to her tents to sleep. She has been a success; and a brave one."

Over the next few years they became even closer, and respected and admired each other. Some of Lawrence's admiration for her creeps into the 'Seven Pillars of Wisdom,' where he describes a war-time trek with an Arab colleague named Auda:

"We … saw a distant corner of the Great Nefudh, the famous belts of sand-dune which cut off Jebel Shammur from the Syrian desert. Palgrave, the Blunts and Gertrude Bell amongst the storied travellers had crossed it, and I begged Auda to bear off a little and let us enter it, and their company."

Gertrude also revealed her own deep admiration for Lawrence. When she arrived to join the Arab Bureau, and found him a part of it she wrote home. At this stage he was unknown on the world stage (but about to change all that). She wrote to Florence:

"You don't know him, he is also of Carcemish, exceedingly intelligent."

Perhaps they got on well because of similarities in their natures, as well as their beliefs. A story about each shows that at times neither had much time for British politeness.

At the Paris Peace Conference they both attended many supposedly important dinners. At one, Lawrence's neighbour is said to have spoken apologetically of his small-talk: *"I'm afraid my conversation doesn't interest you much."*

Lawrence replied bluntly: *"It doesn't interest me at all!"*

Gertrude Bell is remembered for similar feelings and a similar moment. She had little time for the subservient wives of many of the important men she knew. *"It's such a pity,"* she is recorded to have said loudly in front of a timid young English bride, *"that promising young Englishmen go and marry such fools of women."*

In 1918 she wrote home from Baghdad, and this time was critical of both the men and the women she saw around her. She was having a gripe about looking after herself, and wrote on January 25 to Florence:

"Do you know what I really want is a wife, to look after my household, and my clothes. I quite understand why men out here marry anyone who turns up!"

Lawrence and Bell also worked closely together at the Arab Bureau during the war, until Lawrence left to go fighting in the desert with 'his Arabs.' Maps were up-dated, and desert knowledge put on paper. A regular 'Arab Bulletin' was produced with intelligence reports and 'Intrusive' policy recommendations. It found interested readers in London and India.

He stayed with her on the way in and out of Kut, when he was part of that extraordinary episode with her other old and fascinating friend Aubrey Herbert. On the way to Basra, Lawrence wrote to Hogarth saying:

"I want to bring Gertrude Bell back with me."

The two worked together again at the Peace Conference in Paris in 1919, where Lawrence was an aide and translator to Faisal. When her father came to join her in Paris, she wrote to Florence saying:

"We had a very delightful lunch to-day with Lord Robert [Cecil] and T.E. Lawrence – just we four. Lord Robert is I think the salient figure of the Conference and T.E. Lawrence the most picturesque. I spend most of my time with the latter and the former is unfailingly helpful."

Lawrence perhaps got unwarranted (and unwanted?) attention, as he appeared in that strange blend of army uniform and Arab headdress. He looks uncomfortable in every photo, as he plainly struggled with his contradictory role.

Bell and Lawrence were together yet again in Cairo in 1921, as advisors to Churchill. Whatever their stated roles, they were in reality lobbyists, refining schemes together and pushing their strong points of view. Their beliefs and expertise had seen them together for a good portion of the six years between her arrival in Egypt to join the Arab Bureau, and the end of the conference in Cairo.

Lawrence even found that the concrete results from Cairo went part way to help him deal with the guilt he felt for his earlier role with the Arabs. He wrote of the Conference and Churchill:

> *"The work I did constructively for him in 1921 and 1922 seems to me, in retrospect, the best I ever did. It somewhat redresses, to my mind, the immoral and unwarranted risks I took with others' lives and happiness in 1917-1918."*

Without doubt, the 'odd couple' were the foremost British experts on everything to do with the Arabs and the Middle East. At this time the legend of Lawrence is more prominent in our minds. It was the success of the *'Seven Pillars of Wisdom'* in 1926, and the Lowell Thomas biography of Lawrence (with associated travelling show) that saw to this.

The *"Seven Pillars of Wisdom"* may not even exist if it were not for Gertrude Bell. In Andrew Norman's interesting book, *"T.E. Lawrence – Unravelling the Enigma"* he states that Lawrence had doubts whether his massive book was good enough to publish and was only persuaded when Gertrude asked: *"Wouldn't you consider publishing it for your friends?"*

The fact that Lawrence was nearly bankrupt, yet had only eight copies printed would seem to confirm this intention. He certainly gave copies to Siegfried Sassoon, Winston Churchill and George Bernard Shaw.

Lawrence and Bell at the Cairo Conference, 1921

Lowell Thomas was an entrepreneurial and self-promoting American academic and traveller. When the U.S. entered the War, Thomas was sent to Europe with cameraman Harry Chase to report. President Woodrow Wilson had known Thomas from their pre-war days at Princeton University, and he needed someone to provide positive propaganda reports for domestic consumption. Many Americans were ambivalent about joining what they saw as a European war. Finding nothing but death and depressing news in the muddy trenches of France, Thomas and Chase transferred to the desert as accredited war correspondents and reported from there. [They provided reports for America that featured no Americans. This wouldn't happen today.]

After the War, Thomas produced and toured with his film 'With Allenby in Palestine and Lawrence in Arabia.' Night after night he would run the film and personally narrate the silent footage. The run in London theatres alone was for a solid six months, and more than once Lawrence himself slipped in anonymously to watch. The show brought such fame that after only two weeks, Thomas said that Lawrence received 28 marriage proposals by mail, and was being hounded by many people. They included: *"representatives of the fairer sex, whom he feared more than a Turkish army corps."*

Lowell Thomas was ever the showman, and saw nothing over the top about a voice-over that called his new hero: *"The George Washington of the United States of Arabia."* No wonder Lawrence was embarrassed enough to send a short note saying:
"I saw your show last night. And thank God the lights were out!"

Thomas also had an interesting twist on Lawrence's supposed shy nature, claiming that: *"he had a genius for backing into the limelight."*

Hundreds of thousands of people eventually saw the show. After England it toured other countries, including Australia. It made the legend of Lawrence of Arabia, and it made Thomas a wealthy man. To cash in on the show he also wrote 'With Lawrence in Arabia.' It won no literary prizes, but in one part he wrote some words that ring true still today. He wrote in 1925:

"We of the West are prone to underestimate the importance of Mohammedism; one day there may be a rude awakening, for it is the creed of one fifth of the world and is an active and proselytising creed, making converts in London as well as equatorial Africa."

Forty years later came David Lean's epic movie, and the legend of this enigmatic character was cemented into modern history for all time. [see note on page 312]

Lowell Thomas and T E Lawrence in a Harry Chase photograph taken in London in 1919.
Thomas needed more photos of them together for his show, and Lawrence was happy to dress up and pose.

Who should we really place on the highest pedestal: Lawrence of Arabia, or Gertrude, who might have been crowned 'Queen of Mesopotamia?' Michael Asher pulls no punches in his *'Lawrence – The Uncrowned King of Arabia'* where he harshly says:

> *"Miss Bell belonged to the long British tradition of dominant ladies, who by dint of privileged birth and determination had managed to extrude themselves into a world of men."*

Asher's title of Uncrowned King of Arabia was not coined by him for Lawrence, but came much earlier from a British general.   [see note on page 313]

The tough summary of Miss Bell showed unnecessary bias. He never described his Lawrence as a short, illegitimate and asexual Irishman!

Gertrude Bell's achievements were at a time when the proverbial glass ceiling was thicker than a dreadnought's armour, which only makes them more remarkable. Sir Mark Sykes (of the Sykes-Picot Agreement) easily surpassed Asher's description. He had dealings with Gertrude for a decade, and reveals what a tough task she had in life. He wrote to his wife that Gertrude was a:

> *"silly, chattering windbag of conceited, gushing, flat-chested man-woman, a globe-trotting, rump-wagging, blithering ass!"*

Gertrude attempted and achieved many things. Achievements that were simply outstanding for any one person. That she was born into wealth gave her the means to do what other women didn't even dream of, but is it reasonable to condemn her for this? Would the world be a better place if she had sat at home embroidering while the servants prepared lunch?

T.E. Lawrence and Gertrude Bell both deserve a decent pedestal, and let them be placed close enough to show their interaction, yet far enough apart that neither is in the other's shadow.

Another thing that Bell and Lawrence have in common is that the pair have so often been dubbed with catchy titles. It was the Bedouins of the Beni Sakhr tribe that gave her an early one back in 1905. They were naturally amazed at this woman. She was at home in their tents, smoking, drinking their bitter coffee and talking in their tongue:

"Mashallah! As God has willed: A daughter of the desert."

Many years later Gertrude herself coined the phrase for one of her titles as: 'Queen of Mesopotamia.' In 1922 she wrote to Florence from Baghdad:

"I opened a parcel in the office the other day and out of it rolled a large tiara. I nearly laughed aloud – it was such an unexpected object in the middle of office files. It's too kind of you to let me have it – I had forgotten how fine it is. I fear in wearing it I may be taken as the crowned Queen of Mesopotamia."

Dick was another to bestow her with grand titles, writing to her when she was travelling as: *"my queen of the desert."* Later biographers were taken with this and have used various permutations. Tyne Television produced a series called *'Mysteries,'* and episode two was called *'Gertrude Bell: The Uncrowned Queen of Iraq.'*

Lawrence himself had never openly sought a crown. In 1916 the British and French had signed the Sykes-Picot agreement. From the time he heard of it, he was in personal turmoil. To the Arabs he was assisting on a path to self-government after victory, and this was where his heart took him. In his head he knew all along that the Sykes-Picot agreement ordained otherwise.

In the first chapter of his near-impenetrable work, Lawrence states that the whole purpose of the *'Seven Pillars of Wisdom'** was to illustrate how the Arabs had fought their own fight to reach a position of independence, and that his personal role was minor in their achievement:

"It is intended to rationalize the campaign, that everyone may see how natural the success was and how inevitable, how little dependent on direction or brain, how much less on the outside assistance of the few British. It was an Arab war waged and led by Arabs for an Arab aim in Arabia.

My proper share was a minor one, but because of a fluent pen, a free speech, and a certain adroitness of brain, I took upon myself, as I describe it, a mock primacy."

Interested readers should also seek out his less common book 'Revolt in the Desert.' It is much more readable than 'Seven Pillars of Wisdom'. Lawrence himself wrote that it was: *"better, so far as form and unity and speed and compactness went, than Seven Pillars. Should I have mightily abridged the Seven Pillars before issuing it to subscribers? Say to a half?"*

The quote of course, shows a strangely blinkered and self-effacing view. Arabs and desert dwellers would have continued to be a collection of disparate tribes, constantly pre-occupied with in-fighting were it not for British encouragement to be otherwise. Lawrence was undoubtedly the foremost of Britain's expeditors.

Perhaps the writing of a mammoth and best-selling book to illustrate his *"mock primacy"* is also a perfect example of him *"backing into the limelight."*

He painted a grander picture of his role in the desert, in the dedication to the 'Seven Pillars.' He so beautifully summarised the years of desert struggle into a few phrases:

"I drew these tides of men into my hands and wrote my will across the sky in stars." [see note on page 313]

As a result of so many years playing this paradoxical role, the rest of Lawrence's life was dominated by guilt. Publicly, he was the heroic Lawrence of Arabia. Privately, he felt he was the man who misled and eventually betrayed the Arabs he loved. The crown of the King of Arabia sat very uncomfortably on his head. He turned down further army promotions, as well as a Victoria Cross and a knighthood.

A private investiture was organised at Buckingham Palace, but Lawrence told King George V that he couldn't accept it while his country was betraying the Arabs via the Sykes-Picot agreement.

His guilt built up to the stage that he didn't even want to be Lawrence any more, and he 'dropped out.' In August 1922, only months after the Cairo Conference where he had been Winston's right hand man, he withdrew from the world and joined the Royal Air Force as Aircraftsman 2nd Class John Hume Ross. Joining the forces under an alias wasn't easy, but strings were pulled and it was eventually done.   [see note on page 313]

In a letter to his friend and biographer Robert Graves he described what was intended to be his withdrawal from public life:

"I was at last able to abandon politics and enlist. My job was done, as I wrote to Winston Churchill at the time, when leaving an employer who had been for me so considerate as sometimes to seem more like a senior partner than a master."

His ploy to avoid the spotlight was a complete failure. The press soon discovered him, and he was chased at every opportunity. (A recent book compares his fame and the level of intrusive harassment he suffered to the modern case of Lady Diana Spencer).

Due to media attention, Lawrence wore the blue uniform of Aircraftsman Ross for barely six months. By March 1923 he had another new name, and his uniform was khaki. He had been remade as Private T. E. Shaw, a soldier of the Kings Army, and was posted to the Royal Tank Corps depot at Bovington. Here he did manage some anonymity, and found the time to re-write parts of *Seven Pillars of Wisdom* and renovate a local cottage.

This anonymity brought no inner peace to Lawrence. Throughout this time he was on the verge of a complete breakdown. While working on his book he wrote and endlessly re-wrote the passages where he was beaten and raped at Deraa in Syria. For this and other complex reasons he eventually came to hate everything about the Army.* After two years he went back to the Air Force.

The uniform changed to blue again, but the name stayed as Shaw. In August 1926 he wrote a brief introductory note before the index of *Seven Pillars of Wisdom.* He simply signed it 'T. E. S.' The surname was said to be in honour of George Bernard Shaw and his wife Charlotte, who were both lifelong friends.

In 1935, he served out his term of enlistment and left the Air Force. Only ten weeks later he was returning to his cottage 'Clouds Hill' on his motorbike. As he came over the crest of a hill on his near-new and powerful 'Brough Superior,' he swerved to miss two young boys and crashed. He fractured his skull.

After lying unconscious in hospital for six days, he died.

---

*Some recent authors have called the rape at Deraa a figment of Lawrence's imagination; that he made up as part of some sad-masochistic fantasy. It is said he even tried to turn it into truth by removing pages from his diary that might have proved he was elsewhere at the time.

Chapter 32 - Gertrude Bell and the Early Days Of Iraq

On the 25th of June in 1926, the new King Faisal held a state banquet to celebrate the official existence of Iraq. The first democratically elected government would sit on July 16. None of this would have happened without Gertrude Bell and her near decade of promoting the formation of Iraq, and she was duly feted at the banquet.

The British essentially foisted Faisal on to the new Iraqis, including a stage-managed referendum. While this was being organised, Faisal toured throughout and spoke to as many of the people as he could. He had a regal presence and was a skilled orator, and the people voted overwhelmingly to have this import as King. It was a novel and uncommon occurrence - a King chosen by referendum. Before and after the referendum, Gertrude was somehow his 'right-hand man.' She coached him to be a King!

That she did her utmost to also make Iraq a proper and stable nation is evident. Here was a woman who wrote the country's first constitution, opened the first lending library, and founded its first archaeological museum. While all this was happening she and people like Cornwallis were advising Faisal on who among the locals might be suitable and reliable enough to form a government. It was men of course, who had to hold the new government positions, and the official British positions such as High Commissioner, but it was still the woman in their midst who knew the most. [see note on page 314]

As things settled, Gertrude spent most of her days in the Archaeological Museum of Iraq, cataloguing finds. She had started the museum to try and limit the steady stream of Iraq's ancient heritage that was leaving the country. Archaeology in those times was different to the science of today. Archaeologists (like Gertrude Bell, for example) tended to be scholarly types from the so-called civilised Western nations. They would go to more primitive, unknown, and sparsely populated regions to excavate. Money was provided by governments, wealthy benefactors, or some well-respected organization like the Royal Geographic Society. These backers expected booty as a result.

Archaeologists thus couldn't dig and explore for the sake of only knowledge and history. They did both of those things, but brought the spoils back to their own countries. Often this was legal where it happened, or in primitive lands with no applicable laws. If laws did exist, local officials would have their palms greased, so that legality wasn't an issue.

Such finds were triumphantly added to private or national collections, with much less concern for context, or for the necessary destruction that all this entailed. The very first pages of this book mentioned Troy, and it is a classic example.

Troy had been known nearly 3,000 years ago from Homer's *'The Iliad.'* A German archaeologist named Heinrich Schliemann identified the site in the 1870's and spent many seasons with teams of labourers 'excavating' the site. This amounted to crudely burrowing down through what is now seen to be nine distinct archaeological layers, leaving the site as almost rubble. [see note on page 314]

Forty years brought little more sophistication in technique. When Woolley and Lawrence had returned to Carcemish in 1914, there was a report of the rapid progress of the dig:

"in part due to Lawrence's rigorous dynamiting."

No doubt this was handy practice for the trains and bridges he would find himself blowing up only three years later!

A Bronze Dedication to Gertrude Bell from the Baghdad Museum

Before the Americans arrived as part of the recent Iraqi War, it was removed from Baghdad for safe-keeping. It may no longer exist. Some researchers seeking it recently claimed that it had disappeared into a region controlled by a fundamentalist cleric. The photo appears in several old books, but none of them credits the source.

As well as founding the museum, Gertrude Bell held the grand title of Director of Antiquities. As part of her duties she would visit sites being dug by foreign archaeologists. There she could retain some of the discovered treasures for the new Iraq. She had little real power, and knew she was best to stay on good terms. On a trip to Ur to see her old friend Leonard Woolley she claimed the best piece found, and took a chance on the rest.

She described the division of the finds:

"it broke Mr Woolley's heart, though he expected the decision. He values it at 10,000 pounds at least. I'm not going to tell the Iraq government lest they decide to sell it and thereby blacken my face and theirs. The gold scarab is worth 1,000 pounds, but Providence (the toss of a rupee) gave it to me!"

So at times she was only a fifty-fifty chance to secure something for Iraq! Photos exist of her at the biblical site of Ur, dividing the spoils with her old friend Woolley.

The cataloguing and labelling of the finds Gertrude had gathered was a laborious and time-consuming task in the hot and old building she had obtained in Baghdad. Her life and situation certainly lacked the interest and excitement that had been part of it since her graduation from university nearly 40 years before. She was becoming tired and depressed.

She wrote in June 1926 to J. M. Wilson. He was a British appointee to the new Ministry of Public Works in Baghdad. She was obviously close to him and was able to be open and honest. Her depressed state is clear when she says:

"I shall probably stay here through the summer and when I come back, come back for good. Except for the museum, I am not enjoying life at all. One has the sharp sense of being near the end of things with no certainty as to what, if anything, one will do next."

The recent project that had inspired and driven her was the creation of Iraq, with Faisal as the King. This was now in place. It was ticked off her list, and it seemed to a lonely Gertrude that her list of life's tasks was done. If marriage and family were on her list, the ink was certainly faded. She finished the letter on a depressed note:

"...it is a very lonely business living here now."

The Only Woman at Gallipoli

Hugh Bell perhaps sensed some of his beloved daughter's increasing loneliness. He took her for a little holiday during the Paris Peace Conference in 1919. Three years later he visited her in her part of the world. This photo was taken in Ziza in 1922. There was no such thing as a passenger airline then, but someone with his money and influence could hitch a ride on a mail plane. A sack of mail is at their feet.

A 1921 Picnic with Faisal (right foreground) and others at the archaeological Site of Ctesiphon.

A Baghdad Garden Party in 1923

Gertrude Bell sits on the couch with her parasol. She is in earnest discussion with the white-robed Faisal, who is now King Faisal.

Chapter 33 - Cutting a Strong Thread

In February 1926, Gertrude Bell's dear brother Hugh (who the family distinguished from his father by calling him Hugo) died of typhoid. He contracted it on a voyage from South Africa back to England, and arrived near death on December 11, 1925. After arriving he made a partial recovery and everyone's hopes were up. This made his death even more of a cruel blow to the family when he relapsed and died. Gertrude was now a 57 year old single woman in a far-off place. Her brother was dead and so were the only two men that she had ever loved.

The museum tasks and her mundane existence continued to wear her down. On top of this, the family fortune that had enabled her to pursue this life and career had waned in the Great Depression, and the family businesses had been crippled by strikes. She was no longer the independently wealthy woman she had always been. She wrote to her father Hugh, and showed that she was sad, depressed, and even weary of life:

" I think it is extremely unlikely that I can afford to come back and out again this summer – it's a very expensive business . . . But it is too lonely, my existence here; one can't go on forever being alone. At least I don't feel I can."

Research for this book led me to many places, and to varied and interesting sources of information.

In March 2010 I was seeking more information about the death of Gertrude Bell and found myself in the National Library of Australia in Canberra. On the afternoon I was there, a wild storm swept across the city. As I waited for books to be brought from storage, I watched torrents of rain run down the windows outside.

With some excitement I donned the white gloves and respectfully leafed through books that were between sixty years and a hundred years old.

When you look through books with a specific interest, with the thought that readers before had a different interest, you cannot but hope for a revelation. That afternoon as the near-silence of the Special Reading Room contrasted with the tempest outside, I was pleased to have two separate revelations.

The first revelation was that books being brought out for me were dishonest. They were deliberately hiding the truth!

The most illustrative example is the two volume work by Elizabeth Burgoyne: *'Gertrude Bell. Her Personal Papers, 1889-1914,'* and *'Gertrude Bell. Her Personal Papers, 1914 – 1926.'* The first volume came out in 1958 and the second in 1961.

She wrote the preface to the second volume in October 1960, acknowledging wonderful access to first-hand material of letters and diaries. The preface mentions a much earlier book: 'The Letters of Gertrude Bell.' This was edited by Gertrude's stepmother Lady Florence Bell, and was published in 1927. The underlining is mine, but Burgoyne states in her preface that:

> *"At the time of Lady Bell's edition expurgation was a political necessity; but I have been able to make full use of all the letters and diaries. <u>I have not omitted anything of importance, either political or personal, nor have I, by using words out of context, anywhere altered their original meaning.</u>"*

Within the first 30 pages (of nearly 400) we hear of a time when Gertrude was in London in 1915. Burgoyne says that:

> *"Now, after agonising over the terrible fighting and loss of life in the Dardanelles, she heard, while lunching with friends, that Captain ------ had been killed. Deathly still herself, she escaped as quickly as she could and made her way to Hampstead. There she found Elsa, who, misunderstanding and thinking it was their brother Maurice who had been killed, burst into tears.*

> 'No,' said Gertrude almost impatiently. 'No – not Maurice.' And she lay down on a sofa, where for a few minutes she seemed to find comfort in Elsa stroking her forehead. Then she turned her head away."

This little aside - just six sentences in four hundred pages – is Burgoyne's *only* mention of some mysterious Captain ------!

We know it was Charles Doughty-Wylie. We know he was the only true love of Gertrude's adult life, and that her writings are full of passionate love letters. Is this all we are to be given? This is in a book that has not *"omitted anything of importance."*

Shame upon on you, Elizabeth Burgoyne!

The preface of October 1960 is followed by Acknowledgements. They are dated February 1961, and thank the many friends and family of Gertrude Bell who provided so much prime source information for Elizabeth Burgoyne's *"full use."*

Shoe-horned between the Preface and the Acknowledgements is an undated Addendum. The sixty words were obviously written after February 1961, and just before the presses rolled to produce the book. Essentially, they confirm that all that follows is a farce. In full, the addendum says:

> *"I am authorised to state that the man who loved Gertrude and whom she loved was Lieutenant-Colonel C. H. M. Doughty-Wylie, known to his intimates as Dick. He lost his life at Gallipoli in April 1915 leading a gallant and victorious charge of the Australians up the hillside, and fell as the top was reached. He was awarded a posthumous V. C."*

Lilian Doughty-Wylie had died that April in 1961, and the addendum could finally divulge the truth. In an older world where an affair was never mentioned, protection of the 'good name' of the three people involved had been all important.

Suddenly, in the climate of London's swinging sixties, the passing of the final member of the trio changed all that.

The first volume is similarly in denial, with Dick Doughty-Wylie essentially a phantom. It offers only Gertrude's letter to Domnul Chirol, when she first visits Konya:

> "You know there is an English v.consul* here now, a charming young man with a quite pleasant little wife. He is the more interesting of the two, a good type of Englishman."

The small asterisk at the bottom of the page says simply that the vice consul was a 'Captain Wylie.' Perhaps this half-a-name was to ensure that people who looked in the index for Doughty-Wylie would find nothing.

Late in the first volume, Burgoyne quotes from Gertrude's personal diaries sent to Dick during the trek to Hayyil. Burgoyne says that Bell: *'completed the story of the journey, again writing it for the man she loved.'* Nowhere does she say who the man was, because she was writing Volume 1 before 1958, and Lilian was alive. The secret still had to be kept. Selective diary extracts then follow, but they are the dry and emotionless bones of the real diaries.

I said earlier in this chapter that on a stormy Canberra day I had two revelations. My first revelation was that many of the older books about Gertrude were not telling the truth. They were supposedly published to reveal the true Gertrude Bell, yet sought to do so while denying her love of Charles. This meant denying his existence in her life, and his influence on her life and subsequent behaviour.

The second revelation I had, was that during the last years of her life she suffered from the ever-increasing ravages of a fatal disease. No other publication has ever come to this conclusion, and I am not sure why. Did earlier writers ignore the evidence, or is this another case of a deliberate cover-up?

The disease was almost certainly lung or throat cancer. So many books mention her poor health, but none has ever put it plainly on the table. She was seriously ill. Smoking was a constant part of her life, and one of her later signatures was always a long and supposedly glamorous cigarette holder.

A description of her office at the Arab Bureau has *"papers everywhere, her ashtray overflowing."* Of her early trip to Bucharest for an extended stay with her Aunt Mary and Uncle Frank Lascelles, the description of her social finishing includes that: *"she learnt how to flirt with her ostrich fan, puff on her cigarette, and dine on caviar and champagne."*

Gertrude was only twenty at the time, and had probably taken up the habit even earlier during the previous years at Oxford University.

In 1919, Gertrude left Baghdad to travel to the Paris Peace Conference. On the way she stopped in Cairo for briefings with General Gilbert Clayton, who was Egyptian Interior Minister. A description set the scene as: *"Sitting in the garden of the British Residence, a splendid neo-classical building on the Nile, Gertrude smoked one cigarette after another while Clayton spoke."*

These examples are imagined or from hearsay, but they are a realistic representation of Gertrude Bell. She had a lifelong, and eventual life-ending relationship with tobacco. In her early travels, cigarettes are an everyday item of life. In *'The Desert and the Sown'* she mentions getting a box of cigarettes from her meagre supplies, as a gift to a host. This was when she was supposedly travelling through the desert, with only the bare essentials needed to sustain her.

For many of her final years she was ill enough to be constantly seeing doctors. The exception to this was when she avoided them!

Avoidance became her option when she knew that doctors in Baghdad would tell her she was too ill to travel home, and doctors in England would tell her that a return to Iraq would kill her.

Gertrude herself admitted to an illness of the throat when she wrote to Dick in 1914. She had returned to Rounton, from her last great desert trek. He was by this time in Abyssinia. Gertrude's letters don't exist, but Dicks replies tell of her admission. Because of the slowness of mails, he assumes she has recovered when he writes:

" Addis Ababa

20 June 1914

My dear Gertrude,

Another enchanting letter from you to me – they warm my heart. But my dear I am so very sorry you were ill in bed, obliged to rest. – how is your throat?

— well long ago please god — but I know they are painful things. The desert took too much of you and the long marching.

It's already long ago since you went to Rounton to rest with Sir V.C. Next week I shall hear from there. Your letters to me are a part of my life now. I'm so glad I've been to Rounton and can see you there."

Gertrude failed to mention any recovery in her next letter, and so Dick mentioned it again in his letter of June 28. He tells us that even as she tried to dismiss the real seriousness of it, she had still described it to him as not just sore, but ulcerated:

….. *"I am so delighted that Lord Cromer is better — good news indeed. And you my dear? You didn't say how was the ulcerated throat & general weariness of going up and down the earth."*

Friends and acquaintances were noticing her failing health also. Not surprisingly, they saw change as the years passed. Vita Sackville-West was a novelist and poet now mostly remembered for promoting the preservation of the stately gardens of England, and her passionate affairs with Violet Markham, and fellow novelist Virginia Woolf. Publicly she was also the wife of Harold Nicolson. Gertrude had met them on their 1914 honeymoon in Constantinople, and saw them again at the Paris Peace Conference in 1919, where Nicolson was in the British delegation.

Vita Sackville-West's own traveller's tale was published in 1926 as *'A Passenger to Teheran,'* when she again talks of being with Gertrude. Sackville-West's encounters with Gertrude were thus ideally spaced over twelve years to observe her decline. Her dismay at Gertrude's deteriorating appearance comes through in her recollection of a visit to Gertrude Bell in Baghdad. Sackville-West says:

"The doctors had told her she ought not go through another summer in Baghdad, but what should she do in England, eating her heart out for Iraq? … but I couldn't say she looked ill could I?

I could, and did."

King Faisal faces the camera, between Gertrude Bell and Iris Davidson.

Nigel Davidson was a British official in Baghdad, and the Davidsons were good friends of Gertrude. Nigel bends forward and is graciously lighting yet another cigarette for Gertrude.

Look back to the picture of Gertrude Bell and T.E. Lawrence on Page 251. I had seen it many times before someone pointed out to me that she has a cigarette in her hand.

Gertrude did muster the strength to return to England for a three month break in the middle of 1925. It was seen as a well-earned rest, and as something of a holiday. The true purpose may have been to update her medical advice. Upon arriving in London her appearance shocked her mother, who wrote: *"she was in a condition of great nervous fatigue, and appeared exhausted mentally and physically."*

Gertrude went straight to Sir Thomas Parkinson (her London doctor) and then stayed for a few days with her old friend Janet Hogarth (by this time Janet Courtenay).

A fly-on-the-wall account of the meeting of the two old friends exists:

"My dear!" cried Janet, as soon as they met. *"How frightfully thin you are!"* Gertrude laughed. *"Oh – I was always a skinny beast! It's inherited. Look at father! I'm all right you know. You can't say I look <u>ill</u>, can you?"*

That's exactly what Janet wanted to say. Gertrude was not just thin. She was a walking skeleton. And her hair had turned completely white, and very scanty. It looked like a floating halo of light, more than real hair. Her nose, always rather large, had gone longer and thinner, with a sharp bony ridge like a paper-knife. Both women were now fifty-six. Gertrude had always looked by far the younger. But now, Janet felt, she looked ten years older than herself. But of course, she couldn't say anything of this kind, and merely remarked: *"I don't think you ought go out there again."*

"That's just what Dr. Parkinson's just told me," Gertrude replied. *"The family have been saying it for the last year. But there's really nothing wrong with me, Janet."*

She then went on to talk about why she would go back, and why England was no longer her real home:

"Most people, I suppose, live through their children and grandchildren. I've missed that part of life, more's the pity. But I've plenty of lives to live through all the same. Thousands of them! No, I have to go back. I just have to. At any rate for next winter. Just till I get my museum properly started. We're on the verge of getting a proper building at last, did you know?" she ended enthusiastically.

Janet smiled sadly. *"Oh, you're incorrigible. You'll kill yourself for these Arabs!"*

"Well – why not? They're as well worth dying for as anyone else, aren't they? – But don't let's be morbid! I'm not going to be a corpse for a long time yet!"

Gertrude had the strength and determination to go back to Baghdad, and perhaps wondered whether she had visited home and family for the last time. She wrote to Florence in October 1925 and said with some finality:

"I feel certain that I have never loved you so much, however much I have loved you, and I am so thankful that we were together this last summer and that we both have the sense of its having been a wonderful experience. So it was, wasn't it darling. ...

Ever, dearest, your very loving daughter Gertrude."

There are two ways to view: *"this last summer."* No doubt Florence thought Gertrude meant it in the sense of the *previous* summer, but did Gertrude realise after some months back in Baghdad that it really had been her *final* summer in England?

The fly-on-the-wall account of the conversation between Gertrude and Janet Courtenay is from a 1967 book: *'A Woman in the Desert'* by Dorothy Cowin. The book is perhaps the epitome of my previously mentioned revelations about cover-up lies, and the denial of illness. Here is a situation where both are combined, even though it was written when Gertrude had been dead for forty years!

Parts of it support my theory of lung cancer, and yet parts of it are a complete denial of genuine illness. They dish up what *should* politely be told in preference to what *could* be truthfully told, and so perpetuate the un-truth.

Soon after the detailed account of Gertrude's conversation with her old friend Janet (finishing with the almost poignant summary of the incomplete nature of Gertrude's life, and the denial of an imminent death) Dorothy Cowin wrote a distressing account of life back in Iraq.

We read that:

"By the end of December (1925) her health had broken down again. This time she really alarmed everyone. It was thought to be pneumonia. ... She was so bad that a doctor was called from Baghdad, and a night nurse. The next morning it seemed she had escaped with pleurisy, and she was taken by train, especially delayed for her, to Baghdad and put in the care of the night nurse."

It was *thought* to be pneumonia, and she *seemed* to have escaped with pleurisy! I honestly think the author knew better of the real situation, but felt she was not in a situation to say.

Gertrude herself was talking it down, and trying to keep it quiet from family when she wrote to J.M. Wilson of the same episode and her 'steel springs' constitution. She wrote:

> *"It seems that I just didn't have pneumonia, chiefly through being made of steel springs. I spent Xmas day in bed, with H.M., Iltyd and Ken nursing me when they weren't out shooting,* and the next day I was so bad that they telegraphed for a doctor and a nurse. You need not mention these details to my family, to whom I have not retailed them."*

A woman of steel she was certainly not. A more impartial (and perhaps informed) description of Gertrude comes from her friend Elsie Sinderson. She was the wife of Dr. Harry Sinderson, who had treated Gertrude throughout the recent illnesses in Baghdad. As the Sindersons were seen off on a world tour by Gertrude, Elsie was moved to tears by Gertrude's state and described her on the railway platform as:

> *"like a leaf that could be blown away by a breath."*

While people around her were noticing her deterioration, she kept up the pretence with her parents. She wrote to her father not long before the Christmas incident of 'near pneumonia' and reassured him with:

> *"You mustn't bother, darling, about my health. You are not reckoning with the immense elasticity which comes of being everywhere sound. Sinbad** says that I have the most surprising powers of sudden recovery so much that he sometimes feels inclined to accuse me of having been shamming."*

The closest Gertrude ever came to being open with her parents was a few weeks later, when she wrote to Florence on January 6, 1926. The opening line has an ominous feel about it when she says:

> *"I've been having a little quiet illness of my own but it's nearly gone. I was quite bad for a day or two, but now they are all saying that they really wouldn't have bothered if they had known the kind of person they were dealing with."*

---

*Her bed-side carers were only the three most important people in the country! H.M. was His Majesty King Faisal, and Iltyd and Ken were the senior British administrators Iltyd Clayton and Kinahan Cornwallis.

** 'Sinbad' was Gertrude's nickname for Dr. Harry Sinderson.

Perhaps she also meant more than she wrote in a letter to her father about his own good health. Nearly three years earlier, on January 18, 1923 she wrote:

"I'm very glad to gather from your letter of Dec. 27th that there's every prospect of my predeceasing you, which is what I should wish to do."

Three years before this interesting line she made an equally vague admission about her imperfect health. It was in a 1920 letter to father Hugh that was all about the early years of British control in Baghdad. Iraq didn't yet officially exist, and Gertrude was a principal assistant to Sir Percy Cox. In the middle of a long letter all about the arrival of Sir Percy and moves to set up some local government, she suddenly threw in:

"I forgot if I told you that I've got bronchitis.

Well, I have, and I don't see much chance of curing it."

Was it far more than bronchitis, and did Gertrude know that it was?

The supposedly 'nice' books on Gertrude are the early ones that pretend Charles didn't exist. In this they somewhat sanitise her life.

They tend to also sanitise her death. They skip across the facts with euphemisms along the lines that she died peacefully in her sleep.

Elizabeth Burgoyne says that one Sunday night, Gertrude went to sleep: *"…. but it was a sleep that merged into one from which, when the hot eastern night had passed, she could not be awakened."*

This is lovely prose, but meaningless, and Dorothy Cowin's version is no better. Only two pages on from the serious attacks of 'probable' pneumonia and 'fortunate' pleurisy, she expounds about Bell family nonsense:

"It was nonsense of her family to urge her to come home before the task was done. [i.e. the establishment of the museum]. *She was not in the least ill: only tired, terribly tired – which after all was only natural, in such heat, and at her age. Perhaps when the museum was really in order, she would return to England – this time for good?"*

In the very next paragraph, after asserting that Gertrude was *"not in the least ill"*, and accusing the family of *"nonsense,"* we are told by Cowin that:

"But it was not to be as planned. Two days before her fifty-eighth birthday, she died, peacefully in her sleep, without even having felt ill."

This, Dorothy Cowin – this is the real nonsense!

Gertrude Bell went to bed on the night of July 11, 1926, and was found later dead in bed with an empty bottle of pills beside her. She was nearly 58. The pill bottle had contained diallylbarbituric acid (or allobarbital), and on the death certificate a Doctor Dunlop wrote 'Dial poisoning.'

If you take an overdose of a primitive and narcotic sedative, you will certainly die peacefully in your sleep. Nowadays we would call such versions 'spin'. In earlier times, as Elizabeth Burgoyne and Dorothy Cowin were plunking on their typewriters it was deemed as respect.

The closest she came to a suicide note was apparently a brief note to her dear friend Kinahan Cornwallis. She requested that he look after her dog. Cornwallis had known Gertrude since he headed the Arab Bureau, and was now representing British interests in the fledgling nation. Beyond his role as a fellow official in Iraq, Ken (as she called him) was also a very close friend. It is said that only later did Cornwallis realise the true import of her last note. It asked that he look after the little dog:

"if anything happened to her."

Possibly the last photo taken of Gertrude Bell. Her arms are like pale sticks hanging out of her dress. Her companion is probably her Baghdad friend Haji Naji. After her death he wrote to Florence: *"It was my faith always to send Miss Bell the first of my fruits and vegetables and I know not now where I shall send them."*

All this brings us back to that letter Dick wrote to Gertrude when she first shocked him with her mention of suicide by morphine. He wrote back:

"My dear don't do what you talked of – it's horrible to me to think of it – that's why I told you about my wife – how much more for you? – don't do anything so unworthy of so free and brave a spirit. One must walk along the road to the end of it. When I asked for this ship, my joy in it was half strangled by that thing you said, I can't even name it or talk about it. Don't do it. Time is nothing, we join up again, but to hurry the pace is unworthy of us all."

Gertrude didn't *"walk along the road"* of life to the end. She finally decided to *"hurry the pace."* After eleven years of grieving over Dick's death at Gallipoli, compounded by seriously failing health, she had finally had enough.

Way back in 1915 she had mentioned to him the two tubes of morphia (which also gave the title to this chapter) when she wrote that they were:

"enough, I think, to cut a thread even as strong as mine."

Now she was older, frail and sick. It took only a handful of white pills.

A full military funeral for Gertrude Bell was held in Baghdad on July 12, 1926. This was a mere three weeks after she had been feted at Faisal's royal banquet. Iraqis (as they were starting to see themselves) came to pay their respects to the person whose vision and untiring work had created their country.

Troops lined the streets for the procession, and solemnly watched the cortege pass by until it reached the gates of the cemetery. Every British official from the High Commissioner down was there to see her buried. Locals came out and lined up, and sheiks from many outlying areas hurried into Baghdad.

The coffin was draped with the Union Jack. Appropriately, it was also draped with the new national flag of Iraq; a flag she had helped design.

King George wrote to the grieving Hugh and Florence:

"The Queen and I are grieved to hear of the death of your distinguished and gifted daughter whom we held in high regard.

The nation will with us mourn the loss of one who by her intellectual powers, force of character and personal courage rendered important and what I trust will prove lasting benefit to the country and to those regions where she worked with such devotion and self-sacrifice. We truly sympathise with you in your sorrow."

One of her most visible legacies in Baghdad was the fledgling Archaeological Museum. She left no real suicide note, but she did leave a will. The £50,000 she left to the museum ensured that it was one of the world's greatest of its type. It was to remain so until the Saddam Hussein years and the Iraqi War, when too many of its artefacts found their way out of the ravaged building.

An earlier chapter mentioned a dinner given by the Royal Geographical Society in April 1927, and some words by David Hogarth about the reliance by T. E. Lawrence on her reports from the start of the war. It was of course, a tribute dinner, held in London nine months after her death. Hogarth went on to praise her in a way that seems strange to us today. Essentially he implied that she was so great, that she transcended being merely a woman. He went on to say of the respect she had in the Arab world:

> "I do not think that any European has enjoyed quite the same reputation. She had all the charm of a woman combined with many of the qualities that we associate with men. She was known in the East for those manly qualities ... I shall not serve any good purpose by trying to say how much I, and many others, have felt her loss. Hers was the brightest spirit that shone upon our labours in the East."

Other speakers included Sir Percy Goodenough. He said it a little better than David Hogarth when he said her achievements were great, regardless of her gender:

> "Her life was an inspiration, her death a grievous loss, but if ever a man or woman left this world victorious it was Gertrude Bell."

Gertrude Bell's grave in Baghdad as it looks today.

Chapter 34 - Family Knowledge

Domnul Chirol wasn't really family, but to Gertrude he was like a favourite uncle and was always a confidante. When she was in France during those dark and cold days of December 1914, she had felt *"near drowning"* without Dick, and obviously wrote to Domnul about it. He must have suggested that she come back to England to be with loved ones. She wrote back:

"My dear Domnul. I shall not come back to England for the present. At any rate I can work here all day long – it makes a little plank across the gulf of wretchedness over which I have walked this long time. Sometimes even that comes to near breaking point."

So Domnul knew all about Dick in 1914, and was maybe the first person Gertrude told. Her step sister Elsa knew of the love between Gertrude and Dick by early 1915, at about the time he was back in uniform and on his way to the Middle East. With the news of his death, Gertrude needed a shoulder to cry on and Elsa was the only one in the family she could run to.

After this day of May 1, 1915 the news of his death and the affair would have slowly leaked out and spread. Because it was so very improper in that era, it was likely to be a story heard from people who had been told 'in confidence' – who then passed it on in the same way!

It seems to me that once the news of his death was known, either Elsa or Gertrude told the whole story to Hugh and Florence. While there is nothing certain about this, the sense of it shows in the correspondence.

On June 2, Gertrude wrote to Florence and may have been still hoping the story of Dick's death was some dreadful mistake. She wrote:

"I really don't know what to do about Charles. There's really no one at the W.O. whom I know. I'll try telephoning to the secretary – whoever he is.

Ever your affectionate daughter Gertrude."

Nine days later she knew the tragic truth, and was obviously shattered. She had received letters of condolence from both Hugh and Florence. She managed only the briefest reply:

"Dearest Mother. Thank you and Father for your letters. I haven't anything to say that's worth, or at any rate worthy of saying, and therefore I don't write. Your affectionate daughter Gertrude."

By August 25, she was feeling no better, and even though the Office of Missing and Wounded kept her fully occupied. Her letters reveal that she was stuck in a slough of sad loneliness:

"Dearest Mother. It's very dear of you to suggest coming up, but you mustn't do it. Nobody does any good really; it sounds ungrateful, but it is so. Nothing does any good. This Sunday, however, will be better than others for we are going to do an immense filing job. I have 100 school teachers coming in to help and at least I shall not be lonely."

By February 1918, nearly three years had gone by. She was living in Baghdad. She had been there since the previous April, but wouldn't have had any idea that it would remain her home even after the war ended, and for the rest of her life. While the subject of her love for Dick was now something in the past, it was still like an open wound. When Dick had spent those last four days with her, she had raged at her reluctance over what didn't happen, and three years had done little to deaden this pain. She wrote to Hugh on February 22nd:

> "Darling Father, Oh Father dearest, do you know that tonight it's just 3 years since Dick and I parted. I can't think why the recurring date should bring back all memories so strongly, but it is so, and I've lived again through the four days of 3 years ago almost minute by minute. Dearest you know I love you but this sorrow at the back of everything deadens me in a way to all else, whether I go home or stay here in the East, or what happens. Yet in a curious way it quickens the inner life and makes one live more on thought and memory, so whether I'm with you or away from you, you're just as real a comfort to me always."

In the same letter she was lyrical and nostalgic in thinking back on her life, and those days in Arabia before the war:

> "today there came in to see me one of my travelling companions of 1914, an Arab of the Dulaim tribe who rode with me for 4 days when I was going back to Damascus. … He sent me longing for the desert. The grass is springing there and the black tents flowing with milk, and man and beast prosper."

Knowledge and evidence of Dick and Gertrude's love must have also been building up in the minds of the Doughty family as things were sorted out after his death. As mentioned previously, a small photo of the original grave was sent to Gertrude by Dick's brother in September of 1915. Hugh Doughty's ship had been at Cape Helles and he had a camera when he went ashore to pay his respects to his brother.

In the covering letter he also mentioned that the family had been passed all of Gertrude's undelivered letters to Dick. She had written them between early April, and the start of May 1915 when she heard of his death. As she was a prolific writer, it is no surprise that they amounted to several packets.*

---

* That several packets were assembled by the Army mail service is also a tribute to that service. One source says that around this time they were handling over twelve million letters a week.

Even without reading them all, it must have been obvious that a serious relationship existed. Dick's brother wrote:

"I am enclosing a packet that I have just opened to be sure what was in it & the other one unopened. My father wrote to you that he would promise for me, that diaries etc. of yours should be returned to you un-read. Should the unopened ones not be your own would you please send it directed to my father & ask him to send it to my sister-in-law. [ie. Lilian]

You were I know a great friend of Dicks. If only he had told me so, when talking of other things he wanted done in case he got killed, we might have saved you some trouble. He died really nobly out here, turning what was really a defeat into a victory."

So some letters at least were opened and read. Dick's family knew all that they needed to know about the love between the two, and they probably imagined what they didn't read. That Hugh made the effort to send Gertrude a copy of his photo of the grave is telling. At least he wasn't in shock at what he learnt about his late brother, and he might well have come to accept Gertrude had Dick survived the War.

Dick Doughty-Wylie never expected that their love letters or Gertrude's diaries from Hayyil would be seen by anyone except himself and Gertrude. His supposed last letter to her was written on April 20, when he wrote:

"My dear. Tonight I pack up all your letters and leave them addressed to you together with the packet sent by you. Tomorrow if the weather moderates I am embarking on the collier, 'the wreck ship' a wooden horse of Troy."

The weather didn't moderate, and the landing was postponed. He was able to write his actual last letter to Gertrude the next day, but it seems that none of that mail went. After his death, all were passed on to his family.

The diaries that Gertrude wrote on the journey to Hayyil would have also ended up with his family. To stop them being found by Lilian, Dick had sent them from Addis Ababa to London. He wrote to her after receiving the second one, and his words show us how important they were to him:

"That other beloved one that I sent to my bankers, that bewildering blinding live thing – like this one its own sister. Yes, it is as far away as you yourself, some incredible way, but the new one I have for me alone, dearer for that, …."

The Hayyil diaries are now held in the Robinson Library, at Newcastle University. It seems the Doughty family eventually sent them back to Gertrude. She did have some other correspondence with his family over the years, and actually sent them two of Dick's letters to her.

These two letters were returned by Dick's father in 1918, with a short note written on a black-edged card. The family was finally feeling able to disperse all of Dick's papers, and again it shows their strong intentions not to pry into the relationship. Hugh senior's note says:

"Dear Miss Bell, with many thanks I am returning the two letters you were so kind as to send me. They are the only private letters we have seen.

Believe me, Faithfully yrs., H.M.Doughty

We have opened letters for ourselves the rest will be sent to the writers."

It is interesting that Dick's father uses that ending *"Believe me."* These are the same words that Lilian used in her possibly 'phantom' letter to Lord Granville. Again, this may actually signal an untruth, because Hugh junior said he opened some of Gertrude's letters back in 1915. Believe me!

The Only Woman at Gallipoli

> THEBERTON HALL,
> LEISTON.
> SUFFOLK.
> 26 May 1915
>
> Dear Miss Bell,
>   With many thanks I am returning the two letters you were so kind as to send me. They are very private letters we have seen. Believe me
>   Faithfully y'rs
>   H. M. Doughty
>
> We have opened letters from ourselves. The rest will be sent to the writers

The front and back of the small card sent by Dick's father, when he returned two of his son's letters.

The Only Woman at Gallipoli

The Commemorative Stained Glass Window in the Doughty Family Church
The church is St. Peters in Theberton, Sussex. It is not far from the family seat of Theberton Hall. Charles Doughty-Wylie is depicted as St. George slaying the dragon.

Afterword

What prompted me to write this book? It was a fascination firstly with the story itself. A fascination that a woman, any woman, could love a man so much as to visit a grave on a foreign peninsula in the middle of a war.

There was a longing also to understand the people of the World War 1 era.

From my unavoidable Australian point of view I sense there was a colonial naivety of the world and the war. Could it ever have been a brief and grand adventure for 'sporting men'? How was it that so many were rushing to serve and willing to face death, for King and Country?

Someone I would like to understand more is my own grandfather, who died seven years before I was born. In an earlier chapter I made brief mention of William James Howell, and his evacuation from Gallipoli in the hospital ship *Glenart Castle*. Like all men who served, there is a bit more to his story, even though he was an ordinary and undistinguished private.

Bill Howell was born near a small coastal town to the west of Melbourne called Port Fairy. His birthdate was 17/9/1873, so that when he enlisted in November 1914, he was forty one years and two months old! A forty one year old man, with an eight year old daughter, and sons that were five, three, and newly born, signed up to be a part of the Great War. Note that the age for enlistment then was from 18 to 38. It was the following June when the terrible losses at Gallipoli and in France (matched with falling enlistments) caused a change. The upper bound was then increased to 45 years. Many older men before this change would have simply written on their enlistment that they were 38. Bill Howell clearly wrote 41, yet was somehow accepted. He also wrote down that he was 5' 6" tall, which was the minimum height. I'm not sure they really measured him that day either.

This was when the patriotic fervour was at its strongest, but it amazes me still that with his circumstances he volunteered to go. Not only did he go, but enlisted to be part of the 3rd Reinforcement battalion of the 8th Light Horse. The 8th would suffer great losses at Gallipoli, including two of the waves of men cut down in the charge at The Nek on August 7, 1915.

He embarked from Melbourne in February, with 52 other reinforcements on HMAT *Pera*. Fourteen of these shipmates were killed at The Nek.

The rest of his story is typical of the end of the campaign. He was taken on strength (i.e. arrived in Gallipoli from Egypt, and reported for duty) on October 25, 1915 and was admitted to the HS *Glenart Castle* on December 8. His evacuation was typical of late in the campaign: more for medical and illness issues than battle wounds. His stay on the Peninsula was only six weeks. The hospital ship sailed, and three days later he was in hospital in Heliopolis, with the evacuation at Anzac Cove now only a week away. By March, 1916 he was back in Melbourne and discharged from the army.

His life went on as before, and my father Ron was born a year after the Armistice, in November, 1919.

I have travelled around most of Australia, and every town has its memorial to The Great War. Many a town is approached through an Avenue of Honour or has an obelisk or statue in Main Street, or memorial gates at the local showground. Somewhere there are always lists of the young men who went off to a war started by others. Those towns without stone memorials have polished wooden honour boards in the local halls. The names are in gold, so that the memories will stay untarnished.

Whatever form the memorials take, they certainly held a special importance in the sense of grieving. For the first time in Australia's short history, there had been thousands killed in an overseas war. For those left at home, the memorials took on an extra special role. This was all there was now. Those boys who had fallen would never be brought home, and few people would ever be able to visit the real grave of the one they loved.

In small towns, the name of everyone who enlisted is shown. Some have an asterisk beside their name. The asterisk at the bottom of the board says 'killed in action' or 'did not return.' I am drawn to the lists. They are not just names, they are people. Too often I read the same surname two, three, or four times on a single board and imagine a local family where brothers, sons, fathers and husbands were never seen again.

In larger communities, where hundreds or thousands enlisted, the lists are only of those who were killed. Every single name is a tragedy, yet these lists underestimate the true impact of that war. They omit the amputees who returned, the shell-shocked, and the men in convalescent homes who struggled on for years with gas-burned lungs. They omit also the families who lived with these damaged men.

Recent travels have shown me these same memorials in other lands. As I suspected the memorials are in every village in Britain, and they also keep the memory of all those young men. I was surprised to see the same memorials in Italy. I recently spent springtime in Tocco da Casauria, the Abruzzo village where my wife's mother grew up. I was doubly taken aback by being there in April. Firstly it was by the magnificent wreaths that were placed on the memorials on April 25, because by coincidence the Italian Liberation Day is the same as Australia's Anzac Day. Secondly, the onset of spring causes thousands of red poppies to flower among the local olive trees. I feel the poppies appear each year to support the wilting wreaths at the foot of the memorials.

Some time ago I came across a modern Australian poem. It turned out it was written by a man who had lived in my suburb of Heathmont, in Melbourne. I think it captures the young men of the time, and the feelings and emotions of their families at home. Personally, I find that it somehow encapsulates my own feelings. The feelings that are so difficult to enunciate:

The Only Woman at Gallipoli

The Anzac On The Wall   by Jim Brown

I wandered thru a country town 'cos I had time to spare,
And went into an antique shop to see what was in there.
Old bikes and pumps and kero lamps, but hidden by it all,
A photo of a soldier boy – an Anzac on the wall.

"The Anzac have a name?" I asked; the old man answered "No,
The ones who could have told me, mate, have passed on long ago."
The old man kept on talking and, according to his tale,
The photo was unwanted junk bought from a clearance sale.

"I asked around," the old man said, "but no one knows his face,
He's been on that wall twenty years, deserves a better place.
For someone must have loved him so, it seems a shame somehow."
I nodded in agreement and then said, "I'll take him now."

My nameless digger's photo, well it was a sorry sight,
A cracked glass pane and a broken frame – I had to make it right.
To prise the photo from its frame I took care just in case,
'Cause only sticky paper held the cardboard back in place.

I peeled away the faded screed and much to my surprise,
Two letters and a telegram appeared before my eyes.
The first reveals my Anzac's name and regiment of course,
John Matthew Francis Stuart – of Australia's own Light Horse.

This letter written from the front, my interest now was keen
This note was dated August seventh, 1917.
"Dear Mum, I'm at Khalasa Springs, not far from the Red Sea,
They say it's in the Bible – looks like a billabong to me.

The Only Woman at Gallipoli

"My Kathy wrote I'm in her prayers, she's still my bride to be,
I just can't wait to see you both, you're all the world to me.
And Mum you'll soon meet Bluey, last month they shipped him out,
I told him to call on you when he's up and about."

"That Bluey is a larrikin and we all thought it funny,
He lobbed a Turkish hand grenade into the CO's dunny.
I told you how he dragged me wounded in from no man's land,
He stopped the bleeding, closed the wound, with only his bare hand."

"He's been in a bad way, Mum, he knows he'll ride no more,
Like me he loves a horse's back, he was a champ before.
So please Mum, can you take him in, he's been like my brother,
Raised in a Queensland orphanage, he's never known a mother."

But struth, I miss Australia, Mum, and in my mind each day,
I am a mountain cattleman on high plains far away.
I'm mustering white-faced cattle, with no camels hump in sight,
And I waltz my matilda by a campfire every night.

I wonder who rides Billy; I heard the pub burnt down,
I'll always love you and please say "hooroo" to all in town.
The second letter I could see was in a lady's hand,
An answer to her soldier son there in a foreign land.

Her copperplate was perfect, the pages neat and clean,
It bore the date November 3rd, 1917.
"'Twas hard enough to lose your Dad, without you, at the war,
I'd hoped you would be home by now – each day I miss you more."

The Only Woman at Gallipoli

"Your Kathy calls around a lot since you have been away,
To share with me her hopes and dreams about your wedding day.
And Bluey has arrived – what a Godsend he has been,
We talked and laughed for days about the things you've done and seen."

"He really is a comfort and works hard around the farm,
I read the same hope in his eyes that you won't come to harm.
McConnell's kids rode Billy but suddenly that changed,
We had a violent lightning storm and it was really strange."

"Last Wednesday, just on midnight, not a single cloud in sight,
It raged for several minutes it gave us all a fright.
It really spooked your Billy – and he screamed and bucked and reared,
And then he rushed the sliprail fence, which by a foot he cleared. "

"They brought him back next afternoon but something's changed, I fear,
It's like the day you brought him home, for no one can get near.
Remember when you caught him with his black and flowing mane?
Now horse breakers fear the beast that only you can tame."

"That's why we need you home, son" – then the flow of ink went dry,
This letter was unfinished and I couldn't work out why.
Until I started reading the letter number three,
A yellow telegram delivered news of tragedy.

Her son killed in action – oh – what a pain that must have been,
The same date as her letter – 3rd November 1917.
This letter which was never sent, became then one of three,
She sealed behind the photo's face – the face she longed to see.

The Only Woman at Gallipoli

And John's home town's old timers – children when he went to war,
Would say no greater cattleman had left the town before.
They knew his widowed mother well – and with respect did tell,
How when she lost her only boy she lost her mind as well.

She could not face the awful truth, to strangers she would speak,
"My Johnny's at the war you know, he's coming home next week."
They all remembered Bluey, he stayed on to the end,
A younger man with wooden leg became her closest friend.

And he would go and find her when she wandered, old and weak,
And always softly say, "Yes dear – John will be home next week."
Then when she died Bluey moved on, to Queensland some did say,
I tried to find out where he went but don't know to this day.

And Kathy never wed – a lonely spinster some found odd,
She wouldn't set foot in a church – she'd turned her back on God.
John's mother left no will, I learned on my detective trail,
This explains my photo's journey, to that clearing sale.

So I continued digging 'cause I wanted to know more,
I found John's name with thousands in the records of the war.
His last ride proved his courage – a ride you will acclaim,
The Light Horse charge at Beersheba, of everlasting fame.

That last day in October back in 1917,
At 4pm our brave boys fell – that sad fact I did glean.
That's when John's life was sacrificed, the record's crystal clear,
But 4pm in Beersheba is midnight over here .....

The Only Woman at Gallipoli

So as John's gallant spirit rose to cross the great divide,
Were lightning bolts back home a signal from the other side?
Is that why Billy bolted and went racing as in pain,
Because he'd never feel his master on his back again?

Was it coincidental? Same time – same day – same date?
Some proof of numerology, or just a quirk of fate?
I think it's more than that, you know, as I've heard wiser men,
Acknowledge there are many things that go beyond our ken.

Where craggy peaks guard secrets 'neath dark skies torn asunder,
Where hoof beats are companions to the rolling waves of thunder.
Where lightning cracks like 303's and ricochets again,
Where howling moaning gusts of wind sound just like dying men.

Some mountain cattlemen have sworn on lonely alpine track,
They've glimpsed a huge black stallion – Light Horseman on his back.
Yes sceptics say, it's swirling clouds just forming apparitions,
Oh no my friend you can't dismiss this all as superstition.

The desert of Beersheba – or windswept Aussie range,
John Stuart rides forever there – now I don't find that strange.
Now some gaze at his photo and they often question me,
And I tell them a small white lie, and say he's family.

"You must be proud of him," they say – I tell them, one and all,
"That's why he takes the pride of place – my Anzac on the wall."

[Details on Jim Brown poet and performer are at: www.theanzaconthewall.com.au]

NOTES

Charles Doughty-Wylie

Page 11: The incident at Adana is now mostly forgotten, as it was greatly overshadowed by later events. In 1915 (and again after the War) the Armenians were forcibly removed from their traditional homes by the government of the Young Turks. They were sent on long forced marches to supposedly re-settle an arid part of Syria. Many perished on the march, and many also died after arrival. Turkey today is very sensitive to what others call the Armenian Genocide. It is hard for outsiders to see it any other way, when government policy caused the death of maybe a million people.

V Beach

Page 24 *'The Sydney Mail'* of April 14, 1915 reported: "Last week the Athens correspondent of a London newspaper wrote – 'The check sustained in The Narrows in the Dardanelles by the Allied fleet is sufficiently grave to make a radical change in the operations necessary. The present pause is but a prelude to an attack by an overwhelming force. The silence being maintained is not a cloak for inactivity.'

Preparations are being made for land forces to operate in conjunction with the Anglo-French ships. These will probably include some of the Australasian troops who went to Egypt."

Page 26: One of the RNAS tasks was to make primitive bombing raids with small bombs, (the results of these were more psychologically alarming to the enemy than realistically damaging). More useful tasks included range-finding for the seriously damaging guns of the warships offshore, and aerial photography for the production of useful maps.

Before the landing, current and accurate maps were on the Allies wish-list. Older maps that were available were greatly improved during the final fortnight. Captured Turkish maps added more details later.

Early in the campaign there was a small RNAS airstrip on the Peninsula itself. It was between V and W beaches, near where today you can see the British 'Memorial to the

Missing'. In a short time Turkish artillery fire made it unusable, and the RNAS retreated to airstrips on nearby islands.

The Naval Campaign in The Dardanelles

Page 31: In August 1914, the Greek government even offered to provide the army to do this occupation. The offer fell from favour when it gained the added proviso that Turkey must attack Greece first. This may well have been added by Greece because Germany was quietly courting Turkey, and the German Kaiser's sister was the Queen of Greece, married to King Constantine! The King may have had a quiet word with PM Venizelos.

The Land Campaign on The Gallipoli Peninsula

Page 35: Much was made in older books of the supposed current which took the ships and landing craft along the coast, and away from the flatter ground around Gaba Tepe.

Newer publications have got over that old humbug. The Anzacs were given control of their own destiny by Sir Ian Hamilton. As the day approached aerial reconnaissance by Samson and his RNAS fliers revealed that the supposedly friendly terrain at Gaba Tepe was heavily defended. A landing there would have been a death trap. The landing point around Ari Burnu was no accident.

Once the men had been transferred into the smaller boats they were towed towards the dark shore. The diary of a Private Keith Wadsworth reveals that the Navy quite deliberately headed to Ari Burnu:

"We could see the strings of pinnaces coming along on either side and as we came closer to the cliffs we all swung around to the left of where we had been heading for and went along the shore for some distance. I believe we did not reach the point where it was intended that we should land, and it would have been disastrous if we had, it is said, and some say that the launches purposely made a mistake. I don't know how true that is.

> *As we skirted the shore, still some distance out, all was quiet, and Lamerton said to me, "So far, so good."*
>
> *"Too good, I grumbled, having then fears that we were going into some trap."*

On two visits to Gallipoli I have swum in the warm waters off Anzac Cove. I have snorkelled over wreckage and picked up spent Anzac cartridges from the shallows. I have never been swept away by any current.

Page 36: In an ironic twist, a large portion of the Anzac Cove beach was destroyed in 2008, because so many wanted to visit the narrow strip of sand. Thousands of young Anzac descendants now attend the dawn service there on April 25, and the access road had to be greatly widened. Bulldozers cut into the slopes behind, and pushed the spoil onto the narrow beach. In 2012 Turkey built some retaining walls near water level, to prevent erosion. This new work was done with a much more sympathetic attitude than was shown four years earlier.

Page 43: The British officer in no-man's land for the ceasefire was Aubrey Herbert (and he is central to another incident later in this book). In his account he wrote: "We mounted over a plateau and down through gullies filled with thyme, where there lay about 4,000 Turkish dead. It was indescribable. … The Turkish captain with me said: *'At this spectacle even the most gentle must feel savage, and the most savage must weep.'* The dead fill acres of ground … It was as if God had breathed in their faces." Burial parties from both sides got busy, while keeping a cautious eye on each other. Herbert went on: "At 4 o'clock the Turks came to me for orders. I retired their troops and ours, walking along the line. At 4.07 I retired the white-flag men, making them shake hands with our men. Then I came to the upper end. About a dozen Turks came out. I chaffed them and said they would shoot me next day. They said in a horrified chorus: 'God forbid! We will never shoot you.' Then the Australians began coming up, and said: 'Good-bye old chap; good luck!' And the Turks said: *'Oghur Ola gule gule gedejek-seniz, gule gule gelejekseniz.'* (Smiling may you go and smiling come again.) Then I told them all to get in their trenches, and unthinkingly went up to the Turkish trench and got a deep salaam from it."

Perhaps the mood that day was similar to the one during the unofficial 1914 Christmas Eve ceasefire in the trenches of France. Men realised that they were fighting an enemy, but that regardless of propaganda, it was an enemy made of men just like themselves.

These men's wallets also held pictures of loved ones left at home.

Page 47: When the War Graves Commission people did get to bury the dead soldiers who charged bravely at The Nek, there was little left to identify individuals. The cemetery today has only five named graves, and 316 un-named. The general trend of Australian and New Zealand historians has been that the Anzacs somehow bore the brunt of many such losses, and seemed to do the brunt of the heroic fighting, but this is of course narrow-minded. It is also untrue in fact.

One published set of figures has Australian deaths at 7,594 and New Zealand's toll at 2,431. French deaths were over 10,000, and British deaths over 24,000 (including Indians and Ghurkas etc. but not Anzacs). To all these can be added nearly 100,000 wounded and sick.

Antipodean publications have been happy to simplify everything to a case of good men (especially Anzacs) attempting to triumph under the command of fools (essentially British officers). Perhaps this is the product of frustrations. Frustrations that resulted from the deaths of so many of that generation, and frustrations that came from a campaign that should have been a victory.

Page 48: As a small child in the 1950's a nick-name for diarrhoea was the 'Turkey Trots.' We must have learnt it from our grandfathers, but I always thought it had something to do with poultry!

April 26 At V Beach

Page 52: Guy Nightingale wrote letters describing the fighting to his mother and sister. Their tone was unsympathetic to the humanity of both sides. Of a Turkish attack he wrote:

"We mowed them down and only once did they get so close that we were able to bayonet them. We took 300 prisoners and could have taken 3000, but we preferred shooting them. All the streams were simply running blood and the heaps of dead were a grand sight."

A newly arrived comrade was shot during a meal, and Nightingale blithely wrote that he:

"fell into the soup, upsetting the whole table, and bled into the teapot, making an awful mess of everything."

The tough exterior he assumed didn't save him from the inner horrors of war. He died at only 43, exactly 20 years after the Gallipoli landing. He was a depressed alcoholic by then, and some reports have him committing suicide to mark the anniversary.

Page 53: The May 5 edition of *'The Illustrated War News'* also announced that for the first time the Germans had used chlorine gas in France. The magazine called it the 'Poison Belt.' More eye-catching with hindsight is a small mention of the submarine war on page 8:

"Sea-frightfulness has developed into threats once more. The passengers of the 'Lusitania' have received, and ignored, a warning that the vessel would be torpedoed or destroyed on her way to Britain; and the German Embassy has issued, without consulting the American State Department, an advertisement to all the principal American newspapers in which it was made plain that passengers take their lives in their hands if they travelled on British or Allied vessels, for such vessels are liable to be destroyed in the 'War Zone.' The passengers, as has been noted, are as much concerned about this as British and Allied shipowners – that is they pay the advertisement no attention."

Page 56: In 2015 my travels took me to Caernarfon Castle in Wales where the Royal Welch Fusiliers Museum includes Doughty-Wylie's medals. Our itinerary had us there late in late April, only a few days before the centenary of his death. It transpired that the medals were going to his home church in Theberton for a commemorative service. I was lucky enough to arrive at the museum on the very morning they were being removed from the display. Actually holding his medals was a special moment for me.

The humblest and plainest medal at top left is the Victoria Cross. The two large medals in the body of the display are the Ethiopian Order of The Star, and the Turkish Order of the Medjidie.

Page 58: Two diary entries seem to me to be left so that future readers of the diaries will know that the failure of the campaign was more the fault of Hamilton's commander on the shore. Hunter-Weston is at one point 'revealed' to have no belief in the campaign, even four weeks before the landing, with Hamilton's entry:

> "29/3/15 Hunter-Weston has written me a letter from Malta (just to hand) putting it down in black and white that we have not a reasonable prospect of success …. It comes now as rather a startler."

During the early days of the landing, Hamilton also neatly excuses himself from any blame for the farcical evacuation of Y Beach, when he says:

"My inclination was to take a hand myself in this affair but the staff are clear against interference when I have no knowledge of the facts – and I suppose they are right. To see a part of my scheme, from which I had hoped so much, go wrong before my eyes is maddening!"

Hamilton had seen the troops evacuating Y Beach through his binoculars, from his flagship off shore. If things were going maddeningly wrong under the direct gaze of the overall commander, why didn't he step in? It was what he was appointed to do.

Another motive for the 1920 publishing of his diary was to wash off some of the mud thrown at him by the Dardanelles Royal Commission. Such was the disappointment of the British, that it was held in 1916 and 1917, while war still raged in Europe.

[For some interesting reading see *'Gallipoli 1915'* by Tim Travers. A late chapter is titled *'Ian Hamilton and the Dardanelles Commission: Collusion and Vindication.'*]

Years of Over-Active Distraction

Page 71: It was two decades after Gertrude's last climb, when George Mallory disappeared on Mount Everest in June 1924. Mallory had made other attempts on Everest in the previous summers of 1922 and 1923, gradually gaining the knowledge and experience required. On a speaking tour of America he was asked why he would risk all to climb the peak, and his answer went into folklore: *"Because it's there!"*

He and his inexperienced climbing partner Andrew Irvine were last seen near the Everest summit in 1924 by other members of their party, watching through telescopes from far below. The two men disappeared from view in swirling cloud, and never returned.

The frozen body of George Mallory was found at 26,760 feet in 1999, courtesy perhaps of a warm summer and global warming. Papers were found on his body, but not the photograph of his wife Ruth. He had promised to leave the photo on the summit if he made it. Search parties are still looking for Irvine, and the Kodak camera he carried. The camera may one day reveal their final achievement.

Irvine himself wasn't a climber at all, but was a tough and fit rower from Oxford University. He was chosen because he had some practical nous to handle the primitive oxygen equipment they carried, and was made of the 'right stuff.'

In May 2010, winds of around 150 km/h stripped snow that had built up for a decade on the North Col of Everest. An Australian climber named Duncan Chessell was then attempting to become the first Australian to reach the summit three times. He was also intending to search for the body of Andrew Irvine and his precious camera. The Melbourne 'Age' of May 20, 2010 quoted Chessell as saying: *"It is my intention to search those areas en route to the summit and take this rare opportunity to find him and perhaps the missing camera."*

In this case, no news is bad news. The body of Irvine and his precious camera are still somewhere high up on Mount Everest.

Gertrude Bell's status as a climber stands up to history. Two years after Mallory and Irvine disappeared, the *Alpine Journal* wrote of her and her climbing exploits saying:

"Everything that she undertook, physical or mental, was accomplished so superlatively well, that it would indeed have been strange if she had not shone on a mountain as she did in the hunting-field or in the desert. Her strength, incredible in that slim frame, her endurance, above all her courage, were so great that even to this day her guide and companion, Ulrich Fuhrer, speaks with an admiration of her that amounts to veneration."

A Love Affair

Page 80: This is the first of many longer quotes from original letters written by Charles and Gertrude that I have 'translated'. I use that term because they write in English (with only occasional Persian words!) but the handwriting of both is nearly illegible. I have constantly laboured over words and phrases, and often sought a second opinion from my wife Lia.

Luckily they were both good spellers, so I have presented the letters exactly as they were written. Winchester School and Sandhurst may have taught Charles a lot, but they certainly didn't teach him punctuation. His letters must sometimes be read several times to extract his true meanings from strings of unpunctuated phrases.

I note that other publications have worked on his grammar, replacing '&' with 'and' as well as inserting things he knew little of (i.e., question marks) but I have kept to my theme of not tampering. Some of these other authors have misread words as well, so the wisdom of using original sources is clear.

Lilian's letters and diaries are also quoted. Her handwriting is the best of the three, and I would rate it as merely difficult.

[On this scale the handwriting of Charles and Gertrude would rate as somewhere between atrocious and impossible!]

Gertrude Bell and Lilian Doughty-Wylie in the Early War Years

Page 103: Here is PART of Gertrude's report that was sent to the Military Operations Directorate, who passed it to Sir Edward Grey (the Under Secretary of State for Foreign Affairs). It made the British believe that the Arabs would help them speed up the demise of the Ottoman Empire:

'Syria, especially southern Syria, where Egyptian prosperity is better known, is exceedingly pro-English. I was told ... that it would be impossible to exaggerate the genuine desire of Syria to come under our jurisdiction. And I believe it. Last autumn an additional impulse was given to this sentiment by the dislike of growing French influence. This dislike is universal. Germany does not count for much either way in Syria. On the Baghdad side we weigh much more heavily in the scale than Germany because of the importance of Indian relations – trade chiefly. The presence of a large body of German engineers in Baghdad, for railway building, will be of no advantage to Germany, for they are not popular.

No Arab chief likes Turkish rule. This man Abdul Qadir, and Sayid Talib, are more powerful in their respective towns than the Turkish vali. The sheikh Muhammarah is not a negligible factor by any means, and is our ally. If Turkey went to war it is possible that the Arab Unionists might take that opportunity to throw off the yoke …'

Page 105: Gertrude's own attitude regarding the importance of officers over ordinary ranks comes through in a letter to Charles about the fighting at Neuve Chapelle:

"When the Cameronians went in to the attack, when they tore out of the trenches, they lost all their officers. All. The men went on with their N.C.O.'s & they went on like lions. The Indians were splendid too … They've lost comparably in officers."

If Only …

Page 115: At the Dardanelles Royal Commission of 1916/17, Lt. Col. Matthews nobly accepted full responsibility for the evacuation of Y. This was harsh, as he had no support at any stage from GHQ. During the 26 hours that he and his men were ashore, they had fought hard and suffered heavy losses. Twice he had called for reinforcements. Hunter-Weston never even answered! It's not hard to imagine that Matthews probably envisaged his shrinking forces on a path to complete annihilation.

Page 116: Charles Bean was the first official Australian war correspondent at Gallipoli, and later in Europe. The first choices of the Minister of Defence had been A.B. 'Banjo' Paterson and Phillip Schuler, but a change of government meant a change of minister. The new scheme called for an election within the Australian Journalists Association. Charles Bean narrowly won the ballot from Keith Murdoch.

Bean was born in Australia, but the family returned to Essex when he was young. When his schooling was completed he won a scholarship to read Classics at Oxford University. Thus we could argue that his viewpoint wasn't purely Australian, and his opinions are worth noting.

His writings during the war led to him being appointed as editor of the post-war official Australian War history. The history came out in twelve volumes, and Bean himself wrote the six volumes concerning the Australian Infantry Force. The responsibilities of his position led him to be diplomatic about British command, but in his own diaries it was not so.

Late in the Gallipoli campaign, when food, water, shelter and sanitation were all plainly inadequate he wrote bluntly that the Anzacs were being *"sacrificed to that pure British incompetence"* because of *"the hopeless weakness, want of imagination, and above all want of courage of the British staff."* Soon after, as the weather worsened, he wrote: *"The British nation has not the brains to make war. It is much better at manufacturing socks … by the same token our winter clothing is not landed yet."*

The next year he was in France, and witnessed the slaughter at Pozieres, and wrote angrily of: *"These stupid overfed fat red-tabs, enjoying their cigars in front of the fire …"*

Two years later he commented about British defeats in April 1918, and looked at the bigger picture. The problems he saw as more than the limitations of Generals Haig and Gough, as he wrote:

"The real cause has been as plain as an open book since Suvla Bay – it is far deeper than the failure of this division or that general. The real cause is the social system of England, …   … the exploitation of a whole country for the benefit of a class – a system quietly assumed by the 'upper class' and accepted by the ' lower class'."

Charles Bean saw first-hand the heavy cost when leadership and command were the assumed roles of the upper class, regardless of any brains or ability. I personally wouldn't argue with the observations of someone of the stature of Charles Bean. Doubtless he was a man of noble ideals and integrity. Three times he turned down a knighthood, and it was at his insistence that the bronze walls at the Australian War Memorial should list every name of the fallen without their decorations. To him they should all be seen as heroes.

A Book Unopened

Page 134: The modern dismantling of Yugoslavia and the atrocities of the Balkans fighting remind us all that compromises to create countries are not arrived at by satisfying all the races and peoples involved. On the contrary, the compromises only ensure that everyone is a little dissatisfied, and the passing of time causes these 'wounds' to fester rather than heal.

The Arab Bureau

Page 138: The Bureau was an Oxford University reunion as well as an archaeologists' reunion. Gertrude Bell had studied Modern History there rather than archaeology, but David Hogarth had been keeper of the university's Ashmoleum Museum, with Leonard Woolley as an assistant. They were archaeologists, and had both supervised Lawrence during his post-graduate days.

A Visitor to the Grave On Hill 141

Page 161: The Doughty-Wylie grave today, as shown on the CWGC website:

In Memory of
Lieutenant Colonel CHARLES HOTHAM MONTAGU
DOUGHTY-WYLIE
V C, C B, C M G

Royal Welsh Fusiliers
attd. as G.S.O.2 to H.Q. Mediterranean Expeditionary Force.
who died age 46
on 26 April 1915
Son of H. M. Doughty, of Theberton Hall, Suffolk, and Edith, his
wife (nee Cameron); husband of Lilian O. Doughty-Wylie.
Remembered with honour
SEDDEL-BAHR MILITARY GRAVE

Commemorated in perpetuity by
the Commonwealth War Graves Commission

Name: DOUGHTY-WYLIE, CHARLES HOTHAM MONTAGU
Initials: C H M
Nationality: United Kingdom
Rank: Lieutenant Colonel
Regiment/Service: Royal Welsh Fusiliers
Secondary Unit Text: attd. as G.S.O.2 to H.Q. Mediterranean Expeditionary Force.
Age: 46
Date of Death: 26/04/1915
Awards: V C, C B, C M G
Additional information: Son of H. M. Doughty, of Theberton Hall, Suffolk, and Edith, his wife (nee Cameron); husband of Lilian O. Doughty-Wylie.
Casualty Type: Commonwealth War Dead
Cemetery: SEDDEL-BAHR MILITARY GRAVE
Citation: An extract from "The London Gazette", No 29202, dated 23rd June 1915, records the following: - "On 26th April 1915 subsequent to a landing having been effected on the beach at a point on the Gallipoli Peninsula, during which both Brigadier- General and Brigade Major had been killed, Lieutenant- Colonel Doughty-Wylie and Captain Walford organised and led an attack through and on both sides of the village of Sedd el Bahr on the Old Castle at the top of the hill inland. The enemy's position was very strongly held and entrenched, and defended with concealed machine-guns and pom-poms. It was mainly due to the initiative, skill and great gallantry of these two officers that the attack was a complete success. Both were killed in the moment of victory."

Lilian Sees Out The War Years

Page 181: The Royal Flying Corps was the predecessor of the Royal Air Force, and had been created earlier in the War. The Royal Navy hung on to its own flying capability until April 1, 1918 when the RNAS merged with the RFC to form the Royal Air Force. 'A' Squadron was then put with 'Z' Squadron to form RAF 222 Squadron. 222 Squadron was disbanded in February 1922.

The Arab Uprising

Page 186: [See the map on Page 188]   The western side of the Arabian Peninsula is called the Hejaz. It is the Red Sea ports of Wejh, Yenbo, Jidda and Lith. Inland are Taif, and the holy cities of Medina and Mecca. Further inland is the forbidding Nejd desert that Gertrude had crossed less than three years earlier. The purpose of the Hejaz railway was for pilgrims to be able to come from the north to Medina (and then on to Mecca) without long and dangerous desert crossings.

Page 189: The Palestine Exploration Fund was originally founded for the exploration of biblical sites, to find archaeology back to the time of Moses and 'prove' the truth of the Bible. Just prior to World War 1 it was waylaid by the British Army to update local maps and be a front for reconnaissance. They could see Turkey siding with Germany and trying to move on the Suez Canal.

Page 189: Consider the methods that Lawrence created. A century on they are the norm for guerrilla warfare, but they were pioneered by Lawrence. His train bombings have become the roadside bomb, and his small attacks by mobile forces were copied in the deserts in WW2 by the British, and later by many including the IRA, Ho Chi Minh in Vietnam, and Mao in China. Covering large spaces with armoured cars, and calling in aeroplane support was a Lawrence idea. His Rolls Royce armoured cars were the first cars ever taken into those parts, and Lawrence came to love the one he called 'Blue Mist.'

[He went so far as to say that such a car, with a lifetime of tyres and petrol, would keep him happy for the rest of his days. After the war, Lowell Thomas says that 'Blue Mist' became Allenby's staff car in Cairo. There are many pictures of Allenby and cars taken after the war, but I have been unable to identify 'Blue Mist.']

Today's Afghanistan War is a conflict where both sides are utilising many parts of Lawrence's methods. In 1927 Basil Liddell Hart was the military editor of 'Encyclopaedia Britannica.' He approached Lawrence to write a brand new entry on guerrilla warfare. Lawrence declined, and said it could be distilled from his 'Seven Pillars of Wisdom.' Hart did exactly that, and credited the author for the entry to be a 'T.E.L.'

The legacy is more interesting when you consider that he wasn't a Sandhurst man, and had no military training. Possibly his PhD on crusader-era castles led him through some history involving small kingdoms and disparate fighting groups. Making something of many separate desert groups was maybe more possible because of this.

The Paris Peace Conference Of 1919

Page 192: Prime Minister William Morris Hughes was also open in his opposition to some Peace Conference motions outlawing racism. This was well received at home where the White Australia Policy was a popular plank of government, but it upset the powerful Japanese delegation in Paris.

There is even a viewpoint among modern Australian academics that the Japanese left the Conference feeling slighted by Hughes. This hardened their attitudes to the world, and the next two decades saw them on an increasingly militaristic path. The culmination was their invasion of Manchuria and their entry into World War Two.

Page 196: That Adolph Hitler would come to power in the shambles of the Depression could not be foreseen, but the Treaty of Versailles meant that the Germans spent the 1920s in despair. It was the rock-bottom foundation that ensured they were desperate to find a way out.

The Only Woman at Gallipoli

On November 11, 2009 the leaders of France and Germany stood side by side for the first time, and laid Remembrance Day wreaths together. It had been 90 years since the Peace Conference, and another World War had pitted France against Germany in the meantime. The realisation had possibly come that the future should bring forward the building of bridges, and not some new divisive version of the Maginot Line.

Page 196: There were English gentlemen that were different. Then there were ones who were eccentric, and then there was Arnold Talbot Wilson.

By the time he was in his twenties he was certainly a well-born gentleman, and was a lieutenant in the army. His service was essentially in India. By his thirties he was an administrator in Baghdad, and Gertrude Bell described him to her parents in a letter from there on 24/5/1918. She wrote that he was:

" – a most remarkable creature, 34, brilliant abilities, a combined mental and physical power which is extremely rare. ... I don't think I've ever come across anyone of more extraordinary force."

Five years earlier he performed a feat which perfectly illustrated both his physical abilities and his willpower. He was returning from India on leave and had little money. He signed on as a stoker, on a steamer going from Bombay to Marseilles.

Naturally, he was taunted by the crew as a gentleman way out of his proper place. He showed them all the man he really was. He worked the first leg to Aden. When a stoker fell sick there, he offered to do his shift as well for the ten day leg to Suez. He did the double shifts, working 16 hours a day, and insisted on (and received) double the pay.

When they reached Marseilles, he bought an old bicycle and rode across France to Le Havre. After crossing to Southampton, he rode home to Worcester!

By the 1930s he was a member of the House of Commons, but was also a supporter of Oswald Mosley, and so of Hitler and Mussolini. As a new World War loomed, he realised the error of his ways and resigned from parliament. By May 1940 he had joined the RAF, probably pulling a few strings to be accepted as such an old recruit. He was killed at age 55, in a Wellington bomber shot down near Dunkirk.

Page 199: Sir Mark Sykes was the member of the British delegation who died from influenza at the 1919 Paris Peace Conference. Interestingly, his body was exhumed by medical researchers in 2007. They were seeking to connect the strain of the 1919 virus with what was then the new Bird Flu epidemic.

Faisal, Oil, and Iraq

Page 203: When His Majesty's Ships *Ocean*, *Triumph*, and *Majestic* were torpedoed by German submarines in May, the *Queen Elizabeth* was quickly moved away to safety. The newest and best ship was not to be risked.

The Cairo Conference of 1921

Page 205: The post-war unrest in Cairo got to a serious stage of near uprising. The Australian Light Horseman expected to leave Damascus for Australia when Turkey fell in 1918. They soon found themselves acting as unwilling policemen in the riotous streets of Cairo. (This was an interesting case of role-reversal, when you recall the unruly carousing of the Anzacs in early 1915.) The Ottoman Empire had fallen, but now the British Empire was swaying and unsteady on its feet!

Page 206: Gertrude Bell was one who could see that troubles with Israel and Palestine were inevitable. In 1922 she wrote in a fairly pro-Arab tone and said:

"The next episode in Arab history is going to be the fury raised by the confirmation of the Palestine mandate by the League of Nations, and there I'm wholly in sympathy with them. ... I abandon the League of Nations – it's nothing but a fraud. ...

I've received, under the seal of secrecy, a masterly memorandum which shows clearly that the Zionist immigrants are working for a purely communistic organisation – a thing every Palestinian and every Moslem abhors. And we pretend to be setting up a Govt. in accordance with the wishes of the people, liars and knaves that we are! ...

But upon my honour the Arabs have got the soul of truth in them and we haven't."

Page 207: Sunni and Shia Muslims have been fighting each other for over a thousand years about the line of succession from Mohammed. When Jerusalem fell to the first crusaders in 1099, it was partly because the two sects wouldn't cooperate in a defence. This continued for about the next eighty years while the crusaders consolidated, and built their own fortresses. Saladin was a Kurdish Sunni who managed to temporarily unite the factions, and recapture Jerusalem in 1187.

Creating Modern Turkey and Becoming Ataturk

Page 212: From the 1920's until recently, Mustafa Kemal was a Turkish hero placed on such a high pedestal that it is hard to explain how high. Perhaps consider the British Empire's adoration of Queen Victoria, or Italy's near-worship of Garibaldi, and then move to a whole new level.

Nearly every town or village square has a bust or statue, and they are never of anyone except the all-conquering Ataturk. Interestingly, that is now changing after 90 years. A basic tenet of his establishment of modern Turkey was that it be a secular state. Religions have been many, and all were accepted and had their place. This decade has brought a shift. As Muslim political parties have come to power, the solid secular notion of Turkey has changed. Kemal was a dedicated nationalist and saw that as something that far transcended any religion. This great attribute is now seen through Muslim eyes as a fault, and there is some dismantling of his lofty stature.

Lilian's Later Life

Page 215: Hayderpasa cemetery was started for British dead during the Crimean war of the 1850's. Britain joined with France and the Ottomans to fight against Russia. Cemetery 'clients' came from nearby Kadikoy. Here was the famous military hospital run by Florence Nightingale. 'The Lady with the Lamp' insisted on unheard-of standards of hygiene and sanitation, and is said to have reduced the mortality rate of soldiers brought in from 70% to around 5%.

In addition to the Crimean graves, there are now 405 graves from WW1, of which 345 have named occupants. Even though Turkey remained neutral during WW2, there are also another 39 graves from this conflict.

Page 217: Elisabeta and Ileana were the first and last born daughters of King Ferdinand I of Romania and his British born Queen Marie. In 1921 Elisabeta married Crown Prince George II of Greece, but within a year she got typhoid and pleurisy. Within another year George I abdicated and George II and Elisabeta were King and Queen of Greece. By the end of 1923 the chaos in Greece caused them to flee to Romania. Elisabeta was educated by English tutors, and during WW1 Elisabeta and her mother Marie did some nursing work, so a new project with Lilian is no surprise.

Princess Ileana was only 22 in 1931, and married Archduke Anton of Austria that year and had six children. In later life she founded a religious order in America and became its abbess.

Did Lilian Imagine Her Gallipoli Visit?

Page 226: The strings of landing craft at Anzac Cove were towed in to shore by teenage midshipmen in steam-powered motor boats. Eric Bush was one of these brave young midshipmen. As a 15 year old he helped launch a steam pinnace from the davits of HMS *Bacchante* near midnight on April 24. For seventy two hours straight he ferried fit men and supplies to shore, and returned with wounded men back to the ships. He kept a journal of his time at Gallipoli. I have seen it but not read it, as it is in a glass case at the Imperial War Museum.

Page 227: R. R. James is more fortunate than later authors in his 'Gallipoli.' It was published in 1965 for the fiftieth anniversary of the landings. He read the diaries of many of the men, but was also able to talk with many veterans still alive at the time.

He was not a military man, but was the son of Lt. Col. W. R. James. His father won the Military Medal in the retreat to Kut in 1916. There were more details of that disaster earlier in this book.

Page 230: The IWM did retrieve a page for me by Corbett Williamson about the final days at Helles, so he did exist and was at Gallipoli. He returned in October 1915 after two months in a dysentery ward on Lemnos, and was one of the last to leave the Peninsula. He finally left carrying a suitcase of papers for General Street. No sooner were the small group on board De Robeck's yacht *Triad* than they heard a massive explosion. The last ammunition dump on shore had been destroyed. His brief memoir makes no mention of happenings in November at all.

Gertrude Bell and T. E. Lawrence

Page 248: Lawrence apparently dressed for the arrival of the famous woman in Carcemish. Not only did he wear outrageous red slippers with curled-up pointy toes, but also a woven Arab belt with long tassels over his left hip. He didn't know it, but for the locals this was the sign of a single man seeking a bride.

When Gertrude left some days later, she had made lifelong friends of Woolley and Lawrence, but was mystified by the hostile send-off from their hired diggers. They assumed that Lawrence had asked for her hand, and that she had refused!

Page 252: It was Sam Spiegel who bought the film rights to 'Revolt in the Desert' from fellow Hollywood mogul Alexander Korda. After a long lunch Spiegel also ended up with the rights to '*The African Queen,*' that Korda was even keener to unload. Spiegel soon offered the role of Lawrence to Marlon Brando, with whom he had only recently finished 'On the Waterfront.' Luckily for us all Brando turned it down, and the lead role ended up with the unknown Peter O'Toole.

'*Lawrence of Arabia*' won seven Academy Awards, including that for Best Picture.

Page 253: Lowell Thomas explains where the title of *'Uncrowned King'* comes from. He says that he was in Jerusalem soon after it had been re-captured, and was in a bazaar. A Caucasian man in Arab robes was strolling through and was making all heads turn.

Later, Thomas went to see General Robert Storrs and the same man was there in the General's office. It was Storrs who did the introductions and said: *"I want you to meet the Uncrowned King of Arabia."*

Page 255: The dedication of *'Seven Pillars of Wisdom'* is actually to an un-named person, that Lawrence calls only 'S.A.' Because of his professed love, there was much conjecture as to who this was.

The full and beautiful sentence of the dedication to S.A. is: *"I loved you, so I drew these tides of men into my hands and wrote my will across the sky in stars."*

Early books that tackled the possible identity of 'S.A.' came to the fact that he was a young Arab boy named Dahoum. The initials were still a mystery. Later biographers cleared this up. 'S.A.' was actually Salim Ahmad, and Dahoum was a nickname given to the baby boy by his mother. It means 'dark-skinned.' Dahoum was only a teenager when befriended by Lawrence in the early days of digging in Carcemish. Lawrence managed to have him around as a 'companion' for many years, including a visit to England.

A friend and biographer of Lawrence named David Garnett wrote cryptically that Dahoum was: *"his most intimate friend among the Arabs."*

Page 255: It was arranged that Lawrence would be enlisted by an officer in the know named Dexter at the Covent Garden recruitment office. Unfortunately he first came across the Chief Interviewing Officer. This was none other than W.E. Johns who would go on to write scores of *'Biggles'* adventure novels. He turned 'Ross' away the first time for having no paperwork, and a second time for coming back with paperwork that was obviously forged. It was third time lucky for Ross, as Johns had now been given the word, and John Hume Ross was soon based at RAF base, Uxbridge.

Gertrude Bell and the Early Days Of Iraq

Page 257: An indication of how central Gertrude Bell was to all that went on in Iraq is in her letter home of August 6, 1924 when she says:

"Thank the Lord I've finished my annual report for the League of Nations – the High Commissioners report I should say, but I write it. I do all the High Commissioner's part and the report for the Ministry of Interior about which I know as much as anyone. I am often surprised at the amount I do know!"

Another view of how vital she was to the lives of everyone around her is seen from some comments Vita Sackville-West made in 'A Passenger to Teheran':

"I felt that her personality held together and made a centre for all those exiled Englishmen whose other common bond was their service for Iraq …. I could not help feeling that there would have been more in the nature of drudgery than of zeal, but for the radiant ardour of Gertrude Bell."

Page 258: Because of Schliemann's crude excavations, modern tourists are often disappointed with what they see, or more with what they *don't* see at Troy. He finally returned triumphantly to Berlin with a fabulous hoard of golden treasure, and kept it most of his life. As an old man he donated it to Germany. The treasure was hidden by the Nazis during World War Two, in underground chambers dug under the Berlin Zoo. The cache was found by Russian soldiers, and disappeared from Berlin in 1945. It is now possibly in Moscow.

The Only Woman at Gallipoli

BIBLIOGRAPHY

Books

Aldington, Richard	LAWRENCE OF ARABIA Penguin Books, 1971
Anderson, Nola	AUSTRALIAN WAR MEMORIAL Treasures from a Century of Collecting. Murdoch Books, 2012
Anderson, Scott	LAWRENCE IN ARABIA Atlantic Books, 2013
Asher, Michael	LAWRENCE The Uncrowned King of Arabia, Overlook Press, 1998
Bean, C. E. W.	GALLIPOLI MISSION Australian War Memorial, 1948
Bell, Lady Florence	LETTERS OF GERTRUDE BELL, Volumes 1 & 2 Selected and edited by Lady Bell, 1927
Bell, Gertrude	AMURATH to AMURATH Heinemann, 1909
Bell, Gertrude	THE PALACE AND MOSQUE OF UKHAIDIR Clarendon Press, 1914
Benchley, Fred & Elizabeth	WHITE'S FLIGHT John Wiley & Sons, 2004
Bennett, Jack	GALLIPOLI, Angus and Robertson, 1981
Brittain, Vera	THE WOMEN AT OXFORD, MacMillan, 1960
Broadbent, Harvey	GALLIPOLI - The Fatal Shore, Viking, 2005
Burgoyne, Elizabeth	GERTRUDE BELL Her Personal Papers, Ernest Benn Ltd. 1961
Bush, Eric Wheler	GALLIPOLI, St Martin's Press, 1975
Butler, Janet	KITTY'S WAR University Of Queensland Press, 2013
Carlyon, Les	GALLIPOLI, Picador, 2002
Cowin, Dorothy	A WOMAN IN THE DESERT, 1967
Davies, Richard Bell	SAILOR IN THE AIR, Peter Davies, London, 1967
Denton, Kit	GALLIPOLI – One Long Grave, Time Life Books in association with John Ferguson, 1986
De Vries, Susanna	AUSTRALIAN HEROINES OF WORLD WAR ONE, Dennis Jones Associates (print on demand) 2013

De Vries, Susanna and Jake	TO HELL AND BACK The Banned Account of Gallipoli, Sydney Loch Harper Collins, 2007
Dolan, Hugh	GALLIPOLI AIR WAR Pan MacMillan, 2013
Ffrench, Yvonne	SIX GREAT ENGLISHWOMEN Hamish Hamilton, 1963
Graves, Robert	LAWRENCE AND THE ARABS Jonathon Cape, 1927
Hastings, Max	MILITARY ANECDOTES, Oxford University Press, 1987 (from: MONS, ANZAC and KUT, Aubrey Herbert, 1919)
Hickey, Michael	GALLIPOLI, John Murray, 1995
Hutton, Isabel Emslie	WITH A WOMAN'S UNIT IN SERBIA, SALONIKA AND SEBASTOPOL, Williams & Norgate 1928
Howell, Georgina	DAUGHTER OF THE DESERT, Pan Books 2007
James, Robert Rhodes	GALLIPOLI, Sydney Angus & Robertson, 1965
King J. and Bowers M.	GALLIPOLI, Doubleday, 2005
Korda, Michael	HERO, Harper Collins, 2010
Lawrence, T.E.	LETTERS OF T E LAWRENCE, selected and edited by Malcolm Brown Dent & Sons, 1988
Lawrence, T. E.	REVOLT IN THE DESERT, Jonathan Cape, 1927
Lawrence, T.E.	SELECTED LETTERS OF T E LAWRENCE, edited by David Garnett World Books, 1941
Lawrence, T. E.	SEVEN PILLARS OF WISDOM, Penguin, 1965
Macdougall, A. K.	GALLIPOLI AND THE MIDDLE EAST, Moondrake, 2004
MacMillan, Margaret	PARIS 1919, Random House, 2002
MacMillan, Margaret	PEACEMAKERS, John Murray, 2001
Moorehead, Alan	GALLIPOLI, Aurum Press, 2007
Nevison, Henry W.	DARDANELLES CAMPAIGN, Nisbet & Co, 1918
Norman, Andrew	T.E. LAWRENCE – UNRAVELLING THE ENIGMA, Hallsgrove, 2003
O'Brien, Rosemary	GERTRUDE BELL, The Arabian Diaries 1913 – 1914, 2000

The Only Woman at Gallipoli

Orlans, Harold	T E LAWRENCE, BIOGRAPHY OF A BROKEN HERO, McFarland and Co., 2002
Ramsay, Roy and Ron	HELL, HOPE AND HEROES Life in the Field Ambulance of WW1, 2005
Reid, Richard	GALLIPOLI 1915, ABC Books, 2008
Richmond, Lady Elsa	THE EARLIER LETTERS OF GERTRUDE BELL Austin & Sons, 1937
Richmond, Lady Elsa	THE LETTERS OF GERTRUDE BELL Penguin Books, 1953
Rodge, Huw and Jill	GALLIPOLI: The Landings at Helles, Leo Cooper, Pen & Sword, 2003
Sackville-West, Vita	A PASSENGER TO TEHERAN, 1926
Snelling, Stephen	VCs OF THE FIRST WORLD WAR Gallipoli, Sutton Publishing, 1999
Stowers, Richard	BLOODY GALLIPOLI, The New Zealanders' Story, David Bateman, 2005
Thomas, Lowell	WITH LAWRENCE IN ARABIA , originally Hutchison & Co. 1925, Reprinted by Arrow Books, 1964
Thomson, Alistair	ANZAC MEMORIES, Oxford University Press, 1994
Travers, Tim	GALLIPOLI 1915, Tempus Publishing, 2001
Unknown	THE GALLIPOLI CAMPAIGN – An outline of the Military Operations Sifton, Praed & Co. 1923
Various Authors	ENCYCLOPAEDIA OF WORLD WAR ONE, Marshall Cavendish, 1986
Wallach, Janet	DESERT QUEEN, Phoenix, 1997
Ward, Major C H Dudley	REGIMENTAL RECORDS OF THE ROYAL WELCH FUSILIERS Volume IV Forster Groom & Co, 1929
Wilson, Jeremy	LAWRENCE OF ARABIA – The Authorised Biography, Collier Books, 1989
Winstone, H.V.F.	THE ILLICIT ADVENTURE, Jonathon Cape, 1982
Woolley, Leonard	DEAD TOWNS AND LIVING MEN, Oxford Univ. Press, 1920
Ziino, Bart	A DISTANT GRIEF, University of West Australia, 2007

WEBSITES

www.cwgc.org
www.findagrave.com
www.forum.axishistory.com
www.gerty.ncl.ac.uk
www.londonmet.ac.uk
www.onesuffolk.co.uk/Theberton
www.rcnarchive.rcn.org.uk

ARTICLES and ARCHIVES

A NEW NUSRET MINE LAYER   'Gallipolian' Issue 126, Autumn 2011
CHARLES DOUGHTY-WYLIE   Letters to Gertrude Bell, dates various, Robinson Library, Newcastle University
DEEDS THAT THRILL THE EMPIRE   by various authors. A periodical magazine of WW1
GERTRUDE BELL   Letters, Diaries, and Photographs dates various, Robinson Library, Newcastle University
GOOD-BYE GALLIPOLI   by W. Corbett Williamson, date unknown, I.W.M, London
LILIAN O DOUGHTY-WYLIE   Letters, Diaries, Photographs and Newspaper articles, dates various, I.W.M. London
LILY DOUGHTY-WYLIE - A Distant Memory   'Gallipolian' Issue 95, Spring 2001
LILY DOUGHTY-WYLIE   by Timothy Daunt, 'Gallipolian' Issue 133, Winter 2013

PROJECT BENEATH GALLIPOLI   Gallipolian' Issue 126, Autumn 2011

SEARCH COULD SOLVE MYSTERY   'Age' Newspaper, May 20, 2010, Melbourne
THE GALLIPOLI DIARIES   Herald Sun, April 20, 2005
V FOR VALOUR   by Steven Snelling, 'Britain at War' June 2014

www.ingramcontent.com/pod-product-compliance
Lightning Source LLC
Chambersburg PA
CBHW081353290426
44110CB00018B/2358